Mission-Based Policing

Advances in Police Theory and Practice Series

Series Editor: Dilip K. Das

Mission-Based Policing
John P. Crank, Dawn M. Irlbeck, Rebecca K. Murray, and Mark Sundermeier

The New Khaki: The Evolving Nature of Policing in India
Arvind Verma

Cold Cases: An Evaluation Model with Follow-up Investigative Strategies
James M. Adcock and Sarah L. Stein

Policing Organized Crime: Intelligence Strategy Implementation
Petter Gottshcalk

Security in Post-Conflict Africa: The Role of Nonstate Policing
Bruce Baker

Community Policing and Peacekeeping
Peter Grabosky

Community Policing: International Patterns and Comparative Perspectives
Dominique Wisler and Ihekwoaba D. Onwudiwe

Police Corruption: Preventing Misconduct and Maintaining Integrity
Tim Prenzler

Mission-Based Policing

John P. Crank
Rebecca K. Murray
Dawn M. Irlbeck
Mark T. Sundermeier

CRC Press
Taylor & Francis Group
Boca Raton London New York

CRC Press is an imprint of the
Taylor & Francis Group, an **informa** business

HUMBER LIBRARIES LAKESHORE CAMPUS
3199 Lakeshore Blvd West
TORONTO, ON.   M8V 1K8

CRC Press
Taylor & Francis Group
6000 Broken Sound Parkway NW, Suite 300
Boca Raton, FL 33487-2742

Printed in the United States of America on acid-free paper
Version Date: 20110608

International Standard Book Number: 978-1-4398-5036-7 (Paperback)

Visit the Taylor & Francis Web site at
http://www.taylorandfrancis.com

and the CRC Press Web site at
http://www.crcpress.com

This work is dedicated to colleagues and friends in Omaha who strive against poverty, illiteracy, crime, and other consequences of persistent segregation that continue to plague the wonderful city of Omaha, who rise to the question *if not you, who?* Thank you, thank you.

John Crank

I would like to dedicate the book to Omaha 360, The Empowerment Network, the Omaha Police Department, and those in my community who give of themselves to make a difference.

Dawn Irlbeck

To Julie, for her love and support.

Mark Sundermeier

Contents

Series Editor's Preface

While the literature on police and allied subjects is growing exponentially, its impact upon day-to-day policing remains small. The two worlds of research and practice of policing remain disconnected, even though cooperation between the two is growing. A major reason is that the two groups speak in different languages. The research work is published in hard-to-access journals and presented in a manner that is difficult to comprehend for a lay person. On the other hand, the police practitioners tend not to mix with researchers and remain secretive about their work. Consequently, there is little dialogue between the two and almost no attempt to learn from one another. Dialogue across the globe, among researchers and practitioners situated in different continents, is of course even more limited.

I attempted to address this problem by starting the International Police Executive Symposium (IPES), www.ipes.info, where a common platform has brought the two together. IPES is now in its thirteenth year. The annual meetings, which constitute most of the organization's major events, have been hosted in all parts of the world. Several publications have come out of these deliberations, and a new collaborative community of scholars and police officers has been created whose membership runs into the several hundreds.

Another attempt to foster better communication between researchers and practitioners was to begin a new journal, aptly called *Police*

Practice and Research: An International Journal (PPR) that has opened the gate for practitioners to share their work and experiences. The journal has attempted to focus upon issues that help bring the two onto a single platform. PPR completed its tenth year of publication in 2009. It is certainly evidence of the growing collaboration between police research and practice that PPR, which began with four issues per year, expanded to five issues in its fourth year, and now is issued six times a year.

Clearly, these attempts, despite their success, remain limited. Conferences and journal publications do help create a body of knowledge and an association of police activists, but these cannot address substantial issues in depth. The limitations of time and space preclude larger discussions and more authoritative expositions that can provide stronger and broader linkages between the two worlds.

It is this realization of the increasing dialogue between police research and practice that has encouraged many of us—my colleagues and I, connected closely with IPES and PPR across the world—to conceive and implement a new attempt in this direction. I am now embarking on a book series, Advances in Police Theory and Practice, that seeks to attract writers from all parts of the world. Further, the attempt is to find practitioner contributors. The objective is to make a serious contribution to our knowledge of the police as well as to improve police practices through this series. The focus is not only in work that describes the best and most successful police practices, but also one that challenges current paradigms and breaks new ground to prepare a police force for the twenty-first century. The series seeks comparative analysis that highlights achievements in distant parts of the world as well as one that encourages an in-depth examination of specific problems confronting a particular police force.

In *Mission-Based Policing*, the authors take a fresh look at the deployment of line officers with impressive results that make this book an important contribution to the Police Theory and Practices series. The authors begin by exploring the redeployment of line officers from "calls-to-service" to the location of serious crime, utilizing geographic deployment based on contemporary crime mapping. They argue that this change from random preventive patrol transforms the focus of policing from *reducing* to *ending* crime, thus reestablishing policing as mission-based. In this book, the authors also report on their research into counter-insurgency to determine if its organizational structure could be adapted to urban policing. They submit that, even taking into consideration negative reactions to modeling the police after the military, elements and strategies of population-centric counter-insurgency are not only applicable to urban policing, but increase its effectiveness. In addition, the authors discuss the five central principles of mission-based policing—focus, effectiveness, deployment, integrity, and mission's end.

It is hoped that, through this series, it will be possible to accelerate the process of building knowledge about policing and help bridge the gap between the two worlds of police research and police practice. This is an invitation to police scholars and practitioners across the world to come and join in this venture.

Dilip K. Das, Ph.D.

Founding president, International Police Executive Symposium, IPES,
www.ipes.info.

Founding editor-in-chief, Police Practice and Research: An International
Journal, PPR, www.tandf.co.uk/journals.

About the Authors

John Crank is a professor of criminology and criminal justice at University of Nebraska at Omaha. He has written extensively in the area of policing. He received the Outstanding Book Award from the Academy of Criminal Justice Sciences in 2003 for his work titled *Imagining Justice*.

Dawn Irlbeck is an assistant professor of sociology at Creighton University. She teaches courses on the criminal justice system, American cultural minorities, social stratification, as well as other courses in sociology. Her primary research interests include racial profiling, policing and minority communities, Latino police officers, and ethnic identity formation. She has recently published on racial profiling and vehicle searches, as well as variations in ethnic identity among Latino police officers.

Rebecca K. Murray is an assistant professor in the Department of Sociology and Anthropology at Creighton University, where she helps facilitate the criminal justice policy track. She has published work looking at the effects of various urban structures on crime and critiquing spatial methodologies. Her most recent work examines the interaction between community groups and formal mechanisms of social control, and the effects of police policies on wrongful convictions. She lives near Gretna, Nebraska, with her husband, Tom, and her two children.

Mark Sundermeier spent 25 years with the Omaha Police Department, retiring as a deputy chief in 2009. During that time he also served as a reserve deputy sheriff with the Douglas County Sheriff's Office. After retiring, he joined the Metropolitan Community College, where he helped to form the MCC Police Department, Nebraska's newest police department. Mark is an adjunct criminal justice professor at the University of Nebraska at Omaha, and is a security consultant for a variety of companies and individuals.

Introduction: Thinking about Crime's End

This book emerged from a single, seemingly straightforward question: What would a police department look and act like if deployment of line officers was based on the location of serious crime? When we first posed this question, we did not realize the Rubik's cube of shifting complexity the answer would entail. Indeed, what we found was that if deployment was changed according to this somewhat uncomplicated—even widely taken-for-granted—notion, then everything we think about police organization and practice also begins to change. Some of the changes are subtle. In total, they are profound.

First, if one redeploys for a serious crime, then it seems straightforward that the purpose of the police would be mission based to fight serious crime. Yet, the idea that police officers would be responsible for a mission is a sharp change from current practices.

Consider contemporary organization patterns: urban police agencies are bureaucracies that are formally guided hodge-podges of somewhat inconsistent security-related goals. Commanders tend to work with community respectables, line officers with many marginal and disreputable individuals, and between the two very different functions is a "line in the sand." Rational observers call the line police discretion, reformers call it police culture, and institutional theorists call it loose coupling. Rare is the functional command structure in police organizations that is effective below the rank of sergeant. For example, line officers are almost never expected to follow the most recent orders received from a command officer. One is left with what is better described as a "cajoling" structure—commanders try to talk line personnel into participation in operations and into anything outside routine patrol or other assigned duties. But once the police are operating under a mission basis, all of this is swept away; line officers act on behalf of the mission according to operational protocol or they are reassigned or otherwise replaced.

We see in the research and literature on policing the mistaken celebration of line-level discretion as if absence of direction were a positive attribute. For too long, researchers have taken the position that those individuals most recent to the position somehow know the most about how to do it "on the street" or are somehow smarter about the real world than more senior officers with extensive career experience. We argue for the integrity of mission and unity of command, which means that line personnel have an occupational responsibility and command expectation to carry out the direction provided by superior officers. It also means that line officers can be expected to act consistently on behalf of what should be the central mission of the organization—doing something about crime—as that strategy is developed, deployed, and modified by senior staff and command officers.

Second, one could reasonably ask *what is it that a police department is going to do about serious crime when it is encountered?* The correct answer, from a mission orientation, is that one tries to end it. By "end" we mean that serious crime is brought down to levels experienced by relatively safe areas in a city. But this question is usually never asked. More commonly, police in high crime areas view their work as trying to "keep a lid" on crime. If one looks for a security model aimed at ending serious crime, it would be difficult to find in the research on urban policing.

We found in counterinsurgency research the sort of organizational structure we sought for urban policing: mission based, strategically organized, and deployed systematically so that it could carry out a strategy through to its logical conclusion. We debated the role counterinsurgency should play in this model; after all, there is a tremendous resistance to modeling the police after the military, both among researchers and in the public generally. Moreover, counterinsurgency faces its own application issues. The contemporary population-centric model of counterinsurgency is under fire for its inability to defeat the enemy in Afghanistan, where after 10 years of war the enemy has strengthened and has attained widespread public support, and where the government is widely perceived as corrupt and weak. However, the population-centric counterterrorism model may be more powerful as a policing strategy, where the government already has attained legitimacy in the general population (though legitimacy in poverty stricken minority communities is often a significant hurdle), where criminals are rarely heavily armed or trained for military discipline, where the crime problem is highly fragmented and complex, lending itself for sophisticated operations, or where local political leadership has a clear interest in protecting its own citizens.

What counterinsurgency offers is threefold. The first two contributions are security based: A strategic orientation that is mission based and a way of thinking through security problems that is at once citizen based *and* is aimed at bringing those security problems to an end. These two factors led us to adopt elements of counterinsurgency strategy, and we emphasize, not military tactics, as the way to think about what should be the mission of police: ending high levels of serious crime in urban areas. The third contribution of counterinsurgency research is that it offers a strategic integration of security and infrastructural development. This research has a more developed notion of citizen well-being than urban settings, where security is almost never integrated in any meaningful or centralized way with broader economic rebuilding and reinvestment. We find in this branch of military thought an effort to integrate security into a broader process of community development, and concrete efforts to carry out those processes in some of the most difficult places on the planet.

The purpose in adapting counterinsurgency approaches, hence, is not because they represent a more aggressive intrusion into high crime areas but because they are developed, comprehensive strategies aimed at the same end most of us would like to see in urban high crime areas—crime sharply reduced with a fulfilling quality of life for the residents. Put differently, we don't want to reject a good idea only because the Department of Defense came up with it first.

Although counterinsurgency provides a systematic way to link mission to strategic outcomes, crime mapping enables rapid feedback, analysis, and deployment. The technology of crime mapping is central to our efforts and has provided ways to tactically deploy the police to where serious crime is and to develop mission subsets, based on problem-oriented policing, to address the specific kinds of crime in high crime areas. Hence, the ability to measure successes and failures, and to immediately adapt to changes in a criminogenic environment, is possible in ways it has not been previously. In important ways, the technology of crime mapping, for its feedback capabilities, is likely the most important innovation in policing since the introduction of the patrol car a century ago. However, redeployment is based not only on rapid analysis of crime post operation but also on the rapid collection of intelligence by detectives whose primary purpose is to facilitate ongoing operations, particularly through an operation–interrogation–redeployment cycle. This also has a military sheen and has been successfully employed in compare statistics (COMPSTAT) operations.

We write with a purpose that we believe is long overdue. We have seen a large number of quite good innovations related to policing, innovations that contribute a great deal to the way police work can be improved. Indeed, if one were to survey the past 40+ years of research since the seminal "Kansas City Preventive Patrol Experiment," one would wonder if policing were even the same enterprise it was in the 1960s. However, were the same person to go into many police departments around the country, he would find far fewer differences. Beyond crime mapping, computer technology, and a slightly improved comfort level with minority and female police officers, anyone would be hard pressed to identify the differences over that half century.

We—researchers and police professionals alike—have learned a great deal about policing since the dawn of the research revolution in police work, but very little of this is apparent in routine police work. Indeed, the prevalent form of policing, as we pass the first decade of the twenty-first century, was put in place in the 1920s when the automobile was still a novel concept. We believe this is in part because no one has really figured out how all these good ideas can be systematically integrated into a better way to do policing. It is time for those of us who are interested in policing to begin to synthesize this vast body of ideas, practices, and research and think about how policing can actually be done in a better way—in a way that is more effective and so earns the legitimacy that is so often lacking in minority communities. Our hope is that this is not the end of the conversation, but the beginning, in which we start to reconsider—from the ground up—how to police better and to police in a way that is capable of more than "keeping a lid on crime."

This book transitions policing away from practices that are ineffective for dealing with serious crime. For instance, the calls-for-service model, adapted to random preventive patrol and today used almost everywhere, locks police into an operational methodology sharply out of date and with widely known crime prevention limitations. The time for tinkering with these patrol models is past; they need to be radically overhauled and largely dismantled as a primary strategy for police services. The solution is actually simple: assign police officers based on serious crime. Made possible by contemporary crime mapping processes, this solution enables line geographic deployment to focus on places with serious crime signatures. Once one begins with this deployment principle, however, almost everything else about policing changes. This book explains those changes.

Part I of the book describes the theory of mission-based policing. The first two chapters discuss central problems with policing in the current era. These problems are not new or undiscovered. They are quite well known. What we seek to provide is a new lens through which to view them, which, simply put, is that police should be strategically reorganized in a way that they can directly address serious crime.

Chapter 1 looks at the ways in which counterinsurgency strategy might contribute to contemporary policing. We believe that the potential contributions are substantial. Doubtless, many will reject our ideas out of hand once we introduce the military comparison. However, a serious comparison enables the integration of some ideas that, from the point of view of citizen politics, are quite liberal. Certainly anyone who actually spends some time in the Department of Defense literature, the Army College publications, and the writings of counterinsurgency principles will conclude that researchers there have achieved a quite remarkable complexity and sophistication of perspective.

Chapter 2 considers contemporary problems in urban policing today. These problems are all well known and thoroughly studied. What we strive to do in this book is organize the problems not in order to scold the police for practices that are largely out of their control, but to lay the groundwork for a different way to think about a crime control institution that we all already respect. In this chapter we introduce our primary and secondary themes: effectiveness through redeployment for serious crime, and legitimacy for long-term strategic success. One will note, in all subsequent chapters, the issues of effectiveness and legitimacy reemerge in one form or another.

The next three chapters present the five central principles of mission-based policing. Chapter 3 discusses the first two principles. The first is the principle of focus: If you want to do something about serious crime, do something about serious crime. This chapter rejects the contemporary tendency to deal with crime by addressing misdemeanors in the style popularized by "broken windows" and carried out as zero-tolerance policing. We view that as a failure of focus, as are programs that do something about crime by doing community-style policing or any one of a number of illusive strategies that deal with serious crime by aiming at a target other than serious crime. The second principle regards effectiveness. This chapter develops what we consider to be the core guardianship role of the police. Guardianship, we argue, emerges from three aspects of police work: background deterrence, which means that police presence in and of itself deters quite a bit crime; focused deterrence, which refers to the specific kinds of tactics police employ to deal with crime; and legitimacy, which is the respect a community holds for the police. For long-term mission success in high crime areas, we argue that all three of these elements must be in place.

Chapter 4 presents the principles of deployment and integrity. The first, deployment, means that if one wants to do something about serious crime, then officers should be deployed to where serious crime is. This principle borrows extensively from COMPSTAT and its signature capability—the systematic use of crime mapping to rapidly respond to crime. In this chapter we present the concept of layered deployment, in which three kinds of crime zones—hot zones, at-risk zones, and safe zones—receive different kinds of policing. The fourth principle, integrity, refers to mission integrity, which is the responsibility of all officers to act in accordance with tactical operations and strategies. The importance of mission integrity is particularly salient in hot zones, and tactical operations represent a component of a broader strategic endeavor. We wed Boba's (2005) command-driven model of problem-oriented policing to a strategic effort to eliminate crime systematically in hot and at-risk zones. Finally, the fifth principle, mission's end, is about the centrality of long-term planning that aims at ending high levels of crime in an area.

Chapter 5 presents the concept of logical lines of operation (LOOs). Borrowed from counterinsurgency, LOOs represent broad strategic areas of action that need to be accomplished for the ultimate success of the mission. Chapter 6 presents the first three LOOs. The first LOO, planning, emphasizes the importance of developing a systematic plan prior to the actual deployment of officers into a hot zone. The planning phase has two components. First is intelligence, which refers to the kinds of information needed to plan for police tactical operations. The second component is legitimacy. This LOO develops two categories of legitimacy planning, the development of a "community revitalization committee" modeled after weed-and-seed steering committees, which will work with the police and the community simultaneously.

The second LOO, security, argues that problem-oriented policing (POP) is the way in which the primary tactical responses to crime should be organized. All POP actions are followed by after-action reports aimed at assessing tactical success. A small cadre of detectives serve as interrogators, who are assigned to the hot zone command and whose purpose is to carry out interviews both during and immediately after operations to identify criminal suspects or take other rapid crime suppressive action. The third LOO, establish or restore essential services, argues that conditions in many urban areas today mimic the harsh conditions found in international conflicts in third world countries— absence of basic services, unemployment, and the like. The mission for this LOO is to provide a support role for local agencies who seek to provide assistance for community members facing these conditions.

Chapter 6 is the final, "rebuilding" LOO. The characteristic feature of hot zones is a long-term pattern of economic disinvestment. Though the police can suppress crime successfully, long-term success hinges on broad community coalitions, private and public, aimed at economic reinvestment in disinvested areas. Here, the police's role is to provide security for broad private and public enterprises aimed at community development, while continuing to focus on serious crime.

One of the central shortcomings of municipal governance is the lack of integration of the urban planning and the security functions, and this chapter recommends tighter liaison of these functions. The concept of business investment districts is presented as the most promising way to reinvest in hot zones, and the role of the police is to provide security operations in support of reinvestment. Boba and Santos's (2007) POP model of construction crime problem solving is presented as an example of the relationship between reinvestment and security.

Chapter 7 looks at the relationship among the LOOs. The relationship is characterized in terms of time sequencing, in which security is established prior to economic development. An analogic model of four stages, again adapted from counterinsurgency research, is used. The first stage, identify the injury, refers to intelligence planning. This is centrally important; failure to adequately identify the nature of crime or comprehend the social, cultural, and physical environment in which crime occurs can result in failure, no matter how elegant the strategy. The second stage, stop the bleeding, refers to security operations aimed at shutting down serious crime in hot zones, which is described by the security strategy developed in the second LOO. Third, inpatient care and treatment is about working with the community to make sure that basic service needs are met. The final stage, recovery, refers to economic reinvestment and is about the way in which the mayor's office and planning department, working with the police and with local businesses, enable a plan of action dedicated to community development. While these stages are sequential, it is recognized that setbacks can occur in any stage, requiring a return to a previous stage. What is important is that long-term mission success remains the focus of the police department.

Part II of the book presents an example of how a police department might be reorganized around principles of mission-based policing. Using the city of Omaha, Nebraska, and the Omaha Police Department as an example, Chapter 8 presents crime maps in terms of hot and warm spots. Three kinds of crime are examined: business, violent, and property. Overlaying the crime types by police precincts and districts, we describe the relationship between patrol beats and crime characteristics. An "all crimes" map is used to actually develop a hot zone, which is a cluster of hot and warm spots that would be the primary focus of a mission-based strategy.

Chapter 9 uses the Omaha Police Department to suggest a reorganization strategy consistent with mission-based policing that would not require the hiring of additional police personnel. The existing organizational structure, presented in detail, is modified in three ways: a Strategic Operations Command is added to the organizational chart, with personnel reassigned from other commands, for the city's hot zones. In the precinct commands, random preventive patrol is abandoned, and officers are reassigned to multidistrict areas according to the overall level of calls for services and other crime needs according to the precinct captain. And under the principle of unity of command, the precincts have a Precinct Mobile Squad whose responsibility is to address at-risk zones in their precincts.

Finally, Chapter 10 discusses issues that might be raised by the concept or applications of mission-based policing. Questions include the following:

Isn't the idea of ending crime utopian?
What might be the command problems across units?
Will we inadvertently increase victimization in relatively safe areas if we move more police into the hot spot areas?
How do we deal with the accusation of racism when we move more police into minority areas?

These and related questions form the substance of the final chapter. We recognize that there are likely many challenges to mission-based policing that we simply have not considered. Yet our purpose has been to try to transcend the world of the "taken-for-granted" by asking what would a department actually look like that wanted to end serious crime and that was organized to do so. Doubtless, many will think that this is too far-reaching a goal, too impossible at task. We, however, are unsatisfied with the idea that we cannot do better in the provision of security for our cities and our citizens. Had we stopped to ask "What obstacles will we face," we doubtless would have never written the book. Instead, we took the other track; we asked "If we could surmount the obstacles, what would that department be like?" The result is the work herein presented and our concept of a different way to police, called mission-based policing.

PART I

TOWARD A MISSION-BASED MODEL OF POLICING

Part I presents the model for mission-based policing. It is designed as practical theory, by which we mean that it is concept driven, but at every step we look toward how the model would be implemented. The model is a strategic structure for what we call crime dissipation, which refers to bringing crime down to levels not meaningfully different from relatively safe areas of the city.

The central argument in Part I is that the primary purpose of the police should be to do something about serious crime. We reverse the logic of fixing "broken windows"—serious crime can be anticipated and addressed by focusing on misdemeanor crime. We argue that is a misdirection of focus. The most destructive crime in our inner cities and poorest areas is serious crime in its many forms. Bringing down serious crime will have a wide variety of beneficial effects, from enhancement of quality of life to the creation of an urban environment conducive to business investment.

To bring down serious crime requires a long-term commitment and an articulated mission. The articulation of that mission can be achieved through logical lines of operation, which carry the mission from initial information operations to the final goal, community reinvestment and redevelopment. Importantly, each stage of the mission process requires security as a central element. Security, focused simultaneously on effectiveness and legitimacy and operationally carried out within each strategic element of the mission, is the core of our model.

We argue that the police should altogether abandon random preventive patrol across a city, and they should also should sharply cut back on the time investment in response to calls for service. Both practices are extensively discussed, and the shortcomings of both are noted. The primary purpose of the police shifts to a command-driven model where the goal is ending serious crime. A hot zone command structure is developed that can accomplish this goal in the highest crime areas. In precincts out of hot zones, a squad structure is developed to deal with crime problems that are significant but do not rise to the level of "hot spots." Selective or automobile patrol is redesigned to deal with areas with high crash numbers, recognizing contemporary findings that high crash numbers also occur in areas where high crime occurs and that suppressing one may have the diffuse benefit of lowering the other.

Of the various contemporary policing models we borrow from, compare statistics (COMPSTAT) is the one closest to mission-based policing. The mission-based model, though sharply different from COMPSTAT in important ways—for example, restructuring a department's command—consequently builds on many of COMPSTAT's core ideas. Crime mapping and rapid deployment, coupled with after-action reports that feed into subsequent operations, are central to our model. However, we abandon the idea that department operations should focus on misdemeanor crime, and we sharply increase the role of information operations that include a legitimacy component. An extended discussion of COMPSTAT is presented, and the model is compared and contrasted to COMPSTAT's features.

Finally, a neighborhood revitalization committee (NRC), modeled after the weed-and-seed steering committees and building on the stronger elements of those committees, is emplaced. The NRC represents a coalition of community principals, local preventive and youth-oriented agencies, the mayor's office (or equivalent), crime control agencies, and the local business community. It seeks to transcend the limitations of the empowerment orientation of weed-and-seed by focusing on long-term economic solutions to local problems, while keeping the empowerment component of local community identity.

1

The Unasked Question

Tell me how this ends. — General David Petraeus

The Unasked Question: How Do We End Crime?

What is the goal of conflict? Certainly it is not sustained conflict. Equally certainly, what we would want to avoid is the intergenerational transmission of conflict, where people grow up thinking the other side is evil. The goals of conflict would reasonably seem to be first, to end the conflict, second, to thwart future conflict, and third, to maintain a sustainable peace. Planning would seem to be a prerequisite, followed by strategically addressing hostilities while adapting to changing circumstances. In order to achieve that sustainable peace, conflict must be addressed, and it must be addressed especially where it is most concentrated and where its damage is the greatest. As such, it seems sensible to locate your forces where the conflict is and where it is most intense, not where it is weak or nonexistent. It also seems sensible to carry out actions in a way that directly focuses on the most dangerous elements of the conflict. In other words, we would want to use our strengths—our manpower, our resources, and our intelligence—to address the conflict in a logically and geographically direct way.

What is astonishing is that, in US policing, we do neither, at least not to any sort of adequate degree. If one looks at long-term planning in police organizations, one will find no concrete police plan in any law enforcement organization in America—nowhere—aimed at ending serious crime. If one were to look at current urban police deployment practices, one would find police deployed in every part of a city, including areas essentially empty of crime, in order to respond to calls for service. At best, we engage a relatively small proportion of officers in repetitive raiding practices in high crime areas—what police call *operations*—and redeploy our forces after raids (or operations) outside of hot spots back to their routine assignments. This tactic effectively returns control of those areas to criminals and gangs who reassert their authority and exact revenge when we leave.

Failure of long-term planning and inadequacy of deployment are nothing new. However, thinking about victory over crime and planning for the cessation of conflict is utterly alien to US policing. To understand this problem, we will begin with a consideration of another kind of conflict, the Iraq War and the efforts of General David Petraeus to bring governmental legitimacy and the rule of law after the initial US invasion and military takeover of the country.

When General Petraeus took command of Iraq in 2006, he viewed the assignment as perilous, possibly a career ender. The early reports of military action in Iraq, talking in terms of a quick victory and equally quick withdrawal, he considered optimistic. Certainly, in retrospect, they were wrong. He was famously quoted as saying *"tell me how this ends"* (Robinson, 2008).[1] The challenge, he recognized, was not military success on the battlefield. The problem was that tactical successes did not easily or straightforwardly turn into lasting peace. To the contrary, after the fall of Baghdad in 2003 the seemingly quick victories in the initial assault on Iraq degenerated into a complex mosaic of insurgency and civil war. Much of Iraq had no basic electricity, the physical infrastructure was vandalized and looted, and the government had little legitimacy. Tactical victories against Saddam Hussein's army, it seemed, had only produced chaos, and Iraq was spiraling out of control. What was needed was some way to reinvest Iraqi citizens in their country and do so during active conflict operations.

In the kind of murky, low-intensity conflict encountered in Iraq, how does one move beyond military engagement to establish economic viability and governmental legitimacy? How does one not only achieve tactical military victories but also a peaceful and sustainable end to conflict? Iraq, from Petraeus's view, was in a civil war and without governmental legitimacy or faith in the rule of law. The US Army could conduct all the tactical raids it desired, and it was quite capable of killing and imprisoning insurgents who resisted. Its military superiority was unquestioned. Yet, without addressing the broader questions of nation state building and peacemaking, there could never be victory (Robinson, 2008).

Having written his Ph.D. dissertation on counterinsurgency in Vietnam, Petraeus understood the complexity of the US endeavor in Iraq.[2] What was it that the United States was trying to accomplish through its military might? How would it know when it had accomplished its goals? In short, *what was the mission?* Moreover, Petraeus needed control of resources, and he needed the authority to make critical changes in current strategy across the theater. His work, conceptually embodied in the *U.S. Army/Marine Corps Counterinsurgency Field Manual* (Petraeus, Amos, and Nagl, 2007), set out the military strategy for success. Success would be achieved through military presence in the civilian population, through rapid action against belligerents, by seeking legitimacy of a democratically elected Iraqi government, through the reestablishment of the rule of law, and by rebuilding infrastructure, economic viability, and therein creating employment for citizens. This was the path to victory, it was the way to nation state legitimacy, and, hopefully, it was the way to a more durable peace. The mission was not military. The mission was the provision of a democratically invested citizenry and viable governance. Security was an essential precondition and accompaniment of each element of that mission.

Toward a Rethinking of Police Strategy

The applicant for police chief sits across the table from the mayor. The applicant asks the mayor *"What's your plan for ending crime here?"* The mayor spills his coffee.

The question "How does this end?" is, in US policing, the unasked question. Central to military planning, and indeed, to most of the private sector, the notion of long-term strategic planning toward end goals and long-term success is central. In policing, it is rarely considered. The inability to solve the crime problem in major urban centers is ingrained in the US psyche and haunts the police, police researchers, and ordinary citizens. Imagine a chief's preemployment interview with a mayor of a major US city, asking what the plan was to end crime. "Crime's gone on long enough here," the chief applicant says. "What are you doing to solve it? What's the plan for ending it?"

One can imagine the mayor stammering, trying to fit the question into his preexisting mindset about crime, poverty, and other deeply entrenched and seemingly unsolvable urban problems. Crime can't just be ended, or can it? That is the question this book addresses. The question, how to end crime, has two closely related components: (1) that the purpose, strategy, and deployment of US policing should be about strategically ending crime, and (2) that a model of policing can be developed whose purpose is to end crime as we know it in major urban centers.

Tell me how this ends is the question that should organize the deployment and strategy of US police organizations. What is it that we do that would achieve a lasting victory over crime (victory defined as the reduction of serious crime in hot zones to levels not significantly different from safe zones or low-crime areas)? The answer lies in the method of deployment of the police, in building a true command structure for the police—not the current "command and cajole" structure that has no command force—and in focusing on crime prevention efforts, recognizing that prevention of crime is integral to establish a lasting peace and a necessary precursor to the rebuilding of communities.

And how do we get there? What, specifically, is the plan? What is the strategy for carrying out the plan, and what are the steps to achieve that strategy? How do we know if the strategy is successful? We do not ask these questions, though problem-oriented policing represents a significant step in this direction. Consider the alternative: We continue down the current path, which can be summed by the phrase "keeping the lid on crime," carrying out an endless succession of arrests that have virtually no impact on crime but instead have significant backfiring effects that sum to the destruction of urban communities. Like General Petraeus, it is time we in policing seek real solutions to profound security problems in our urban centers by asking the question how does it end?

What's Wrong with American Policing?

There is something wrong with US policing. It is not that officers who carry out the work of law enforcement are doing a bad job. Given the unpredictable and dangerous work they're tasked to carry out, they're doing a pretty good job. Neither does the problem lie in some short-coming of command: Commanders are responsible to a wide munici-pal audience for the actions of their organization and are often widely involved in many different activities in their communities. It is not a failure of the police to recognize crime as an important concern; they are doing what they have been taught and what citizens ask them to do, and though we might identify shortcomings, police represent and enact the will of the state, formalized through peace officer standards and training academies.

The problem with policing doesn't lie within the law either: It is not that officers' hands are tied by overly cumbersome due process protections, which officers may grouse about but grudgingly respect. It is not a failure to be tough on crime given the opportunity, which officers occasionally seek too energetically. What's wrong with US policing is actually quite simple: *It is not geographically deployed to fight serious crime*. It is deployed to respond to citizens' calls for service, which rarely have much to do with serious crime. All we think we know about US policing—what we think of as effective practices, the role of discretion in police work, what constitutes good policing and good police, and especially what we think about the administration of patrol officers—flows from this deployment model and from the organizational design that has emerged to support this model.

This book presents a new model of policing. The model is devel-oped from four contemporary innovations in urban security: compare statistics (COMPSTAT) crime mapping, Boba's model of problem-oriented policing, the weed-and-seed programs sponsored by the Department of Justice, and Department of Defense (DOD) counter-insurgency security practices developed from US stabilization opera-tions in Iraq and Afghanistan. Each of these innovations is discussed later in this book. The model we propose takes these innovations and combines them in a way that focuses urban policing in the United States on serious crime and away from its current emphasis on calls for service, and then uses a crime dissipation platform to launch revital-ization efforts. By *crime dissipation*, we mean the permanent lowering of crime in an area from "hot zone" levels, which refers to levels sig-nificantly higher than those in the surrounding city, to normal levels, by which we mean a nonsignificant difference between levels in the city and levels in the hot zone. The core argument of this model is (1) that the police should deploy, on a permanent basis and at high levels, officers to hot zones, and (2) that they should be mission focused on serious crime in those hot zones. By *mission focused* we mean that a command-driven model of police deployment identifies the dissipation of crime as the primary mission—the central organizing feature of its mission-set—and that all activities are strategically organized around operations intended to reduce crime.

Central to this book is our belief that the police *can and should* play a role in doing something about "root causes" of crime. However, we also believe that root-cause problems cannot be addressed until security is established. This view reverses traditional criminological thought that social conditions have to be fixed prior to doing something about crime. Long-term crime dissipation requires that economic opportunities are adequate and service supports are in place in order to dissipate crime in hot zones. This work needs to be carried out under adequate security protection and the police need to be at the security center. However, it also requires the leadership of the city government and, as needed, grants from the federal government, just as federal support provides economic assistance for recovering areas in counterterrorism operations.

This model is not to be interpreted as a guide for strategic deployment to crack down on high crime areas. It must be emphasized at the outset that the "iron fist" of the model, the permanent deployment of large numbers of officers to high crime areas as a first priority, is balanced with a central concern for justice and for legitimacy, *as they are perceived by inhabitants in high crime areas*. For this model to succeed over the long term, strategic police intervention must be followed by the rebuilding of local infrastructural supports and the enabling of economic viability. In other words, the iron fist is married to municipal–federal–local efforts to rebuild areas after they are secured. The reduction and dissipation of crime are not the end goals of this proposal, but rather the end of the beginning, the establishment of areal security, from which significant and steady redevelopment of physical and economic infrastructure can proceed.

Legitimacy and effectiveness are notions that may seem to pull against each other. In order for efforts to be effective, they may sometimes be furthered by aggressive police practices, and efforts to reinforce the legitimacy of government, on the other hand, may be facilitated by reaching out to the community and engaging in a variety of activities that do not seem to do much about crime. Yet both are important. As counterinsurgent researchers have noted, long-term successful stability operations require both legitimacy and effectiveness. Figure 1.1 displays a graphic adapted from Parker (2007: 4).

In Figure 1.1, legitimacy and effectiveness are both characterized as axes on a quadrant. In Parker's original figure the legitimacy and effectiveness axes were used to characterize counterinsurgency operations and indicated that actions are carried out by anti-insurgent forces that continually seek to increase both legitimacy and effectiveness over time. By increasing both, the ability of the opposition to claim greater legitimacy is eroded. In an urban policing example, as presented in Figure 1.1, we have retained the counterinsurgency conception but reframed the model for police activity. We can see in the figure two central principles of the policing model proposed in this monograph:

1. Effectiveness without legitimacy results in strategic failure from lack of local support.
2. Legitimacy without effectiveness results in strategic failure from inability to protect citizens.

Hence, a successful strategy must operationally plan for effectiveness, and it also must operationally plan for legitimacy.

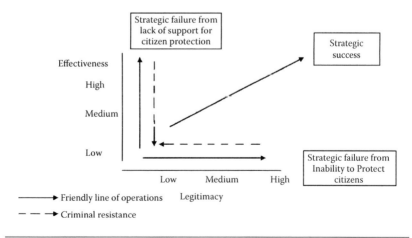

Figure 1.1 The relationship between efficiency and effectiveness in successful stability operations.

Consider efforts to act tactically against a powerful gang. In a hot zone a gang may claim greater effectiveness in protecting locals and intimidate the local population into accepting their presence. However, some gang suppression efforts focused on identification and regular contact of gang members and leaders have been somewhat effective at reducing gang influence. However, one must also address legitimacy issues as well. If the police are seen as a heavy handed presence that is as likely to bring the same quantity of pressure against local nongang youth for minor infractions as well as gang youth, the community may pull together in efforts to protect their young. Moreover, many community service organizations work with gang members and do not want to let the police have access to their records or their contacts, which would undercut their own legitimacy with gang members and in the community. The police will often need to work with such groups, while respecting their need for professional distance, in order to maintain legitimacy with gangs. Operation Cease-Fire, discussed below, represents an attempt to address these issues tactically.

Legitimacy and Effectiveness: Operation Cease-Fire

Operation Cease-Fire, administered by the Chicago Project for Violence Prevention (CPVP), was developed to mitigate gun crimes, especially gang-related shootings and retaliatory violence in hot spots (Skogan, Hartnett, Bump, and Dubois, 2008). Central to the CPVP strategy were "violence interrupters," who:

> worked the street in the night, talking to gang leaders, distraught friends and relatives of recent shooting victims, and others who were positioned to initiate or sustain cycles of violence. ES-2.

Interrupters were recruited from the hot zones in which they worked. They were:

> "culturally appropriate messengers" who were enough street savvy to maneuver through an often rough-and-tumble environment, and they often had to pass muster with gang members. ... They gained legitimacy because many had themselves "lived the life." The archetypal Cease-Fire staff member had been in trouble, turned his life around, and now wanted to help others do the same. ES-3.

Operation Cease-Fire was able to significantly lower crime in the hot zones in which it had violence interrupters and counselors. Success was measured by comparing changes in program statistics to comparable areas where Cease-Fire was not operating. Its successes stemmed from two sources. The work of the outreach workers (the violence interrupters and counselors) was able to sometimes break the cycles of violence that characterized the areas they worked in. It was also successful because the workers were themselves at-risk individuals, many of whom had previous prison records, and the employment in the program itself provided them with alternatives to the illicit economy of local street hustles.

One of the central problems with Cease-Fire was its failure to obtain buy-in from the Chicago Police Department. Staff tended to avoid the police, fearing that association would delegitimize them with local gangs. And police distrusted the staff, concerned that program practices could lead to crime opportunities among a generally unsavory lot. This example shows the difficulties of establishing legitimacy in a high crime area. Local groups, such as Cease-Fire, derive their legitimacy from working with gang members because they "know the street," because some of the group's members have been gang members before or have relatives involved in gangs, and because they are perceived by local community members as genuinely understanding and caring about the community. They cannot maintain their connections to and legitimacy with gangs and at the same time make their knowledge and records available to the police. However, outreach groups can work toward a common cause with the police on community anticrime boards, where each works with the other in service of broad community goals. Consequently, the police must be attentive to the way they carry out their work both in terms of the need to suppress gang activity and the avoidance of actions that undercut their legitimacy, backfiring by increasing community secrecy about gang activity.

A Military Contribution to US Policing

"*What do you need here?*" McChrystal asked.

A translator turned the general's words into Pashto.

"*We need schools!*" one Afghan called back. "*Schools!*" "*We're working on that,"* McChrystal said. *"Those things take time."* McChrystal walked some more, engaging another group of Afghans. He posed the same question. *"Security,"* a man said. *"We need security. Security first, then the other things will be possible."* (Filkins, 2009)

"Security first, then the other things will be possible" is the phrase that clarifies the military mission in contemporary US counterinsurgency efforts in Iraq and Afghanistan. Those "other things" include adequate schools, infrastructure, economic development, and rule of law, and they have become part of the military counterinsurgency mission. The thread that weaves through the "other things" and ties them together is security. It is, however, a particular notion of security that is termed *population-centric*. The term population-centric refers to the fact that the goal of counterinsurgency is not the destruction of the enemy but the protection of resident populations, contested by the enemy for shelter and support. This section is about the military conception of security, as understood from a counter-insurgent population-centric model, and how that model can contribute in a novel and significant way to the reduction of crime in US cities.

The notion that military concepts and practices have something to contribute to US policing will doubtlessly alarm many readers. Liberals will fear that any proposal to introduce military practices in an urban policing setting will legitimize violence by the state against its citizens. Images of Kent State University (where the national guard, under command directive, killed four unarmed students during an anti-Vietnam rally in 1970) crystallized the political left's fears of military intervention in domestic affairs for several subsequent generations. The political right, on the other hand, is staunchly opposed to any effort to increase any image of US military action into the nation's affairs. The combined and potent political symbols of "state's rights" and the "right to bear arms" under the Twelfth Amendment mobilize conservative support against a broader military presence, particularly if it were seen as a federal intrusion into local issues or usurpation of "states rights." Those who espouse these concerns, both of which are political staples of US governance, fail to understand the breadth of contemporary counterinsurgency practices, the issue to which we turn next.

Breadth of Counterinsurgent Military Practices

Military or DOD practices and urban policing or Department of Justice (DOJ) practices are different in a variety of ways. Consider their respective scopes of operation. The operative goal of urban police is, for the most part, keeping a lid on problems. At the street level, this means that officers go from call to call, individually solving a large mass of public order problems, doing so relatively rapidly—depending on the frequency of calls for service—and then moving on to the next problem. Urban police officers, consequently, tend to deal with most individuals in nonarrest ways that provide short-term solutions, what Caldero (2006) once described as "in your face policing." Officers tend to move from one problem to the next, driven by calls for service, developing quick solutions to conflicts between people, usually through threats about future police actions if the problem continues. Police, for example, may tell a drunken man, who is having a family beef with his wife, to leave the premises. He is summarily instructed that if he does not leave, or if he returns later, he will be arrested.

If someone is arrested, the police are the front end of an adjudication and incarceration process that invokes a sequence of decision-makers in other organizations, and the responsibility of the police in that particular case recedes as a felon moves further into the criminal justice system and into incarceration. However, postincarceration, individuals may again come to the attention of the police. Indeed, a high level of recidivism is one of the enduring and unsolvable features of modern penal practices.

Police success in their work is summed up by the aphorism "keep the lid on things," which means to try to provide enough police presence, given existing budget constraints, to keep crime from getting worse. Hence, the role of the police is ubiquitous in its public setting but brief in the everyday lives of the citizens with whom it comes into contact, and it plays a quite limited role in criminal justice processes due to its focus of energies on maintaining general public order.

Contemporary counterinsurgency is much broader in scope. Like urban policing, central to its purposes is the establishment and maintenance of security. However, the work of counterinsurgency, under contemporary population-centric models, extends through the "clear and hold" initial conflict stages to the reestablishment of local governance, rebuilding of infrastructure, facilitation of employment, and facilitation of viable and legitimate governance. In other words, counterinsurgency, unlike urban policing, views as central to its work the continual development of long-term viable infrastructure and governance in areas occupied by US forces, and in which security is only one, though the central, continuing element. The prescription for counterinsurgency success is, as noted above, the "establishment of a lasting peace." This is a substantially higher mark than "keeping the lid on things." This can, and we believe should, be the mark set for contemporary urban policing in high crime areas as well.

The fundamental difference between operational scope, comparing urban police and counterinsurgency, is presented in Figure 1.2. Two models of policing are shown: the current US policing model and a counterinsurgency model hypothetically applied to the police. The counterinsurgency model is adapted from and summarized

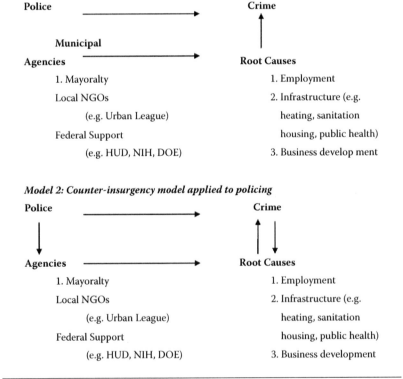

Figure 1.2 Comparative security models applied to a domestic urban setting.

in the *U.S. Army/Marine Corps Counterinsurgency Field Manual* (Petraeus, Amos, and Nagl, 2007; see also Kilcullen, 2008). The urban policing model is developed from the authors' knowledge of existing practices and represents a typical police agency in an urban setting. Both share the same underlying variables: the police, the root causes of crime (with a list of examples beneath), and a list of municipal agency types (such as the Urban League) that deal with the root causes.

The difference in the two models is symbolized by two arrows added to the *counterinsurgency model*. The first added arrow extends from the police to agencies responsible for dealing with root causes. According to this model, the police not only engage in crime directly, but have practices that are integrated into the agencies that are responsible for dealing with the social conditions and urban problems across the area. To borrow a phrase from the military, the police, under this model, are engaged in a "full spectrum" fight against crime, not simply or only in an "enemy-centric" repetitive raiding (or operations) approach characteristic of contemporary urban policing.[3]

The second added arrow extends from crime to root causes. This arrow is intended to emphasize the notion that security is a prerequisite for economic investment, viable infrastructure, and governmental legitimacy. The recognition that security is essential for economic development, central to counterinsurgent efforts, is almost absent in contemporary research on crime control, which views root causes as either causal to crime (liberal view) or irrelevant to crime (conservative view). The counterinsurgency model recognizes that crime must be addressed in order to do something about root causes, whether the cause is economic investment, education inadequacies, or the stabilization and enhancement of real property.

These two added arrows also suggest three programmatic changes in American policing:

1. Police work directly with youth services and other community agencies as well as the mayor's office on "root cause" issues. The provision of security focused on those issues would not be on an ad hoc or operational basis but would involve permanent assignments based on strategic assessments of crime.

2. Police provide security throughout an area with the goal of permanently securing, so that community and city groups, whether representing the mayor's office, nongovernmental offices, or federal investment, can address the root problems.

3. Because the ultimate goal is the establishment of a lasting peace (defined as crime rates not significantly different from safe zones), specific police practices are primarily crime preventive in orientation, and only secondarily are they reactive.

The strength of the counterinsurgency model is that the US military, and it alone, has significant experience in developing full spectrum practices and protocols aimed at a lasting peace. Full spectrum means that one begins with areas that have serious security problems and transitions those communities through imposed security, to self-security, to economic reinvigoration, and finally to long-term stability with an emphasis on the legitimacy of government and rule of law. There is no parallel organization, program, or government protocol in contemporary urban life that takes on a task of this reach, let alone succeeds in it. It is our argument that those features of the counterinsurgency model that have been thoroughly studied, and that have emerged from a history of both successful and unsuccessful interventions, can provide the missing link between what is already known about policing and crime prevention and what is necessary (but missing) in order to achieve the reachable goal of crime dissipation in urban areas.

On Comparing Counterinsurgency and Policing

One might argue that policing should not be compared to counterinsurgency, and for some good reasons. Insurgencies are organized resistance, and heavily armed insurgents can inflict significant casualties on an occupying force. While this can happen in urban policing in the United States, it is unlikely. To the contrary, the outcome of most serious crime is not insurgency against the police, but victimization of citizens.

We contend, however, that the fragmented nature of criminal activity, spread as it is across myriad micro settings and absent central organization, creates a highly complex criminogenic environment without focus or leadership. In this sense, high crime environments are more difficult to deal with than counterinsurgent settings. Moreover, with regard to gangs, a limitedly systematic organization can take on the characteristic of an organized insurgency, but the presence of many gangs involved in turf conflicts and ongoing armed violence, common in urban areas in the United States, is a significant and highly decentralized threat to public security.

Urban areas where gangs flourish are rife with crime accelerants, such as poverty, economic decay, available building structures suitable for crime activity, lack of employment, proportionately large numbers of youth, easy access to drugs and alcohol, and broad and largely uncontrollable access to firearms. In these areas, resident youth are highly recruitable by gangs, analogous to recruitment by insurgents in state conflicts. Research tends to show that such areas often have high levels of robbery, family violence, and other kinds of violent crimes. Many of them have endured long-term residential segregation and poverty intensification by segregationist practices and from contemporary mainstream hostility, which are additional crime accelerants.

Urban high crime areas are consequently analogous to mosaic insurgency conflicts; no single strategy can resolve an entrenched and enduring crime problem. One could reasonably call such areas, which also tend to be hot spots for violent crime, mosaic crime environments. The central problem in both is the same: how to establish permanent security and stabilization in an area with substantial infrastructural and economic problems, and in which a basic absence of security precludes infrastructural and economic development. Consequently, though the central threat dynamics of urban policing and military counterinsurgency differ, both share a high degree of complexity and can be described as complex "mosaic conflict" security problems.

The Issue of Discourse

An additional strength of using the counterinsurgency model is that it provides a different discourse through which to consider crime. Currently, crime prevention and control practices are emotionally freighted by the terminology of conservative or liberal discourse. Practices consequently become symbolic targets in US political life. Notions such as community policing and due process protections, for instance, tend to be rejected out of hand by conservatives, not so much for what they mean, but because they presage liberal views on crime control. Liberals, on the other hand, tend to reject without forethought zero-tolerance policing, three strikes laws, and broken windows, not for what they try to achieve, but because they herald a conservative crime control argument.

A counterinsurgency discourse recombines and reconstitutes the liberal and conservative discourse in new and unexpected ways. Consider the counterinsurgency term *accelerant*. This is defined as local community or regional features that intensify insurgent activity. Accelerants are problems faced by local citizens that consequently have to be dealt with in population-centric stabilization operations. Accelerants in counterinsurgency include living conditions, the presence of armed insurgents in the community, and the like. Applied to urban police, examples include gangs (symbolically meaningful to conservatives) and poverty (symbolically meaningful to liberals). Both are accelerants in that they contribute to crime, and consequently, addressing both is part of the strategic structure of crime prevention. A military discourse, consequently, carries the potential to recombine politically polar terms under a common anticrime strategy.

The counterinsurgency discourse offers one of those rare historical moments to reconsider crime practices, both conservative and liberal, and to identify and consider, with lessened political bias, those that address specific crime problems the most effectively. This book will consequently include many elements that are quite conservative as well as elements that are quite liberal. That is because we implicitly support a greater appreciation of *both* conservative and liberal practices and conceptions in order to solve the riddle of crime in US society.

Overview of Core Elements in Mission-Based Policing

The question that drives this book is: *What would a department look like that was organized and deployed to bring an end to the high levels of serious crime in major urban areas?* The answer to the question, though simple in principle, is complex because of its far-reaching implications for policing. It requires a rethinking about virtually everything regarding how police work is currently carried out. What we slowly realized as we worked on this book, and what we want to try to convey at this early point, is how far police organization and practice is from such a crime-fighting model. The dominant model of policing that we have today is a political model. It is designed around making the greatest number of citizens relatively happy with their police officers, and to do so in a highly charged political environment that characterizes most urban landscapes. If citizens are happy with their police, then the mayor is happy and the chief is happy. Consequently, police officers are everywhere concerned with how fast they can respond to calls for service, how quickly they can take a call and write a report when needed, and then how quickly they can move on to the next call. And they are deployed around a city so that they can respond to the greatest number of citizens. Indeed, for many departments, the signature measure of how well they are doing is not reported crime levels but the average speed with which they respond to calls. To be sure, departments have serious crime units, homicide units, and the like. But these are secondary to the primary budgetary expenditure in all organizations, which is the development of a district or precinct overlay of the city so that officers can be assigned to maximize the speed of their response to calls for service. Moreover, we will argue that even units specifically designed to fight crime are not organized in a particularly effective way, in that they are based on a repetitive raiding model of operational activity.

We decided to present a different model, one that is actually designed so that police organizations can do something about serious crime. This book is dedicated to the proposition that the high levels of serious or hot spot crime characteristic of poverty stricken urban areas can be permanently lowered. This simple and straightforward idea, once located at the heart of the police function, changes a great deal about police work. Those changes are represented in several areas of organizational behavior, identified and briefly discussed below.

The Core Idea: A Mission Basis for Police Work

The most important element of this model is providing police departments with a mission that is tangible and measured. When we look at police departments today, we note that they have a number of goals related to public service, crime control, and public order, and often have mission statements that speak to these varied (and often amorphous) goals. When we speak of mission, we are not alluding to police adhering to their missions of "to protect and serve" and the like, but to concrete, measurable missions that are more aligned with military missions. Indeed, police are multiservice agencies, providing a wide variety of services such as suppressive enforcement, highway safety, event security, licensing, organization of neighborhood watch and citizen patrols, and many others. They are complex bureaucracies, and their complexity derives both from their efforts to sell their legitimacy to the public and from their efforts to do something about crime. These various organizational goals often exist in uneasy alliance, with emphases varying depending on budgetary constraints, the political will, and the chief's prerogatives. The notion of a mission, on the other hand, means that the organization is focused on a *particular* long-term outcome, and that its work is strategically organized at each step to reach that outcome.

The mission we speak of is *lowering serious crime in high crime areas to levels no higher than safe areas of a city, and doing so on a permanent basis.* By serious crime we mean violent felony crime and property felony crime. By high crime areas, we refer to hot spots as developed in works such as Braga and Weisburd (2006). By safe areas we mean the average crime levels of areas outside of hot spots. By lowering crime, we mean that there should be no significant or substantive difference in levels of crime between areas that are identified as hot spots and other areas of a city. To achieve their mission, the police should be deployed according to the geographic distribution of serious crime rather than the ubiquitous calls-for-service model characteristic of contemporary district-based deployment.

The notion of mission-directed organizations has been elsewhere noted. In management literature, the mission-directed organization has been described as a "management by missions." For instance, Cardona and Rey (2008) describe a mission-based management model, according to which organizational elements are strategically aligned to accomplish specific tasks in pursuit of an overarching goal. This model, management by missions, is defined as an organization that engages all elements of a company in order to achieve a corporate mission. The corporate mission is operationalized through specific objectives that are viewed as vital for the mission. The purpose of the management by missions philosophy is to ensure that all elements are working in a way that facilitates specific mission achievement (Cardona and Rey, 2008).

The concept of a mission-directed policing has also been noted in police research (Willis, Mastrofski, and Weisburd, 2007). Braga and Weisburd (2010: 231), referring to Willis et al., note that "there is a greater need for environmental support for a focused mission for local police in the United States and the need to establish reliable and well understood crime control technologies that the police will employ."

However, the notion of a mission basis for municipal police work has not been systematically developed. This is in part because the notion of "mission" itself has been identified by many departments (and other organizations) as a philosophy rather than a goal, and as such, has kept departments from identifying and employing missions that are able to be fully achieved, or even measured. This book endeavors to develop such a model.

We have selected the counterinsurgency model of mission organization over the management model suggested by Cardona and Rey because it is strategically aligned to address three important features of any long-term solution to crime in urban settings. First, legitimacy is central to any effort to permanently lower crime, and legitimacy is seen as a cornerstone of counterinsurgency. Second, economic revitalization of areas suffering long-term disinvestment also needs to be addressed. The "management by missions" corporate model only deals with specific corporate objectives. The counterinsurgency model, on the other hand, recognizes that many different elements of public life have to participate in the mission for long-term crime dissipation to occur. Third, a mission, to succeed, requires that all elements in the organization work toward the same goal and do so for an extended period. This means that commanders develop strategy and review tactics, and that line personnel carry out the decisions that commanders make. The mission model is consequently a command-integrity model: line personnel are responsible to the command structure of the organization, up the chain of command. The highly discretionary, low visibility character of contemporary policing ceases under this model, replaced by a command-driven model focused on strategic adaptation to the long-term goal of permanent reduction of serious crime in high crime areas.

Philosophy: Principles Aimed at Fulfilling the Mission

The philosophy that provides the intellectual and ethical foundation of the mission model is described by five principles. Those principles are:

1. The principle of focus. In order to do something about serious crime one should focus on serious crime. This principle seems almost banal until one considers the extent to which contemporary policing (and a sizable quantity of academic research) has tried to do something about serious crime by focusing on misdemeanors. This principle is realized by having police carry out operations specifically designed to address serious crime.

2. The principle of effectiveness. The police can have a significant and permanent effect on crime. This chapter draws from the work associated with environmental criminology to argue that effectiveness derives from a guardianship role, which includes elements of deterrence and of presence in hot spots.

3. The principle of layered deployment. Police should be located where crime is, which refers to hot spots, and is driven by the geographic analysis of serious crime. This is a "layered" rather than "hot spot" model of deployment in that a command is developed that "layers" deployment for serious crime on top of existing patrol activities, though those activities are also reconceptualized.

4. The principle of mission integrity. All elements in the chain of command are responsible to the mission. This means that all of the officers are responsible for carrying out the operations, tactics, and strategies enacted to achieve the mission. This is a sharp reconceptualization of police work; it means that officers follow orders of commanders. Nor is this principle limited to hot zones, but extended across the organization, so that precinct commanders in relatively safe areas also have command responsibility and control for the deployment and activities of the officers under them.

5. The principle of mission's end. The mission is to end crime at the levels and intensity that it is experienced in hot zones. The principle of mission's end is that all aspects of assignment, deployment, command integrity, and mission coherence are

guided by the principal mission, and that planning at every stage focuses on what it takes to successfully achieve, and thereby end, the mission. This principle mandates that a strategic structure be emplaced that can encompass the complex ends that the mission requires, which is our next topic.

Strategy: The Steps Taken to Fulfill the Mission

Mission-based policing uses the logical lines of operation security model. Logical lines of operation are an adaptation of the traditional military notion of physical lines of operation, modified to apply to conflicts in which descriptions of positional reference on a battlefield are not helpful. They provide a strategic framework through which the mission can be accomplished. Each line of operation (LOO) focuses on a substantively different strategic concern and hence represents a stage toward achieving the mission. Though the LOOs cover substantively different areas of the urban environment and make use of different resources, each has a significant security component. The four LOOs in our model are:

1. Information operations. Information operations, developed from intelligence led policing, anticipates all practices. Intelligence is developed during initial and ongoing strategic planning, tactical planning, and operational activity.
2. Security operations. Security operations represent the specific activities carried out in hot zones and are based on a redesigned problem-oriented policing concept based on squad deployment.
3. Establish and restore essential services. This represents the integration of police and urban planning, both of which focus on addressing the social problems that act as accelerants for serious crime.
4. Security for economic development. This addresses the final phase of the security/planning linkage, which is about economic rebuilding of areas suffering long-term disinvestment processes.

Tactics: The Operational Practices Aimed at Achieving Strategic Success

Tactical deployment is summarized by the phrase *enforcement-initiated problem solving*. This deployment model recognizes the value in the highly focused problem model developed by Goldstein (1977), but also argues that problem solving has to be focused on the way in which it ultimately addresses crime. Hence, this tactical model has three elements: crime control and suppression, problem solving, and squad deployment.

Tactical deployment also is located inside an intelligence cycle. Deployment occurs after operational planning, and information gained during deployment furthers subsequent operational planning and problem-solving assessment of success. Hence, each crime response or problem-oriented policing (POP) deployment is not a stand-alone operation, but occurs within an intelligence loop that constantly monitors squad activity and assesses its effectiveness toward achieving the overall mission.

Organizational Design: The Organizational Structure for Strategic Success

Command reorganization for mission-based policing is located along two organizational dimensions: the creation of a hot zone command, and the realignment of precinct commands. The hot zone command is a command unit, organized at a level equal with a precinct command, that is assigned specifically to deal with serious crime in hot zones. Precinct commands are realigned. By realignment we mean that the precinct commands are not reorganized, but are expanded to include a deployable squad for crime events and adapted to command integrity. Additionally, patrol assignments to particular districts or to clusters or districts are always command dependent and are flexible, driven by command responsiveness to changes in crime as well as to citizen calls for service.

Both hot zone and precinct commands operate under the principle of command integrity. Command integrity means that line officers take orders from unit commanders and on up the chain. The principle of *unity of effort* applies here, which means that all elements of the department that are pertinent to the mission act together, and their actions flow from coherent and shared planning.

Deployment: The Principle of Assigning Officers to Areas to Most Effectively Carry Out Tactical Operations

The basis for deployment of line personnel changes from the contemporary model, which is district based so that officers can respond to calls for service and create a city-wide sense of omnipresence, to deployment based on the frequency, quantity, and seriousness of crime. The mission-based model relies on the analysis of hot spots and the permanent redeployment of police according to hot spot analysis. The location of hot spots becomes the first priority of deployment. Priority deployment is carried out by operators whose primary work is the establishment of security in hot zones. By hot zone we mean hot spots that tend to cluster together. Second priority deployment is for officers in at-risk zones, where crime is still high but not as dynamic as in hot zones. Third priority is in response to calls for service and is based on the ongoing assessment of needs from precinct commanders.

Endnotes

1. This quote is attributed to a conversation Petraeus held with an embedded journalist, Rick Atkinson, in March or April 2003 (Robinson, 2008: 88).
2. The title of the dissertation was "The American Military and the Lessons of Vietnam: A Study of Military Influence and the Use of Force in the Post-Vietnam Era." Petraeus received his Ph.D. from Princeton University's Woodrew Wilson School of Public and International affairs in 1987.
3. Discussed later, repetitive raiding refers to the practice of carrying out an operation from outside the area and securing it, only to leave it and have it fall back into enemy hands. Enemy-centric approaches here lead to repetitive raiding, believing that the enemy is vanquished, only to find he or she has retaken the town in the intervals between operations. Most police operations have the character of repetitive raiding.

2

THE RELATIONSHIP BETWEEN POLICE AND CRIME

Consider the police from a citizen's perspective. What do citizens think is the relationship between police and crime? When citizens think of US police, they look to them as enforcers of the law. Indeed, the term *law enforcement* is often used in place of *policing* when the occupation is mentioned. There is little doubt in the public's mind that the purpose of the police is to do law enforcement, which means to do something about crime, especially serious crime.

The United States employs a lot of police to do something about crime. According to recent statistics on policing, in 2003 there were an estimated 683,396 full-time sworn officers in the United States, not including federal employees (see Bureau of Justice statistics, 2006). At a median average annual salary of $45,780, the cost of police officers to the United States is about $31,285,868,880. US police officers are collectively paid just over $31 billion annually to do something about crime.

With all that investment in law enforcers, why can't they do something about crime, beyond just "keeping a lid" on it? Here's the challenge: Is there any place in the United States where we can look at crime and say "There! The police have finally gotten rid of all that nasty crime in that place. Praise the Lord!" The answer is, without belaboring the emphatic point, "no." To the contrary, the characteristic feature of crime is its persistence. Once an area becomes a high crime area—a hot spot, in contemporary parlance—it tends to stay a hot spot.

Police do not ignore hot spots. To the contrary, they deploy operations aimed at specific crimes, crime types, and criminals in hot spots. Yet, operations do not have much long-term effect. The police move into a hot spot with a large visible display of authority, make a lot of street contacts with a few arrests mixed in, and then they leave. The hard cases, street smart criminals and gang leaders who are at the center of crime activity, melt away when the police come in, and then they return when the police leave.

We recommend a new way to prioritize police work that we, again adapting counterinsurgency language, call *persistent presence*. First, however, we will frame the problem of "deployment" in greater detail.

Framing the Deployment Problem: Police and Calls for Service

We think of police as law enforcers, so it would seem that we would want to put them where crime is. This is the deployment issue as we see it: What is the best way to deploy police across a city in order to best respond to serious crime? The answer to the deployment problem is surprising, and even more surprising is that it has not been reconsidered in any sort of fundamental way in nearly a century.

Think of the deployment problem this way. If I ask a citizen what the basis for the geographic deployment of the police is, the citizen will invariably answer "crime." If I ask a police commander what the basis of deployment is, she or he will start to say "crime," then hesitate a moment and say "calls for service" or something like that. Unfortunately, the geographic deployment of officers on a calls for service basis—the foundation of contemporary policing— sharply curtails their ability to do something significant about serious crime.

Here is how the calls for service basis for deployment works. Cities are covered in grids, often called sectors. Omaha, Nebraska, for example, is a city of 800,000, organized into 78 sectors. Officers are assigned to those sectors in order to respond to 911 calls and assist citizens as needed. Departments take pride in their ability to respond to calls for service from citizens in a quick fashion, so sector deployment is tied to the goal of rapid response to citizen calls.

Citizens, however, do not actually use police for serious crime. Citizens use police to solve problems that they do not know how to deal with. Egon Bittner (1974) referred to this as the *something-ought-not-to-be-happening-about-which-something-ought-to-be-done-NOW!* function of policing. Unfortunately, that *something* is far more likely to be a barking dog or noisy neighbor than a burglar or armed robber. Statistics on police calls for service consistently show that minor issues, including service and misdemeanor calls, vastly outnumber serious crime calls.

So what explains the ubiquitous use of the calls for service model? It is deeply rooted in the history and traditions of modern policing. August Vollmer, widely described as the patriarch of modern policing, developed the model of random preventive patrol (RPP), according to which police officers drive around more or less unpredictably within specific areas, creating the impression of "omnipresence," which means that criminals will never know where police officers are—they could be anywhere and everywhere. This model was developed concurrently with the widespread expansion of the patrol car in the 1920s, and RPP became central to police work as the way to do vehicular patrolling.

In 1968, AT&T began providing citizens with an emergency call number, 911, that was intended to boost the rapidity of the police response to imminent victimization, and by implication to better enable them to respond to serious crime. By the beginning of the twenty-first century, over 95 percent of US addresses had enhanced 911, which meant that the police could automatically locate a 911 caller's address based on the telephone number from which the call originated. The 911 systems dovetailed comfortably with random preventive patrol: officers could be assigned to do RPP in a sector—a relatively small geographic area—and could also respond to calls for service in that sector. When a city was fully under the sector "blanket," whereby no part of the city is left without RPP and rapid response, no citizen call would be overlooked. Today, US policing is largely locked into that model; officers drive around within sectors, seek to act therein as an "omnipresent" deterrent to crime, and respond rapidly to calls for service. What's the problem with this? Both RPP and calls for service are important for the public persona of police, and the public might expect that the force would be able to address crime and calls for service simultaneously and seamlessly. Because crime happens "out there" where citizens are, and also is widely perceived to happen to those citizens, it seems like a quick call from a frightened citizen would be a good way for police to find and respond to crime.

There are, however, two primary problems with this way of thinking. The first is that calls for service is an inadequate (though commonly used) proxy for serious crime deterrence. The second problem is that the calls for service model quickly depletes police resources. Because of these problems, calls for service actually *impedes* crime reduction efforts.

Calls for Service Is a Misleading "Measurement" of Crime

The calls for service model is inherently misleading; it seems like it would be a good proxy for serious crime deterrence but it is not. In local newspapers, serious crime occupies a revered place in the pantheon of hot stories. What citizen is not fully aware that, if something bad happens, he or she should call the police? The 911 call, to them, may be the only available lifeline. The field of academic research has tended to reinforce this view. Numerous researchers have used calls for service as a measurement of crime (for example, see Bursik and Grasmick, 1993; Sherman, Buerger, and Gartin, 1989; Warner and Pierce, 1993). Across these different groups, citizens, academicians, and the police themselves, the view that calls for service is the way to do crime fighting is pervasive and largely unquestioned.

As previously noted, calls for service may actually act as an impediment to the ability of the police to deal with serious crime. Importantly, calls for service tend to be weighted toward minor public order and service calls (Table 2.1). Indeed, data show that the *majority* of calls for service have been for lower level maintenance or social service calls (Reiss, 1971; Scott, 1981; Wilson, 1968). Table 2.1 shows

Table 2.1 Citizen Calls for Service, by General Problem Types

PROBLEM	NUMBER OF CALLS	PERCENT
Violent crimes	642	2
Nonviolent crimes	4,489	17
Interpersonal conflict	1,763	7
Medical assistance	810	3
Traffic problems	2,467	9
Dependent persons	774	3
Public nuisances	3,002	11
Suspicious circumstances	1,248	5
Assistance	3,039	21
Citizen wants to give info	1,993	8
Internal operations	633	2

Table 2.2 Frequencies of Top Ten Calls for Service

NATURE OF CALL	COUNT	PERCENT
Traffic stop	186,123	10.8
District assignment	79,032	4.6
Domestic violence (suspect present)	77,420	4.5
Burglar alarm	71,686	4.2
Silent 911 call	71,620	4.2
Residential burglar alarm	62,889	3.7
Drug activity	54,195	3.1
Civil disturbance	50,087	2.9
Suspicious activity	34,750	2.0
Theft report	34,312	2.0

the distribution of calls for service in the Police Services Study, carried out in three metropolitan areas (Scott, 1981; in Walker and Katz, 2008: 8-9).

Table 2.1 shows that calls for service are weighted away from violent and serious crimes. Indeed, only 2 percent of all calls are for violent crimes. The second category, nonviolent crimes, includes both felony and misdemeanor property crimes, and accounts for 17 percent of all calls. We see in this table that, while calls cover a wide array of requests important to citizens, only about 19 percent (the first two categories) account for felony and misdemeanor crimes.

Table 2.2, a more recent study carried out in Cleveland, shows a similar pattern of calls for service. These data are for all calls for service for 2001–2003 (Holcomb and Sharpe, 2006).

Table 2.2, showing the top ten reasons for calls for service, again shows that less serious concerns make up the large bulk of calls for service. In this study, violent crimes—as a category—are not listed in the top ten, though data on domestic violence may include violent crime.

Also important are two calls not listed in Table 2.1: those representing silent 911 calls, and those representing alarm calls (residential burglar alarm, and business burglar alarm). The three categories represent unknown 911 calls, and combined represent 12.6 percent of all calls.

What the data in Tables 2.1 and 2.2 do not tell us is how police are actually dispatched to respond to calls. We need to know how police actually respond to crime. A study of Baltimore's east district, carried out in 2002, provides that data. The Baltimore data on dispatched calls are presented in Table 2.3 (Moskos, 2007).

Table 2.3 provides a great deal of detail on dispatched calls. First, we note findings similar to those reported in Table 2.2, with regard to alarm calls. In Moskos's Baltimore study, alarms accounted for 8.3 percent of all calls. However, we also see that 94.4 percent of all alarm calls needed no police response. Similarly, we note that 911 silent (no voice) calls accounted for 5.6 percent of all calls, and in nine of ten cases did not need a police response. More serious "index" crimes—burglary, stolen auto, aggravated assaults, assaults involving shooting or cutting, rape, and carjacking—tended to show a high level of crime committed response, ranging from 31 to 75 percent. However, in total these calls accounted for only 5.3 percent of all calls, and half of these were burglary calls, which had a 49.1 percent "no need for response designation." Police dispatched "crime committed" or "report required" calls accounted for approximately 1.76 percent of all calls, in other words, less than 2 percent of all *dispatched* calls were calls that might be considered verifiably serious crime calls. Moreover, as noted, this number may be inflated, since all domestic calls, which are included in these cases, require a report, and these include unfounded calls (see the last note of Table 2.3). Finally, it should be noted that Baltimore's east side is a high crime area, hence it is most likely to show the worst that crime has to offer in the city.

Tables 2.1 through 2.3 show that, in a variety of settings, when dispatchers receive, and police respond to, calls for service, they are most likely responding to a call that has little or nothing to do with serious violent crime. In other words, a great deal of time is spent in responding to calls that places officers out of service and removes them from opportunities to deal with serious crime.

In addition, distinguishing between serious and nonserious calls can be difficult. When a citizen calls 911, her or his call is sorted as to kind, severity, and immediacy of need, first, by the caller him- or herself (who tends to overstate seriousness and immediacy of threat), then to an operator who passes the calls on, then to a dispatcher who decides what to do with the call, and finally to the patrol unit that responds to the call. Citizens may, intentionally or inadvertently, supply misleading information about the situation depending on their perception of the danger of the circumstances, their lack of knowledge

Table 2.3   Calls for Service in Baltimore's Eastern District

CATEGORY OF DISPATCHED CALL	DISPATCHED CALLS			
	PERCENT OF ALL CALLS	NO NEED FOR[a] RESPONSE	SOME POLICE[b] SERVICE	CRIME COMMITTED/ WRITTEN REPORT REQUIRED[c]
All calls for service	100% (113,205)	38.9% (44,003)	35.4% (40,093)	25.7% (29,109)
Drugs	25.6% (28,959)	13.9% (4,027)	67.2% (19,462)	18.9% (5,470)
Disorderly	10.5% (11,874)	28.6% (3,398)	64.9% (7,707)	6.5% (769)
Other[a]	8.8% (9,953)	39.3% (3,910)	26.0% (2,584)	34.8% (3,459)
Alarms	8.3% (9,353)	94.4% (8,833)	3.7% (346)	1.9% (174)
Common assault	6.9% (7,865)	41.3% (3,252)	23.7% (1,867)	34.9% (2,746)
911 no voice	5.6% (6,341)	90.1% (5,764)	7.3% (462)	1.8% (115)
Larceny	3.8% (4,346)	28.0% (1,219)	12.8% (556)	59.2% (2,571)
Family disturbance	2.9% (3,277)	25.6% (839)	37.1% (1,216)	37.3% (1,222)
Auto accident	2.6% (2,990)	23.8% (712)	30.5% (912)	45.7% (1,366)
Burglary	2.3% (2,639)	49.1% (1,297)	12.0% (341)	37.9% (1,001)
Armed person	1.9% (2,168)	57.9% (1,255)	29.7% (641)	12.5% (272)
Destruction of property	1.8% (2,059)	27.9% (575)	14.6% (300)	57.5% (1,184)
Aggravated assault	1.4% (1,580)	48.0% (759)	20.4% (322)	31.6% (499)
SELECTED OTHER CATEGORIES				
Gunshots	0.9% (980)	59.4% (582)	32.8% (321)	7.9% (77)
Stolen auto	0.9% (969)	37.9% (367)	7.4% (72)	54.7% (530)
Assault, shooting	0.3% (324)	51.9% (168)	1.9% (6)	46.3% (150)
Assault, cutting	0.3% (312)	29.2% (91)	5.4% (17)	65.4% (204)
Rape	0.1% (120)	39.2% (47)	4.2% (5)	56.7% (68)
Carjacking	0.04% (48)	20.8% (10)	4.2% (2)	75.0% (36)
Not listed above	15.1% (17,048)	40.5% (6,898)	17.3% (2,954)	42.2% (7,196)

[a] *No need for response:* These calls are not legitimate. If no written report is required, police may assign an oral code. There are six oral codes: (A) call unfounded, (B) unable to locate complainant, (C) no such address, (D) no police services needed, (E) [suspect] gone on arrival, and (F) call abated. For most categories, codes A through E are included in this column. For the categories narcotics, armed person, and disorderly, codes A though D are Included in this column, and code E is included in the following column. Gunshot calls coded D are also included in the following column as, by custom, the oral code for gunshots refers to the presence of a victim rather than the existence of gunshots.

[b] *Some police service:* These calls are coded abated, a catch-all oral code. Some of these calls are legitimate. Calls coded abated may (narcotics) but usually do not (auto accident) involve a crime. While no police report is written, calls coded abated imply some need for or effect from police services, even if minor.

[c] *Crime or report:* A written police report is required for any property damage, injury, victim, arrest, and all domestic calls. A call in any category can be domestic. In this column, categories with a large number of domestic calls, family disturbance, larceny, destruction of property, common assault, and other Care inflated due to the inclusion of unfounded domestic calls.

about the legal system, or to manipulate police presence for questionable reasons (Klinger, 1997). Further, different communities and
neighborhoods develop different expectations of when and why police
should be called. Consequently, calls for service may not only match
up with actual crime, but may vary according to differences across
neighborhoods. This is particularly the case with regard to differences
in neighborhood income levels, where relatively high socioeconomic
neighborhoods tend to bring in calls to the police for minor incidents.
Hence, general ideas about the relationship between calls for service
and police response tend to develop independently of actual crime
(Johnson and Rhodes, 2007; Klinger, 1997).

Calls for Service as a Drain on Police Resources

Unfortunately, calls for service can actually *impede* officers from
addressing crime. As noted previously, calls for service deployment, as
a budgetary item, create an enormous drain on police resources, leaving fewer resources to fight serious criminal activity. Consider one of
the more significant calls for service problems: "unknown-compelled"
calls for service. In recent years, the police have tried to adapt their
response to calls for service by prioritizing calls, giving the highest
priority to the most serious calls and immediately dangerous circumstances. This means that less important calls often get dropped to
the bottom of the "to do" list, and conversely, that more crucial calls
involving serious crime are prioritized. There are, however, some calls
that police are compelled to respond to, not knowing whether they
are low, medium, or high priority or even if they might be complete
mistakes agree altogether. The most pervasive of these "unknown-
compelled" calls stemming from home alarm systems.

In most US cities, it is policy to send police to intruder alarms.
Unfortunately, false alarms are far more common than real crime
alarms, and they detract considerably from the ability to deploy officers correctly (Gilbertson, 2005). The city incurs an additional expense
for police response to false alarms, and the alarms take officers out of
service when they could be dealing with actual crime. Unfortunately,
there is no way to know if alarms are false or not without dispatching
an officer. Every alarm carries the unknown possibility that it might
not be false. These are called *unknown-compelled* calls for service, and

they represent a potential public relations nightmare for police depart-ments. As Tables 2.2 and 2.3 show, these calls account for about 8% of the total volume of calls. Moreover, as the data in Table 2.3 show, nine of ten of these calls are unfounded. Yet, what if a bank alarm goes off, one that has already been found to be false several times before, but this time it is for real? The idea that the police might not respond quickly to any alarm, regardless of whether the alarm indicated a real threat, strikes at the heart of the public's perception of police, upon whom they can rely to be there for them, consistently.

Rapid Response as a Measure of Police "Lateness" to Crime

Police departments take pride in their ability to respond to citizen calls for service in quick fashion. What is overlooked in that model is that typically, except for a very few calls where rapid response actu-ally matters, response time is simply a measure of how late police arrive. That is, response time is always inherently reactive; it occurs after a threat appears, and almost always after the incident is over. This occurs for two reasons. First, with regard to property crimes, which are far more prevalent, the time interval between when the crime occurs and when a call is made to dispatch can be lengthy, up to days, for instance, in the event of someone returning home and discovering a burglarized house. Second, with regard to violent vic-timization, people tend to call friends or family first, and then call the police. Even for violent victimization, the time interval between discovery of the crime itself and the call to the police averages about a half hour, making a fast response time virtually irrelevant (Cordner, Greene, and Bynum, 1983 as reported in Walker and Katz, 2008). Consequently, no matter how much the police decrease their response time, they will always be limited by discovery, reporting, and process-ing time (Figure 2.1).

Discovery time:	The interval between crime commission and discovery
Reporting time:	The interval between discovery and when citizen calls
Processing time:	The interval between call and dispatch of patrol car
Travel time:	Time from dispatch to when officer arrives at scene

Figure 2.1   The structure of response time.

Yet, in spite of these limitations that inhere in emphasizing the importance of police response time, if the police fail to respond quickly when a real call comes in, they can expect a complaint to a city councilperson, a story in the local news and, if very unfortunate, on national news channels, followed by the rolling of administrative heads up to and including the chief. It is an unfortunate model, and it is singularly ineffective when it comes to addressing serious crime. The resources poured into answering unknown-compelled calls for service and in sustaining rapid response times cannot be overstated. The budgetary resources necessary to acquiesce to such a high level and consistent public service demand are significant.

Operations in a Calls for Service Model

How can the police, working within the limitations of the calls for service model, do something proactive about serious crime in high crime areas beyond simply driving around randomly, waiting for citizens to call them to report crimes that have already happened? The answer is that they have developed specialized operations within high crime areas. For instance, a police department may assemble a small unit, made up of three or four officers who focus specifically on open market drug sales in a particular area. These officers, who are likely assigned to RPP in that sector already, will take a few hours out of their normal patrol schedule, or work overtime, to carry out the focused operation. In a word, the typical proactive response to high visibility crime problems is to develop an operation.

By carrying out an operation the police can bring more pressure to bear on high crime areas than is otherwise available through budgeted salaries. Operations are budgetarily manageable because they are relatively short lived and supplemented with overtime money and the odd collection of small state and federal grants of limited duration, but are widely available for the police. These grants typically carry the stipulation that they cannot be used for routine expenses, hence are particularly attractive for the funding of special operations. An unfortunate side effect, however, can be the tendency to rely on operations as the way of addressing hot spot problems, because operations are finite and measurable, thus easily reported within a grant funding period. Commanders know that budgeted funds will be used primarily to stage officers in districts and to respond to radio calls, and consequently will use "extra" grant money to carry out highly focused operations. A second unfortunate side effect is that, when the grant money is gone, the special operation is abandoned. The history of federal funding of community policing has shown that community policing practices, supported and developed under National Institute of Justice solicitations, tended to rapidly disappear once the grant moneys ended (Crank and Langworthy, 1996). Any short-term effect on crime from the operation, consequently, is quickly lost after the end of the grant funding cycle.

One could consequently say that contemporary police managers, dealing with crime hot spots and hot shots, have an "operations mindset." We call this way of carrying out operations a *short-term, repetitive raiding strategy*. This means that the police raid an area, criminals disappear, and then when the police leave, criminals come back, business as usual. Then the police do it all over again. The raiding mindset is one of the reasons crime flourishes in the United States: It creates the image that police are doing something about crime without really dealing with hot spot crime. Unfortunately, the repetitive raiding strategy can also contribute to the longevity of crime in a particular area. As criminals evolve in a particular neighborhood, they learn to survive under the variability in the security conditions they face. Raids become a factor in their activities, one to which they adapt, recognizing that the raid is a temporary condition and they can "hang low" and wait it out. Information Box 2-1 lists a variety of backfiring problems associated with the use of repetitive raiding operations in a calls for service model.

The operations method of policing hot zones is a combined effect of current deployment practices, budgetary shortfalls, and the desire of police to actually do something about crime. In addition to government grant dollars, operations tend to be limited to funding from that part of the budget that is left over after funding geographic deployment according to principles of random preventive patrol and calls for service. Therefore, such operations tend to make use of overtime since staffing is primarily for calls for service. Hence, the principal budgetary investment in policing is to deploy officers around the city so that they can respond to calls for service in a timely way, and so that the chief can tell the mayor that no part of the city is absent police services.

INFORMATION BOX 2-1:
BACKFIRING EFFECTS OF OPERATIONS

Operations enable the police to proactively focus limited resources on crime problems while maintaining a calls for service model. However, operations have several backfiring effects, which means that they have a variety of unintended outcomes that ultimately hinder their ability to effectively do something about serious crime. Seven effects are listed below.

First, citizens in the operational area may have the mistaken impression that the operation actually does something about crime, lulling them into dangerous complacency.

Second, scant municipal monies are spent on practices of questionable success.

Third, citizens, seeing crime staying at the same level, question police effectiveness.

Fourth, the criminals learn about police practices and ways to evade them.

Fifth, an inadvertently heavy handed police action may delegitimize the police in the operational area.

Sixth, the action of *leaving* an operational area effectively returns control to criminals and gangs, who can solidify their positions by seeking revenge on supporters of the police. This creates additional victims, and in itself undercuts police legitimacy.

Seventh, the police themselves begin to question their effectiveness and the ability to do something about crime, while at the same time get frustrated at the intransigence of particular areas to respond to police presence.

We argue that both the calls for service model and its adjunct practice, operational "raids" into high crime areas, are fundamentally flawed models if one wants to do something about serious crime. A persistent presence model is superior. The term *persistent presence* was coined in counterinsurgency research and refers to the stationing, over long-term periods and at adequate staffing levels, of security personnel within those areas that require the greatest security. The notion of persistent presence and its role in achieving permanent levels of crime suppression will be developed throughout this book.

The Problem of Underdeployment in High Crime Areas

Police are overdeployed to areas where there is virtually no crime, locked into the calls for service model, and are underdeployed to areas where crime is the highest, while tied to an operations mindset. Consider a bit of common sense wisdom held by police researchers, mayors' offices, and often by the police themselves. Adding more police will have little *additional* impact on crime. This is a corollary of the argument that the police have little impact on crime. We counter that adding more police can actually have a substantial effect on crime. This assertion flows from the notion that police guardianship is in part a quantitative variable, and that an increase in the number of guardians will increase crime prevention efficacy.

Research on the effectiveness of police size on crime is usually carried out as a measure per one thousand citizens. The problem with this research is that of the censored variable. Censored variables are those whose effects are difficult to gauge because their effects are not linear and the full range of the variable is not measured. This applies to adding more police to deter crime. Our position is that cities have not added enough police in high crime areas for sustained periods to make a large and enduring difference. *What if we added substantially more police on a long-term basis to hot zones?* The logic of permanent presence—significant numbers of officers on permanent assignments inside hot zones who carry out focused operations inside those zones—suggests that effectiveness can be derived from significant increases in deployments. There is indirect support for effectiveness of a higher police-to-citizen ratio in the counterinsurgency literature. Information Box 2-2 briefly reviews that research.

The take-away from this section is that the counterinsurgency literature suggests that much higher levels of police presence are needed in high crime areas. That counterinsurgency and urban policing in high crime areas both can be described as mosaic conflicts was discussed in Chapter 1. Moreover, some elements, particularly the disorganized

INFORMATION BOX 2-2
FORCE LEVELS: COMPARING COUNTER-
INSURGENCY AND POLICING

Consider counterinsurgency research, where the upper end of the variable for measuring security force has been assessed. The US counterinsurgency forces use the recommended number of 20 security personnel per 1,000, considerably higher than the 2 officers per 1,000 widely cited in US national estimates of municipal police department size. Petraeus and Amos (2006; see also Quinlivan, 1995) observed that:

A better force requirement gauge is troop density, the ratio of security forces (including the host nation's military and police forces as well as foreign counterinsurgents) to inhabitants. Most density recommendations fall within a range of 20 to 25 counterinsurgents for every 1,000 residents in an AO. Twenty counterinsurgents per 1,000 residents is often considered the minimum troop density required for effective COIN operations; however as with any fixed ratio, such calculations remain very dependent upon the situation.

Research has compared use of force ratios across US military and US urban policing settings. McGrath (2006), using historical data to estimate military to civilian force ratios, suggested that 13.26 officers per 1,000 citizens provides the best force planning number. He also looked at deployments in major American cities. Assessing levels in 5 cities, he noted that force sizes ranged from 3.3 (Los Angeles) to 4.9 (New York), both numbers proportional to relative population densities, with an average of 4.1 officers per 1,000 citizens.

nature of serious crime, actually make the conflict more difficult to address tactically. Substantially higher levels of police forces permanently stationed in high crime areas are needed if our goal is to actually do something about serious crime.

Framing the Command Problem of Current Deployment Practices

If the police are geographically deployed to do something about crime, then they need a set of rules for crime fighting. The current rule book is a department's standard operating procedures (SOP) manual. The SOP is a department's statement of policy as it applies to all personnel, and it provides direction for a wide variety of police activities. For instance, the City of Cocoa Beach Police Department has a detailed protocol for its Citizen Observer program. It provides definitions and rules regulating the use of observers and the relationship between observers and police officers. It provides guidelines for the training, uniforms and equipment, and the volunteer registration process.[1] The Louisville (Kentucky) Metro Police Department has detailed protocols on the interdiction practices, definition of, and case criteria for narcotics interdictions.[2] And the San Antonio Police Department has a complex (and intimidating) set of protocols for recommending changes to unit SOPs.[3]

Beyond the SOP, the line officer's primary command responsibility is to his or her sergeant. Research generally shows, however, that sergeants do not place heavy demands on line officers beyond the expectation that they carry out their assigned patrol activities in a way that does not bring negative attention to the unit. There is little other guidance besides the calls from the dispatcher, assistance from other officers, and personal efforts to position oneself for promotion (from recognition for making the extra effort) and for overtime pay (by timing the extra effort to coincide with the end of the shift, thus requiring overtime pay to do the paperwork).

Discretion and the Problem of Command Control

A characteristic and ubiquitous feature of contemporary policing is an absence of command control over the behavior of line officers. Officers tend to operate with a great deal of discretion, which means that they can make personal decisions about the best way to respond to calls for service, how to respond, whether to arrest, or whether to take some other course of action. When not responding to a call for service, they make decisions about where to drive in their sector, how fast to drive, whom to talk to, whether to stop someone, and whether a situation requires additional investigation. In brief, they have wide discretion in almost all of their work.

Once on patrol, line officers are largely beyond regulation—police work is consequently best understood as "low visibility decision making"—selecting courses of action with little command oversight in largely unpredictable situations. Therefore, decisions to engage in crime prevention and suppression are largely self-regulated. To the extent that there is guidance, it is largely in terms of the SOP, which tends to provide guidance for officers in their interactions with citizens with a set of negative prescriptions, telling officers what they should not do, with little substantive direction for describing what they should do. One person referred to the SOP manual in his department as a list of "one hundred years of screw-ups."

Who, then, controls line officer crime-fighting behavior? To be sure, the police are under a broad accountability blanket from training protocols and from due process requirements that condition police–citizen interactions. However, they do not operate under direct command protocols. That is, patrol officers who are assigned to a specific beat are not given a set of orders for which they are directly accountable. They are not responsible to an articulative "mission." Experts in the study of police culture have commented that their work is more like learning how to "keep one's head down and avoid trouble" (Crank, 2003). Sergeants exert some control over what officers do. However, researchers have noted that lone officers quickly become aware of what activity they need to perform to make sergeants happy.

One can see in the structure of the operational shift the absence of command control. Officers on a particular shift gather together at the beginning of a shift and, for perhaps 15 minutes, receive a presentation about current hot spot problems, criminals, and areas of concern from the shift commander. At the end of this presentation, officers go to their patrol cars, take up activity in their beats, and are invisible to command for the remainder of the shift. Their work is determined by their preferences within their areas and is heavily influenced by opportunities for arrests, overtime, and by calls from citizens. As Black (1980) has noted, citizens largely determine what officers do. Caldero has referred to this way of policing as "in-your-face-problem solving," where officers use personal authority, sometimes aggressively, to rapidly solve citizen problems and then move on to the next problem. Black (see Crank, 2003) recognizes the high levels of discretion that street officers have that cannot be brought under command control.

Where command does have an influence over and interest in is the way line officers respond to radio calls; however, it is often manifested as an interest in the rapidity of their response time, not the actual response itself. Unfortunately, this involvement may contravene efforts toward good policing outcomes. Instead of line officers focusing on the current call for service, the next call becomes prioritized, as pressures on line officers become the clearing of the first call to get "back into service." In other words, Caldero's concerns about rapid-fire, "in-your-face" policing are actually reinforced by command preoccupations with response time quickness.

The command role in the current deployment model is consequently poorly designed for crime fighting. One could say that command prerogatives are *disarticulated* from line activity, which means that commanders have few organizational opportunities and limited oversight capacity to affect what line officers actually do.

Detectives and Crime Fighting

One might argue that the detective function in police departments is that organizational element that is clearly oriented to fight crime. Yet, a close look at detectives reveals that they are inefficient at fighting crime and are similarly hamstrung by the limitations of the calls for service structure of policing.

The job of detective is treated as an assignment in some departments and as a rank in others. Generally it is a preferred position; detectives tend to work favorable hours and are better salaried than line officers. When a serious crime occurs, one can anticipate that detectives will show up, gather evidence, and work with the prosecutor's office in the development of a criminal case against a suspect. The detective role is one that "knits" the police department into the criminal justice process. The detective builds the case, typically initiated by line officers, that will carry a particular individual through the various stages of the criminal justice system: prosecution, probation or incarceration, and ultimately, release and recycle.

Researchers have noted that the primary activity of detectives is evidence development for a prosecutor. Evidence development is important for *known* cases. Known cases are those where the suspect is known and evidence is available for his or her prosecution. The detective can put the case together in a way that maximizes the likelihood that a prosecutor will successfully adjudicate the case. Where a suspect is unknown, or evidence is simply not available for the prosecution, the adjudicatory role is ineffective. Put simply, detectives do a good job "solving" solvable cases.

Because case loads in most agencies are fairly heavy in proportion to the detective bureau, officers tend to work on cases for a limited period. Unlike the television shows of a forensic detective painstakingly returning to a case for weeks, interviewing suspects in faraway places and developing the thinnest of evidentiary leads into a robust case, most cases that are not known are quickly abandoned. In most major cities, the ratio of reported cases to available detective time is so out of synch that most cases will get only a nominal review before being open-filed.

The detective role, consequently, has virtually no impact on crime, and it has no proactive crime focus. The essence of detective work is reactive; they are always working with cases for crimes that have already occurred. Moreover, they are working with known suspects, many of whom are already likely in custody.

Hence, the detective role, like the line officer role, has limited effectiveness in doing something about serious crime. Both are heavily reactive in that they deal with known cases and existing crimes. Neither role is designed in a way to "get out in front" of crime.

This book develops the argument that both the line officer and detective roles can be straightforwardly redesigned into a more effective crime prevention tool. Many line officers will be redeployed to hot spot areas to carry out specific commands under an articulated mission. The role of the detective will be to focus on interrogation and rapid evidence review to facilitate specific deployment missions in hot spot areas. This is what we will refer to as the intelligence element of crime prevention, which is the rapid development of facts and information to develop leads on criminal activity. This notion of detective work blends current detective practices with the intelligence component of contemporary counterinsurgency practices and will become one of the cornerstones of the model of policing developed here—mission-based policing.

Endnotes

1. http://www.cityofcocoabeach.com/Cityhall/Volunteers/Citizen_Observer_Application.pdf
2. http://www.drugendangeredchild.org/PDF%20Files/SOP%20820%20Narcotics%20Investigation.pdf
3. http://www.policevolunteers.org/PDF/SanAntonioHandbook.pdf

3
REDESIGNING AMERICAN POLICING, PRINCIPLES 1 AND 2

Focus and Effectiveness

What if the primary mission of the police were to do something about serious crime? If the police were refocused on a primary mission of crime fighting, with an organizational design based on the geography of serious crime, policing would radically change. It is that change in model—a model we call mission-based policing—that is presented in the rest of this book. Mission-based policing is based on five principles: the principle of focus, the principle of police effectiveness, the principle of serious crime deployment, the principle of mission integrity, and the principle of mission's end. The first two are discussed in this chapter, which continues our emphasis on developing a strategic and sustained police response to serious crime.

The Principle of Focus

The first change principle is the most important. We call it the principle of focus. This principle flows from contemporary crime prevention research, in which effectiveness derives from tying specific goals to articulable means for achieving those goals. The principle is this: *If you want to do something about serious crime, then focus on serious crime.* In practice, this means focusing on serious crime—not disorder, not the community, and not citizen needs—in order to have an effect on serious crime. There are two components to this element. First, the mission must be organized around serious crime. Second, it must be carried out where serious crime is.

Focus Element 1: Organizing for Serious Crime

First, we will discuss the organization for serious crime. Integral to the first principle is that the police mission is organized around serious crime, constructed strategically to deal with serious crime, and the police need to be tactically deployed to where serious crime is. It may seem odd to use compare statistics (COMPSTAT) as a model for dealing with serious crime, in that it was heavily used for misdemeanor crime, quality of life issues, and zero-tolerance policing. However, we believe that the model would be quite effective for serious crime. A discussion of the mission model similarities and differences with COMPSTAT will be presented at this point.

COMPSTAT: A Precursor to Mission-Based Policing   Consider an important crime fighting program developed in the past twenty years: COMPSTAT. COMPSTAT has been described as the most important innovation for US policing in the late twentieth century (Kelling and Sousa, 2001). COMPSTAT emerged from the New York Police Department's (NYPD) efforts to develop a more effective crime fighting focus (Silverman, 2006). The NYPD was "reengineered" so that precinct commanders were held accountable to central headquarters for crime that occurred under their commands. Computer mapping facilitated managerial control by providing real-time information on criminal activity across New York City. Armed with these numbers, police commanders established crime reduction benchmarks. For instance, the benchmark of a 10% reduction in crime was established—and achieved—in 1994. The following three elements were integral to COMPSTAT:

> *The Weekly COMPSTAT report.* The weekly report provided straightforward statistical descriptions of crime patterns and provided patrol commands with more specific crimes and arrest data for their command (Henry, 2003). The report was circulated to patrol commands and to NYPD executives, providing a data-structured accountability measure over police crime suppression activity.
>
> The COMPSTAT report, providing current data on criminal activity, was enabled by crime mapping technologies, which have become increasingly central to police activity. Crime

mapping provided "real-time" inspection and analysis of criminal activity, together with a detailed description of the kinds of crime, suspects, and crime patterns.

The Commander Profile. The commander profile was an adjunct report to the weekly COMPSTAT report. It contained information on

> command's population and demographics, the number and ranks of personnel assigned, the number and categorized type of civilian complaints made against officers, the number of vehicle accidents involving Department vehicles, and a host of other information by which the commander and the state of his or her command can be assessed. (Henry, 2003: 253)

The Crime Control Strategy (CCS) Meetings. CCS meetings were held twice a week and provided a forum for NYPD executive leadership to meet with local or midlevel commanders. A "state of the command" briefing required commanders to present current practices and explain their current and proposed impact on crime. Local commanders could bring line officers with them who were involved in crime suppression activity (Kelling, 1995).

The Command Accountability Loop   The crime mapping technology used to guide command meetings enabled the integration of COMPSTAT crime suppression strategy. Real-time crime mapping transited through a seamless command–midlevel accountability loop:

1. Line officers carried out crime suppression and coded it into computers.
2. The information technology unit uploaded information into the COMPSTAT database and downloaded it into the weekly report.
3. Executives met with local commanders to review the data.
4. Local commanders adjusted precinct activity according to current data. This command accountability loop enabled rapid dissemination of information integral to the review of crime, adaptation of practices, and response to real-time crime measures.

COMPSTAT, by many evaluations, proved to be an effective organizational response to crimes it addressed and also was associated with sharply lower levels of crime across New York City.

Issues with COMPSTAT   Below we discuss several issues that have been brought up with regard to COMPSTAT. It should be emphasized that these are all addressable problems and are to an extent largely interpretive. However, they provide a sensibility through which to think about the relationship between COMSTAT and mission-based policing.

COMPSTAT and Line Officer Accountability   One of the problems suggested by evaluators of COMPSTAT was an inability to hold line officers accountable for their actions. COMPSTAT focused on the middle and top of the chain of command. This means that it sought, through a command-driven model, to hold middle managers responsible for crime suppression in their jurisdictions. However, there is little evidence that accountability translated to any improvement in crime effectiveness on the part of line officers. Many line officers had little direct information about what actually happened at COMPSTAT meetings. Willis, Mastrofski, and Weisburd (2007: 148) noted in their three-department assessment of COMPSTAT:

> When asked "How often does your supervisor discuss what happened at COMPSTAT meetings?" 61 percent of those officers we surveyed in Lowell responded "never" (43 percent) or "every few months" (18 percent); for Minneapolis, 34 percent responded "never" (14 percent) or "every few months" (20 percent); and for Newark it was 42 percent (8 and 34 percent, respectfully).

Given that one of the celebrated strengths of COMPSTAT is the real-time delivery of crime information through crime mapping, the failure of a significant part of the police department to be excluded from the informational loop suggests that COMPSTAT was not working as well as it could have. Willis et al. (2007: 166) suggested that, because of this limitation, COMPSTAT was largely ceremonial: its reputation "sent a powerful message to the community, just as it did with the rank-and-file, that key personnel were being held strictly accountable, even though the results of their efforts were unclear."

COMPSTAT and the Quality of Life Problem   A second criticism of the COMPSTAT model concerned its application to what is called quality-of-life policing. *Quality-of-life policing* means that the police can do something about serious crime by taking on quality-of-life problems, largely by generating arrests for misdemeanor violations or through enforcing code infractions. Quality of life is widely noted as a central element of the COMPSTAT strategy (Weisburd and Braga, 2003). By focusing on disorder, the police are theorized to address serious crime in the following ways:

1. Those contacted or arrested were at times involved in more significant crimes.
2. At times those contacted or arrested also had outstanding warrants for felony crimes.
3. Interrogation could sometimes provide leads for more serious crime.

However, we believe there are two important problems with a disorder focus on crime control. It is indirect, and it undercuts police legitimacy.

Indirectness   Quality-of-life or "disorder" policing is an indirect approach to addressing serious crime. A disorder focus is indirect in several ways:

1. It does not focus directly on serious crime but instead takes another crime category—misdemeanor—and theorizes a relationship to serious crime.
2. Sometimes the arrest will indeed result in a quality hit in the sense that a serious crime felon will be identified. However, in many cases the misdemeanor arrest will come to no more than that, one more misdemeanor arrest, a loss of officer time that could have been spent in more serious crime matters, and a lack of a clear strategy that ties misdemeanor arrests to an articulable crime pattern.
3. It is a shotgun approach to serious crime—in a broad sweep of misdemeanants, inevitably some criminals who had committed serious crime would be identified.

4. It overfocuses on minor crimes. This concern was noted within the Minneapolis Police Department. For instance, Willis et al. (2007: 163) noted that officers stated that COMPSTAT "focuses on the minor offences, hoping for it to turn into something bigger ... wasting time to stop people for loitering and not answering calls."

Legitimacy   A second concern with the public order focus was that the NYPD failed to take into consideration long-term legitimacy concerns associated with crackdowns on public order problems (see, for instance, the DVD *Rudyland*).[1] Consider the following:

1. Sherman (1993) has observed that the problem with such crackdowns is that they tend to backfire, leading to a lowering of legitimacy in the long term and inadvertently contributing to crime increases.
2. COMPSTAT operations are sometimes perceived as a heavy-handed police strategy. The COMPSTAT program, for instance, has been described in some quarters as "The New York police department against 65 committed squeegee hucksters." Though the quote may not be technically accurate, it carries the implication—and the public perception—that the NYPD was overapplying force on a relatively minor area of crime control.

Legitimacy concerns are a part of the reason why we believe that quality-of-life policing, under the mission-based model, may strategically be a bad idea. Central to the mission-based model is the long-term development of police effectiveness in serious crime, which necessitates positive public perceptions. The establishment of security is only the first step in the development of an adequate economic infrastructure and the successful reinvigoration of depressed areas. Legitimacy—the belief, by the majority of citizens in hot spot areas, that the police and city government are respected and are welcomed for their contributions to local areas—is undercut by a heavy-handed police presence focusing on nonserious crime and citations.

A focus on misdemeanor crime may have a role in mission-based policing. That role, however, depends on how any specific misdemeanor enforcement is tactically tied to the mission of serious crime dissipation in hot zones. The question asked by mission-based policing is: Will a particular kind of misdemeanor or city code violation focus directly impact a serious crime practice, pattern, or cluster? For instance, a city violation crackdown on apartment complexes might be clearly tied to drug distribution and sales within a particular complex.

Finally, an issue with COMPSTAT is that it sought to "overlay" a command-driven mission-based model of policing over an existing calls for service model. That overlay resulted in a blended model that continued to be undermined by many of the central problems of a calls for service model of policing. As echoed by Willis et al. (2007: 171), "random preventive patrol and the calls-for-service apparatus that dominate the organization of patrol work in most urban police departments were largely unchanged by COMPSTAT reform."

Willis et al. (2007) called for sweeping revisions, including a fundamental change in beliefs about the efficacy of random preventive patrol, the need to allocate resources where crime was, and that police managers have the independence to carry out the kind of work needed to achieve effective crime prevention. We have taken those recommendations to heart in the mission-based model of policing by (1) focusing on unity of command and the permanent deployment of police to crime-intensive areas or hot spots and (2) deemphasizing calls for service deployment in favor of tactical responses to crime.

Figure 3.1 presents a comparison of COMPSTAT and mission-based policing.

Focus Element 2: Being Where the Crime Is

The second component of the principle of focus is that the police must be where serious crime is. Perhaps the most compelling argument for relocating the police in high crime areas is presented by Braga and Weisburd (2010) in their work "Policing Problem Places." In this work, the authors develop the important principle that the police, to be effective, should be primarily focused in hot spots. This work provides compelling evidence for the notion that a relatively small number of places—called hot spots—account for a disproportionately large quantity of crime. Moreover, research has consistently shown positive effects from focused police interventions in high crime areas.

MISSION-BASED POLICING	COMPSTAT
Rapid operational deployment tied to crime mapping.	Rapid operational deployment tied to crime mapping.
Intelligence planning guides operations.	Intelligence planning guides operations and strategy. It "looks farther" than under COMPSTAT.
Emphasis on long-term mission outcome. Mission is tied to articulated strategy. Strategies are articulated to mission.	Emphasis on the here and now. In fairness, there is strong emphasis on long-term goal, i.e., reduction of crime. Not wedded to a particular strategy, but assumes that the result of many short battles will be winning the war.
Insistence on continual reference back to mission as a measuring stick to decide whether it is appropriate to spend resources on a project.	Insistence on rapid response to any outbreak of crime. Two similar crimes are a possible trend, three similar crimes are a series.
Territory gained must continue to be occupied until evidence shows need no longer exists. Will be considered at risk for relapse for a much longer period of time than under COMPSTAT.	Rapid deployment of resources permits vacating territory where nothing is happening for the moment.
Accurate and timely intelligence. To that is added the strategic information concept of using both in-bound and out-bound information as a mission tool.	Accurate and timely intelligence. Focus on in-bound information to develop operations.
Serious crime operations.	Quality of life operations.
Effective tactical response, gauged in terms of crime suppression, legitimacy, and contribution to strategy.	Effective tactical response, gauged in terms of crime suppression.
Rapid and permanent deployment to hot zone area, along with reallocation of resources away from cool spots.	Rapid deployment to a hot spot, on top of a calls for service model.
Congruency of mission, congruency of command. Restructuring of command.	Uses the existing command structure, which requires networking and cooperative relationships to work, as existing command structure is left intact.
Relentless follow-up and assessment.	Relentless follow-up and assessment.
Legitimacy planning is an operational component.	Legitimacy is not addressed.

Figure 3.1   A comparison of COMPSTAT and mission-based policing.

Braga and Weisburd (2010) also discuss an issue central to directed patrol: that crime does not tend to displace, but instead that a diffusion of benefits characterizes effective police practices. This is a critically important finding for advocates of directed and proactive police practices; it undercuts the (somewhat cynical) argument that when police focus their energies on a particular place, all they accomplish is moving the problem elsewhere. To the contrary, the notion of diffusion of benefits means that, when the police are effective at addressing a particular crime problem, the areas contiguous to the crime problem may also show a lowering of crime.

Of similar concern to police professionals is the stability of hot spots. To what extent are such areas stable over time? That is, is a spot hot one year, then cool the next? This is particularly important when police are allocated to a particular area based on crime levels and frequency. The investment of scarce budgetary dollars needs to be based on some predictability of effort. As Braga and Weisburd (2010: 25) noted, "Only a very strong continuity in crime hot spots would support a large scale commitment to hot spots as a focus of police operations." Information Box 3-1 discusses their findings.

What kind of policing should be used to address hot spots? The authors noted that three strategies are commonly employed. They are:

1. Traditional incident-driven approaches, which include preventive patrol, investigation, and rapid response to calls for service.
2. Enforcement problem-oriented policing (POP), which includes directed patrol, crackdowns, and automobile searches.
3. Situational POP, which involves understanding the causes of crimes, developing nontraditional solutions, and collaboration.

Of concern with the enforcement-oriented approaches—numbers 1 and 2 above—is that they "tend to concentrate mainly on the time and location of crime events, rather than focusing on the characteristics and dynamics of a place that make it a hot spot for criminal activity" (160). The authors, however, noted that (in a specific intervention) the strongest crime prevention benefits were driven by situational prevention strategies that modified the criminal opportunity structure at the crime and disorder hot spots (Braga and Bond, 2008). Misdemeanor arrests for disorderly behavior generated much smaller crime prevention gains in the treatment places.

The authors conclude that POP is the most favorable tactical response to crime in hot spots. Their review of POP, however, is not wholly favorable. They note that POP is often difficult to develop in practice, and that it is often too complex for line officers, who are usually tasked to develop solutions. (In the next chapter we will present an alternative POP model that is more appropriate for hot spot

INFORMATION BOX 3-1:
STABILITY OF HOT (AND COOL) SPOTS.

How stable are hot spots? Braga and Weisburd (2010), discussing a variety of pertinent research, stated that hot spots were remarkably stable over time. They cited evidence from research conducted in Seattle. An assessment of crime incidents over 14 years showed that about 50% of the crime was found in about 4.5% of the street segments used to analyze stability. This was on a year to year basis.

To further assess stability, the authors looked at developmental trends of street segments. These trends should show the extent to which each area trended away from or toward different levels of crime. About 30,000 street segments were grouped into 18 trajectories, areas with similar developmental trends. Importantly, the authors found a high degree of stability for both hot spots, and for areas that had very low crime rates as well.

The finding that low crime places tend to remain low crime is particularly important for the mission-based model. It suggests that police forces can be moved from low crime to high crime areas without facing a sudden spike in criminal activity. However, any such reallocation would require constant monitoring to ensure that, over time, crime did not trend up. Consequently, any reallocation of forces away from safe areas should also entail the capacity for rapid response should such an area face an unexpected surge in serious crime.

policing.) What one finds, they observe, is more like "shallow problem solving" than problem-oriented policing. They conclude that "While it is difficult for police agencies to implement the 'ideal' version of problem-oriented policing, we believe that even 'shallow' problem solving better focuses police crime prevention efforts at crime hot spots." Consequently, this work, while providing a compelling argument for the focusing of police resources and activity in hot spots, does not clarify the policing modalities that should be used to carry out hot spot policing.

The Principle of Police Effectiveness

The second principle is that the police can have a significant and long lasting impact on crime. There are several elements to this principle.

Effectiveness of the Police Derives from Their Role as Guardians

This notion of guardianship is drawn directly from Felson's (1994) work on crime prevention. Felson asserted that, for crime to occur, three elements have to coincide: a likely offender, a suitable target, and an absence of capable guardians. Felson's work marked an important milestone in criminological theory. He argued that most crime was routine and followed routine patterns of human behavior. These routines could be disrupted or mitigated by addressing any one of the three elements. One of the strengths of his perspective is its ability to remove the intention of the offender from criminal outcomes by manipulating the other two items, making the target less accessible or emplacing capable guardianship.

Research following Felson's work has looked at a variety of factors related to all three elements of crime. When guardianship is investigated, researchers tend to look at the way in which informal guardianship practices can be used to lower the likelihood of crime in specific areas. However, scant research has specifically looked at the police themselves as guardians or has sought to alter police behavior in order to increase its guardianship capability. The mission-based model, perceiving the police first and foremost as guardians, does this.

Moreover, contrary to contemporary research that specifically argues for effectiveness in terms of what police do, we perceive police guardianship effectiveness also as a quantitative measure of presence. It's not only *what* the police do, but *that* they are present in the right places at the right time. Police guardianship in and of itself can mitigate crime. In the following section, we will explore the various components of police guardianship.

Components of Effective Guardianship: Deterrence and Legitimacy

Guardianship works, in part, because it has a deterrent effect. Research suggests that police deterrence has two components: background effects and focused or proactive effects. Guardianship also works in part from public perceptions of police legitimacy. These effects will also be considered here.

Guardianship Effect 1: Background Deterrence   By background deterrence, we mean that any police presence provides a certain level of deterrence simply because they are there. Strategies such as random preventive patrol, response to calls for service, and any other particular activity, though not in themselves particularly effective when compared to focused, articulated interventions, will deter some crime.

Consider, for instance, random preventive patrol (RPP). RPP is intended to provide a deterrent effect by enabling a police presence spread more or less uniformly across a city. Yet, since the evaluation by Kelling et al. (1972) of the Kansas City Police Department, RPP has been viewed as an ineffective way to do policing. The criticisms of RPP in the current era are many, for instance, that it ties up department resources, or that the overall police presence is so widely spread across the urban landscape that most citizens rarely see a police officer.

We differ from this critique and in doing so reconsider the way in which the deterrent effects of RPP should be considered. RPP is limitedly effective, not because it is random, but because it places guardians in the general area where crime occurs. It is proportionally effective to the effect generated by response to calls for service, which also provides a background deterrent effect because it provides guardians in an area. Hence, the police, from our perspective, essentially changed one strategy for placing guardians in an area with another—calls for service were maintained and arguably enhanced, while RPP levels were manipulated across the service areas being studied. We argue that what counted as a deterrent was not *what* the police did—RPP or response to calls for service—but *that* they were there.

There is some evidence for the importance of a background deterrent effect. Historical research has suggested that uncontrolled police manpower experiments, instances in which officers strike across a city, tend to result in dramatic escalations of crime. Sherman (1997), for instance, noted that "The police strike evidence ... is fairly consistent in showing the effect of this natural experiment: crime rates skyrocket instantly." Citing Clark (1969), Sherman observed that "The 1969 Montreal Police Strike resulted in 50 times more bank robberies and 14 times more commercial burglaries. This body of largely anecdotal evidence suggests that police presence creates a substantial deterrent effect" (Sherman, 1997). That deterrent effect, in other words, is substantially important to security in urban areas. Uncontrolled strike experiments, perhaps more than any other evidence, stand as powerful testimony to the substantial impact a police presence has on crime on a day-to-day, routine basis.

Guardianship Effect 2: Focused Deterrence   By focused deterrence, we are referring to the general class of police activities Sherman (1997) called "directed patrols." Directed patrols are the concentration of patrol activities in hot zones, and in which patrol is focused on an articulable crime problem. Citing Koper (1995) and Sherman and Weisburd (1995), Sherman (1997) observed that directed patrols had a deterrent effect on crime. This effect was not particularly long, sometimes being measured in minutes. Nevertheless, Sherman concluded that directed patrols is a police-based crime prevention strategy that worked. Another form of focused patrol activity, hot spot policing, also has shown consistent positive effects. Citing a variety of experimental designs, Weisburd and Eck (2004: 9) noted that "policing that is focused on hot spots can result in meaningful reductions in crime." This conclusion is supported by several research studies, summarized in Braga (2001).

From the mission-based perspective, directed patrols, though recognized by Sherman as an example of "what works," represent the kind of raiding strategy we discussed in Chapter 2 (see Figure 2.1). That is, raids enable security forces to briefly occupy a hot zone, but once they leave the zone it rapidly falls back under the influence of criminal and gang elements. For this reason, the deterrent effect, though significant, quickly diminishes over time.

Operations that are followed up by continued activity in hot zones, on the other hand, seem to have longer deterrent effects. Eck and Wartell (1996) found that operations that were followed up by continued contacts with landlords could lead to sustained crime benefits for longer periods of time. This research suggests that a continued presence in the hot zones can substantially improve crime control.

The effectiveness question is: How can we wed the elements of background and focused deterrence so that crime is lowered for substantially longer periods of time? The answer is that directed patrols have to be conducted by officers already deployed on a permanent basis inside the hot zones, not from the outside. This means that a large physical presence has to be assigned to the hot zone, which will provide a high level of background deterrence in the hot zone, and this physical presence has to be mobilized to act tactically against specific crime problems. In this way, directed patrols are carried on against specific crime targets, but the police presence does not leave after the operations. It simply changes form as officers develop different tactical responses to the crimes they are addressing.

Deterrence, Legitimacy, and the Problem of Arrest

Citizens must recognize the moral legitimacy of the police in order for the police to sustain the long-term presence required for mission success. Deterrence represents the ability of the state to intimidate potential law breakers; it works by threat of sanction, show of force, and fear of arrest. The problem is that deterrence, particularly acted out in terms of the heavy-handed or unfocused use of arrest practices, can backfire. Sherman (1997) described research into the reactive use of arrests that had significant backfiring consequences for youth; they tended to adopt a defiant posture, leading to long-term increases in crime.

Consider the routine use of arrest, central to notions of deterrence. Arrests serve the short-term purpose of removing an individual who is likely a threat to the public safety from the streets. However, arrests also carry significant backfiring effects. An arrest may mobilize onlookers to support the arrested, those who may be friends or family members. If the person is the same race as onlookers and the officer is a different race, then the arrest may be perceived as racist especially if the offence is viewed as trivial. If a person being arrested resists, the media-portrayed image of police rough treatment, regardless of its legality, may be seen as brutal. Arrests may cost the arrested time and money, in court fees, court appearances, and fines, negatively affecting family members and potentially costing the arrested her or his job.

Consider the community consequences of imprisonment, a frequent outcome of arrest (Information Box 3-2):

INFORMATION BOX 3-2: IMPRISONING COMMUNITIES

What is the relationship between penal sanctions and crime? One way to answer this question is to look at communities and assess the way in which crime changes in response to changes in penal sanctions. Clear (2007) asserted that, when crime is relatively low, penal sanctions – jail and prison – can have a positive effect on communities. That is, arrests and sentencing will tend to lower crime. However, a threshold can occur, when the imprisonment rate is too high, at which point imprisonment itself will contribute to crime. This effect is most likely to be found in communities already suffering significant urban problems such as poverty, absence of adequate medical care, very low property values, absence of business infrastructure, lack of jobs, and deficient school systems. In these neighborhoods, the criminal justice system can become part of the urban problem, not part of the solution.

How is arrest and incarceration a problem in these neighborhoods? Consider the family. One fourth of juveniles convicted of crime have children, and prison and jail both increases divorce rates and breaks their bonds with their children. It contributes to the collapse of marriage as an institution—for black males over 23, the likelihood of marriage drops by 50% after incarceration. Similarly, 46% of the prison population is divorced, compared to 17% of the regular population. Additionally,

1. Economic impact: Loss of income, costs of visitation, telephone calls, mail and money for prisoner.
2. Relocation of family, changes in educational districts, reduced time for maternal parenting due to additional employment.

3. Children's social maladjustment, depression and hyperactivity, antisocial behavior, drug use, mental health issues.

4. Male homosexual activity in prison: increases transmission of diseases such as AIDS and brings those back to the community.

5. Community-level increases in gonorrhea, syphilis, and chlamydia.

6. Economic wage impact: prison is linked to a 33% loss of lifetime wages.

7. Sharp erosion of local labor markets.

8. Neighborhood crime reduces the value of a home about 37%.

9. Residents resist going in businesses where ex-felons congregate.

10. Finally, there is no financial reward for conforming to the law. There are substantial financial rewards for violating it.

The overall impact on communities is devastating. Not only is the impact of incarceration substantial, but the reentry population—estimated at about 650,000 in 2010, adds substantial additional burdens. They tie up the limited interpersonal and social resources of their families and networks, weakening their ability to import resources from the outside world...they influence their peers and networks to isolate and insinuate themselves from mainstream social processes. They also increase the supply of motivated offenders. (2007, 159)

Consequently, the prisonization process "contributes to crime by sending large numbers of people from impoverished places to prison, and then returning them" (2007, 159).

In addition, one can list the following personal consequences of imprisonment.

1. Those imprisoned, for all the problems they may have had going in, will have worse psychological problems and anger issues coming out.

2. They will have a new set of "friends."
3. They will have had significant exposure to a broad range of crime practices.
4. They will be desensitized to the prison experience.
5. They will have forfeited many of their opportunities to lead a "straight" life, making a criminal lifestyle more attractive.
6. They will bring the prison mentality back to the communities where they live or to which they are released.
7. If they have children, the children may emulate them and resent the criminal justice system for putting their parent in prison.
8. Gangs may recruit them and emulate them, providing an escape from poverty.
9. A breadwinner may be removed from the family, creating additional hardship and deeper poverty for the family members.

In other words, whether or not someone deserves prison, it has devastating backfiring elements that undermine any good that might come from the prison experience. *Because of all these problems with arrest, it needs to be abandoned as a routine deterrent practice.* Arrests should be used only as a matter of last resort, when all else fails to quell criminal activity, and even then arrests should be mission-justified, not simply treated by police as "business as usual." It must be emphasized that the purpose of mission-based policing is to lower crime, and the use of criminal sanctions is only one component of that equation. Arrest should be carried out primarily in conjunction with articulated crime prevention or focused patrol activities.

Guardianship Effect 3: Legitimacy   The third piece of the puzzle—the key to long-term police effectiveness—is the moral dimension of effectiveness, which is legitimacy. Legitimacy is described by Sherman (1997) in the following terms: "The claim is that a legitimate police institution fosters more widespread obedience of the law itself. ... There is even evidence that the police themselves become less likely to obey the law after they have become disillusioned with its apparent lack of procedural justice."

Discussing Skogan's (1996) Chicago research, Sherman noted that community policing had the largest effects on serious crime in areas where the police were most responsive to citizen concerns. Moreover, Paternoster and his colleagues (1997) noted that repeat domestic violence was lowest among arrestees who said the police had treated them with respect. Recidivism appeared to be substantially lowered by the simple act of police taking the time to listen to the concerns of an offender.

Police legitimacy appears to be a fuzzy idea, peripheral to doing something about serious crime. Yet, when we look at places where the police have no citizen-based legitimacy, in countries where police support totalitarian regimes, for instance, we can better understand the importance of a police force that is tied in concrete ways to public expectations of their actions and demeanor. In such countries, the rule of law is replaced by rule by fear and intimidation, police secrecy, and the absence of basic due process protections for citizens. Legitimacy, understood in this context, is at the core of the police function.

Problems of legitimacy are seen in many US urban areas today. Central to crime control are both witness participation in the evidence gathering for cases and in citizens' reporting of crimes. However, where there are legitimacy issues, citizens will not cooperate with police, witnesses will not come forward, and witness testimony is absent from criminal cases. This problem is widely cited in many urban areas. Moreover, police become less effective crime enforcers in areas where citizens do not notify them that crimes have occurred. Such circumstances render the police's reactive function almost irrelevant.

Tyler and Legitimacy   In a paper reviewing research on police legitimacy, Tyler (2004) asserted that legitimacy was central to effective crime control and order maintenance. His central points are summarized in Information Box 3-3.

Police crime fighting effectiveness is one of the ingredients of police legitimacy. Certainly, a bumbling, inefficient police presence cannot acquire legitimacy. The effectiveness of the police appears to have been

INFORMATION BOX 3-3:
TYLER AND LEGITIMACY

People, Tyler asserted, are more willing to cooperate with legal authorities when they believe that those authorities are legitimate. This includes both deferring to their decisions during personal encounters and generally obeying legal rules in their everyday lives. Furthermore, people are more cooperative in helping the police to deal with crime in their communities when they view the police as legitimate. (2004: 90) Tyler made the following three points.

[1] First, the police need public support and cooperation to be effective in maintaining public order, and they particularly benefit when they have the voluntary support and cooperation of most members of the public, most of the time.

[2] Second, voluntary support and cooperation are linked to judgments about the legitimacy of the police. A central reason people cooperate with the police is that they view them as legitimate legal authorities, entitled to be obeyed.

[3] Third, a key antecedent of public judgments about the legitimacy of the police and of policing activities involves public assessments of the manner in which the police exercise their authority. Such judgments are central to public evaluations of the police and are independent of assessments of police effectiveness in fighting crime.

These points, Tyler noted, suggested "the importance of enhancing public views about the legitimacy of the police and suggest process-based strategies for achieving that objective" (p. 84).

To effectively maintain social order, Tyler continued that the police must be widely obeyed (Tyler 1990). However, he noted that it was "impractical for the police to be everywhere all of the time." Consequently, the police "must rely upon widespread, voluntary law-abiding behavior to allow them to concentrate their resources on those people and situations in which compliance is difficult to obtain" (p. 85).

enhanced in recent decades by police management and technological innovations, together with increases in police professionalism. On this issue, Tyler (1990: 86) observed:

> evidence suggests that police innovations in the management of police services may have contributed to the widespread declines in crime reported in major American cities during recent decades. ... Furthermore, indicators show increasing professionalism in policing, including declining rates of complaints against the police and lower levels of excessive police use of force against community residents.

However, effectiveness alone is not enough. Studies of public perceptions of and cooperation with the police consistently show that citizens' attitudes and police performance are only loosely associated. That means that effectiveness in performance, in and of itself, is inadequate for gaining citizen cooperation. In a related study of residents of Chicago, Tyler (1990) found that legitimacy has a significant influence on the degree to which people obeyed the law. He found, in this research, that this could not be explained by the likelihood of being caught and punished for illegal behavior.

A follow-up study was carried out on two samples of residents in New York City. Sunshine and Tyler (2003) found that "the legitimacy of the police significantly influenced compliance with the law. They [also] found that those residents who viewed the police as more legitimate were more willing to cooperate with them both by reporting crimes or identifying criminals and by engaging in community activities to combat the problems of crime" (cited in Tyler, 2004: 89).

Tyler concluded with the following summary statement:

> (findings of the research assessed in this article indicate that) people consider both performance in controlling crime and procedural fairness when evaluating the police and the courts. The major factor, however, is consistently found to be the fairness of the manner in which the police and the courts are believed to treat citizens. ... Sunshine and Tyler (2003) find support for this argument in two surveys of the residents of New York City. In both studies, residents who thought that the police exercised their authority in fair ways were also more willing to comply with the law and cooperate with the police. (2004: 93)

The clear implication of this conclusion was that the police need to take seriously both legitimacy and effectiveness and to engage the public in efforts that aim at improving their perceptions of both.

Finally, one should not assume that prison releasees or former—or even some active—criminals will reject the idea of a sharply heightened police presence, done right. The idea of focusing on areas where a great deal of crime occurs will also mean putting the police in areas where a large ex-offender population lives. It is no coincidence that the largest number of registered sex offenders can be found in the impoverished areas of any town; to the contrary, it reflects the sharply lower property values of those areas. Their reduced earning capacity as both ex-offenders and modern-day untouchables relegates them to the areas of the community already under the most strain. Thanks to public sex offender registries, it is easy to map and demonstrate this effect. The less well-known effect, but still instinctively understood, is the concentration of all types of ex-offenders into these same communities. Mission-based policing, with an emphasis on guardianship and continual police presence, gives communities what every resident, regardless of past criminal history, wants and needs, that is to say it provides reliable safety and security. And for criminal fence-sitters and gang "wanna-be's" it might provide the reason they need to stay out of trouble.

That effectiveness should be balanced by efficiency is central to all security efforts. We have noted parallels between policing and counterinsurgency previously in this book. One can see such a similarity on this balance as well, as indicted in Information Box 3-4.

From the broad body of research and writings on legitimacy, we have developed the notion of what we believe is the "guardianship" role of the police most likely to promote crime prevention effectiveness: that of background deterrence, carried out from the presence of large numbers of officers located inside hot zones; that of focused deterrence, which are operations carried out by officers assigned in hot zones with articulable crime prevention targets; and that of legitimacy, which is a prerequisite for winning the "hearts and minds" of citizens and thus for establishing long-term support among the local population.

Guardians and Broken Windows   The beneficial effects of guardians has been noted by Wilson and Kelling (1982). They argued that the absence of citizens in public areas, spurred by public order problems,

INFORMATION BOX 3-4:
LEGITIMACY IN COUNTER-INSURGENCY

One can witness the importance of legitimacy in security efforts by looking at an analogous security problem: the establishment of governmental legitimacy in counterinsurgency. Consider the difficulties faced by US troops in Afghanistan in the wake of the 2009 re-election of President Karzai, who is widely perceived by Afghani citizens as having stolen the election through ballot fixing. One of the central elements faced by US security operatives in Afghanistan, when seeking to establish security in areas previously held by the Taliban, was winning the "hearts and minds" of locals (see Kilcullen, 2009). The seeming illegitimacy of the president sharply undercut the ability of US troops to argue they were acting in the best interests of Afghani locals. The loss of legitimacy meant that the Taliban and Al Qaeda would be able to more easily acquire recruits, to mix with the population, and to carry out attacks against the government. What we see in this discussion is that the failure of legitimacy—the inability to promote the notion that government, through its security apparatus, can act on behalf of citizens—is a lynchpin for successful security efforts. Our position is that legitimacy is just as important for urban security practices in US cities as it is for international counterinsurgency efforts.

contributed to an increase in crime. The police, they argued, had to take on a guardianship role; they had to act aggressively against public order problems in order to prevent further neighborhood decay and the onset of serious crime. The "broken windows" paper, understood this way, is a narrative of guardianship of public places, made meaningful by the "broken windows" metaphor.

Subsequent research on Wilson and Kelling's notion of public decay has generally not been supportive. Skogan (1980, 1990), for instance, has noted that the best predictor of long-term serious crime was not an earlier onset or condition of misdemeanor activity, but instead was the earlier economic viability of neighborhoods. Others have questioned the accuracy of the historical references that Wilson and Kelling used to locate the "watchman-style" policing in historical context. On the other hand, the "broken windows" perspective has emerged as a widely accepted and popular theory of policing in US police departments (Caldero and Crank, 2010). Moreover, zero-tolerance policing, a style of policing associated with "broken windows," has established itself as a promising police strategy for dealing with crime (Braga, 2001).

We believe that the "broken windows" conception of misdemeanor-induced community failure is limitedly effective for dealing with serious crime. The concept of guardianship overall is sound, but it needs to be grounded in legitimacy as well as effectiveness. And it needs to be applied to serious crime. Research simply has not provided evidence supporting a strong link between misdemeanor crime and subsequent serious crime (Skogan, 1990). Put simply, the best way to deal with different kinds of serious or felony crime is by focusing efforts specifically on serious and felony crimes, not misdemeanors.

Toward a Hot Zone Command: Permanent Presence through Holding and Securing We consequently recommend that a hot zone command is created that focuses specifically on (1) carrying out operations in the hot zone, but operations strategically aligned for specific long-term crime dissipation goals, and (2) maintaining a substantial and highly adaptable police presence in the hot zone at all times. In other words, this command recognizes that both *police presence* and *what they do* suppress crime. Chapter 9 discusses a specific set of recommendations for organizationally charting and staffing such a hot zone command. The point of this command is to break the competitive raiding strategy characteristic of contemporary police practices in high crime areas and transition to a "secure and hold" strategy aimed at providing permanent security. Assigning a permanent presence would have several legitimizing effects, which are listed in Information Box 3-5.

In sum, the act of holding and securing is integral to guardianship. An occasional police presence cannot establish the kinds of community connections and trust that are needed to forge long-term positive

INFORMATION BOX 3-5:
LEGITIMIZING EFFECTS OF
"SECURE AND HOLD"

1. It would reduce the reliance on raiding strategies, which tend to provide very short term deterrent effects and which can be counterproductive, creating the impression that police are ineffectual.
2. It would provide the kind of presence needed to effectively maintain security in a hot zone.
3. Security would provide protection for economically vulnerable local businesses, a security issue extensively discussed in future chapters.
4. Importantly, it would take away the territory from criminals and gangs who inhabit those zones.
5. Again taking a recommendation from counterinsurgency efforts, it would force criminals to come to police controlled areas to carry out their work, rather than vice versa, which characterizes contemporary raiding operations. This would be a significant tactical advantage for police officers in their efforts to establish not zone security.
6. Deployment at this level would enable the carrying out of focused patrols while also conducting other operations at the same time, thus attacking crime problems from several different tactical directions at once.
7. Local citizens have to be convinced that, if they testify, that the police will be densely present to protect them from retaliation. Failure to do so in the current era delegitimizes the police. Citizens will be able to see officers in order to engage in routine banter, out of which valuable intelligence might be developed.
8. Criminals cannot "game" police operations, timing them so that they can duck out of site during an operation (with a quick cell phone call) and then flow back in as soon as operations are over. The ability of criminals to reassert control over an area undercuts public respect for the police.

community relations. In all these ways and more, a sharply increased and proactive permanent presence, in the style we describe as "holding and security," can facilitate legitimacy as well as effectiveness.

Endnotes

1. John Philip. (2001). *Rudyland.* Directed by Matthew Carnahan. Produced by Downtown Production, Firewater Films.

4

REDESIGNING AMERICAN POLICING, PRINCIPLES 3 AND 4

Deployment and Integrity

The principles discussed in this chapter are the principles of deployment by crime seriousness and the concept of mission integrity.

The Principle of Layered Deployment

The principle of layered deployment recognizes that the police should not neglect their other missions, but should prioritize their efforts to combat serious crime by being where serious crime is and focusing their energies directly on serious crime problems in those areas. This is not an abandonment of other missions, but a substantial reprioritization and restructuring of them. It is a shift away from current practices, which prioritizes (1) deployment in distributed beats intended to maximize access by citizens through calls for service and (2) omnipresence through random preventive patrol. This principle is based on and driven by hot spot analysis of crime intensity.

The deployment model is based on a crime analysis that identifies and prioritizes

1. The highest crime areas as "hot zones," which are clusters of hot spots and "warm" spots
2. Intermediately high areas of crime as "at-risk" zones, which tend to be areas close to hot spots, though sometimes they are stand alone areas
3. Areas where crime is "cool" as "safe" zones

Officers who are assigned to hot zones are called *operators*, and their primary work will be the establishment of security. They will be a separate command within the organization, and their leadership will be at the same level as a precinct commander. Officers assigned to at-risk zones will be called *supporters*, and their primary work is security maintenance against outside threats. A squad of supporters will be assigned to each precinct squad who will seek out serious crime problems in at-risk areas. Their work will be crime suppression within that precinct. Finally, the primary work of *responders* is comparable to the traditional beat officer, creating an omnipresence and responding to calls for service. Each of these is discussed below.

The Deployment Model

The deployment model is a layered approach, described by the response blanket, support squads for at-risk pockets in relatively safe zones, and the hot zone command.

Hot Zones   Hot zones, identified by hot spot mapping technologies, are areas whose level of serious crime is substantially higher than the surrounding community. They are conceived as areas absent adequate levels of security and in which the primary purpose of the police will be to establish security. Hot zones are where the greatest number of officers are concentrated. In the model developed herein, hot zones will have their own command, formed to work in conjunction with the department's serious crimes (or other local designation) command. Importantly, all zones—hot, at-risk, and safe—will receive staffing from responders, who will handle misdemeanor calls, public service calls, and isolated serious calls. Hot zones will be staffed by operators. The term, adapted from military special forces, refers herein to their motivation, intelligence, training, and adaptability. Operators are deployed as squads or split-squads. (A split-squad is one in which an operator squad may be halved to respond to two separate simultaneous problems, if a tactical need arises.) Operator squads are provided latitude to determine the immediate operational form of interdiction, prevention, and suppression objectives and to change an operational deployment should local information warrant a rapid change. However, all actions must always be in support of strategic goals and will be command reviewable.

Effectiveness, for operators, depends on being in sufficient numbers at the right place and also entails doing the right kinds of things.

The "right things" may be counterintuitive to a traditional officer, for instance, forgoing an arrest if it might interfere with broader strategic objectives. Individual operator units will be organized according to traditional deployment principles—sergeants for squads assigned to a particular area during a shift, and lieutenants for the areas across the shifts. A captain or deputy chief will serve as commander of all operators across a city, depending on the local organizational structure of command.

Operators should substantially reconstruct the criminogenic landscape of hot zones.[1] The operators, because they are flexible and adaptive themselves, working on the basis of mission objectives and fueled by intelligence, will be a significant force multiplier over the traditional deployment model. Operator activities are the focal or "action" point of the mission strategy within a hot zone, and all operator activities have to contribute to long-term crime prevention and dissipation. That contribution—their activities—is command driven, and operator tactical decisions always support strategic command prerogatives.

Information Box 4-1 presents what we believe are some of the advantages accrued by designing an operator role for police officers in hot zones. One might compare the similarities of Box 4-1 to Box 3-5 in the previous chapter. The substantial overlap shows how the effectiveness of an operator function can be used to facilitate police legitimacy.

At-Risk Areas   Some areas will be lower in crime activity than hot zones, yet will need a tailored police presence because of their potential for crime activity. These are called at-risk areas, conceived as areas where security has been established but in which crime activity is not yet adequately controlled. At-risk areas are characterized by crime that is higher when compared to the rest of the city, but not at the level of hot zones. Unlike hot zones, security is not openly contested, but significant security problems nevertheless remain. At-risk areas are of two types. First are transitional areas surrounding or connecting hot zones. Second are areas that are not contiguous to hot spots. Fixed permanent patrols, guided by the crime signature of the area, will be assigned to these areas at a level that is adequate for mission accomplishment.

These areas tend to be relatively small, typified by isolated problem areas. These areas will be policed by "support" squads, directed patrol squads that focus specifically on serious crimes and do not respond

INFORMATION BOX 4-1:
BENEFITS FROM THE PRESENCE OF A
PERMANENT OPERATOR FORCE IN HOT ZONES

1. Likely offenders are disinclined to commit crime if they know a police officer has a reasonable chance of finding them quickly or if they keep seeing police officers on the way to and from crime.
2. Convenience store robberies are unlikely to occur if a police officer is within sight of the store and is staying in the area.
3. Gang members—that large crowd of occasionally involved players—will be disinclined if they perceive a heightened arrest presence, or if they find they must continually deal with a police officer in their face.
4. Criminals from outside the area who come into it for drugs will be disinclined from the larger presence. Open air drug markets can be quickly extinguished.
5. Police will provide a visual role model for pro-social behavior for younger children.
6. Citizens will not be as vulnerable to revenge if they can quickly contact a police officer, and if they know that the police are already close by and able to assist on a 24 hour basis.
7. Police officers will become familiar with the area, will have better or at least more knowledgeable relations with locals, and have a keener sense of who belongs and who doesn't. They will be more likely to recognize dangerous outsiders and insiders.
8. Because the presence is permanent, outside crime producers will themselves be less likely to raid the hot spot areas.
9. There will be an increased street presence of individuals on the streets who are acting legally. The increased presence of police on the streets acting as guardians will in turn lead to increases in citizens on the streets, thus amplifying the guardianship role.

to calls for service. They will also be deployed to any area that seems to be heating up, that is, where there is a recent or sudden escalation of crime. They are layered on top of the responder blanket, so that these zones will also have responders. This ensures that safe areas that receive lower levels of routine patrol will have rapidly deployed forces in the event of any increase in crime. Depending upon need, they can answer calls or support the activities of the operators. While supporting the activities of the operators, they are also expected to suppress crime within their specific precincts. Support officers will also be positioned to address crime outflow from hot zones, particularly in instances or specific areas where crime displacement is an issue. On the other hand, recent evidence regarding a diffusion of benefits would suggest that at-risk areas contiguous to hot zones that experience significant drops in crime might see a drop in crimes as well.

At-risk areas that are independent of hot zones will be addressed at the precinct level, under a squad specifically assigned to the precinct and who will "float" according to precinct command needs. At-risk areas that are geographically contiguous to hot zone issues will be under the hot zone command, or if they are in a different precinct, will be under that precinct command though guided by principles of unity of command.

Safe Zones and the Response Blanket The foundational layer is the "response blanket," which covers the city. Responders will be assigned to this blanket coverage and will respond to calls from citizens. This blanket coverage differs from traditional random preventive patrol (RPP) assignments in two important ways:

1. Officers in this coverage are called responders and are assigned according to the relative frequency, not only of calls, but of time of day for calls. It should be emphasized that this assignment is no longer the primary department mission; the primary mission has shifted to the dissipation of serious crime. Officers consequently may be assigned to multiple districts or whatever corresponds to a patrol beat.
2. RPP, tied to a district, is no longer practiced. Omnipresence is achieved through high visibility response to calls for service, and through multibeat or multidistrict patrol.

The work of responders is not "business as usual." The work of responders, while in principle seeming to be the most consistent with traditional police practices, changes in an important way. Responders are operating in what we call safe zones, and their work is traditionally seen as routine: in response to a minor disturbance call, an officer addresses citizens' concerns while displaying a positive and supportive attitude. This is the primary work of responders that, although challenging, is already well understood and is the default practice in most departments. Officers hence are focused on rapidly resolving the instant problem and returning into service for the next call.

We transition the focus of respondents to outcomes. By outcomes, we mean that an officer should think about how the instant situation can be resolved on a more durable basis. This sort of consideration requires more time and hence requires command deemphasis on service turnaround time. This work, which can be characterized as problem solving, lacks the complexity and effectiveness of full-blown problem-oriented policing (POP), but can provide some beneficial outcomes when their purpose is to lower the likelihood of follow-up (see Braga and Weisburd [2010: 182–85] for a discussion of this way of thinking about POP). Officers respond to incidents from the level of misdemeanor to repeat serious incidents, according to need, with an eye toward patterns. These officers routinely will review crime-mapped data to seek effective solutions as needs require.

The Operator Concept

We have developed three types of officers for the layered approach to mission-based policing: operators, supporters, and responders. In the most general sense, operators are individuals who have substantial experience and who are both capable and energetic to imprint their own solutions on crime problems.

Gladwell (2008), in his study of individuals who had exceptional skills, suggests that expertise has been obtained after ten thousand hours of practice. This principle—expertise through practice—applies equally to the capacity to do police work well. Ask any police commander who her or his best officers are and almost invariably (s)he will point toward those with five or more years of experience. Policing, commanders recognize, is a complex activity, a dance between often competing systems of crime control and public legitimacy, and to do it well takes years of experience. On the street, clear "bad guy, good guy" views of the world do not always lend themselves to successful crime control, a lesson that takes a great deal of experience to learn. Recruits often have a tendency to see the world in terms of black and white, where the grays—the nuances of policing done well, developed from a large skills base learned from many different experiences with different kinds of people—become more evident with experience.

This particularly applies to the operators in our model. The quantity of preservice police training varies nationally, police training ranges from two hundred to over one thousand hours (Connolly, 2010). This is a preentry level, and the upper end, as Connolly notes, keeps recruits in seats for up to half a year when agencies would like to be deploying officers. However, recruit preservice training does not provide the skill and systems knowledge necessary to be an operator. Importantly, operator assignment is merit-based, requiring time in service, but also chosen through competitive selection processes. Operators should develop their skills along a career track, which is a planned path of attaining skills, expertise in a variety of areas, and broad understandings of the working environment. Training will be developed in the following areas:

1. Crime control skills: Operators must possess investigative skills associated with detectives, the technical skills needed to respond to violent citizen behaviors, and the systems knowledge normally associated with command rank. Because these officers work both *as a team* and under the principle of *unity of command*, they learn coordination and control skills traditionally associated with Special Weapons and Tactics (SWAT) activities.

2. Crime prevention skills: Operators will also need training in the central concepts of routine activities, and applications of POP in terms of crime prevention, environmental criminology, and Crime Prevention through Environmental Design (CPTED) programs. This will also include training on "reading" the environment and tracking changes (keeping written records) in it.

3. Knowledge of the overall structure of mission policing: The operator must buy into the philosophy of the department and

the strategic means of reaching the mission goals. They will be provided training in the "grays"—assessments of scenarios and likely long-term consequences of lines of actions. This training specifically focuses on the relationship between individual actions and logical lines of organization (LOOs) end states (see Chapters 5 and 6).

4. Study and practice in "doing legitimacy well": "Doing legitimacy well" is seen as a skill that is developed through practice after the acquisition of a knowledge base, like other aspects of police work. Officers will be trained in terms of the balance between public pressures within hot spots (1) in how to protect victims by getting offenders under control, (2) through skills training to take the position of community members in stressful circumstances, (3) in the importance of communication and how audiences interpret information, (4) through learning how to communicate effectively and clearly, and (5) learning why perceptions of community legitimacy are essential for strategic success. Counterinsurgency literature has explored the importance of legitimacy, often phrased in terms of winning the "hearts and minds" in terms of mission success to a substantial extent, and officers will be provided with and expected to study this literature.

5. Technological platform skills. Platform skills require that officers be knowledgeable about technologies upon which the capacity for crime analysis and criminal response are based. They learn to work with the data-entry report forms necessary to provide rapid information to commanders. They read and interpret data mapping and learn how to carry out basic data analysis. They can overlay crime data onto images of the physical plant of the city so that they can assess the environment for problem solving and for problematic characteristics of the environment.

The career background of an operator can include previous work as a support officer or detective or related role where an officer has had the opportunity to demonstrate aptitude and attitude and where she or he has observed strategic operations. When an officer has performed well as a supporting officer, she or he will move into the pool of officers who can be assigned into the operator ranks. The department command should spend a significant amount of time directly communicating with operators and those on the operator career path and should plan on spending a very significant amount of time, money, and effort on operator training.

Deployment and Crime Mapping   Deployment is tied to the use of technology to track crime. The value of technology to command-structured crime suppression was at the center of New York's compare statistics (COMPSTAT) program and has since established the value of computerized crime mapping for the analysis of crime patterns and characteristics. Crime mapping has been established not only as an efficient real-time method for modeling crime, but also for problem solving under a problem-oriented policing strategy (Boba, 2005).

The widespread use of data-driven incident management and identification is a large, significant change that characterizes contemporary policing (Weisburd and Lum, 2001). A wide and virtually unlimited variety of crime information can be developed on a real-time basis. The strength of crime mapping is threefold:

Real-time response. The police can respond to crime in real time, in terms of what is actually happening in the field. This is helpful for tactical response to crime clusters and in providing direction for the deployment of units to hot spots. Moreover, real-time crime analysis, if tied to deployment practices, can lead to rapid response at an organized level not available under traditional patrols.

Environmental crime analysis. Real-time analysis dovetails with environmental crime research, showing that crime is specific in time and place and is best understood and countered through an understanding of the dynamics of "place"—the concrete characteristics of locations that may have criminogenic features. Such criminogenic features can refer to structures and spaces that facilitate crime access and getaway, may channel people in a way that increases victimization opportunities, or may inhibit guardianship oversight. Crime mapping can identify such places, and thoughtful applications of environmental criminology can carry out the work of mitigating their crime appeal.

Hot spot specification. Crime mapping also shows consistently that crime is not randomly distributed but rather spread out in hot spots, and these hot-spots have crime signatures that uniquely identify them. This body of research has noted that a small number of locations account for most crimes. From this work, researchers have coined the term hot spot (Weisburd and Braga, 2003), which refers to areas with high levels of crime. The corresponding body of research on hot spots shows that a focusing on problems in those areas can have large impacts on crime and, through a diffusion of effects, may also lower crime in areas contiguous to hot spots.

Figure 4.1 provides a comparison of the respective work of operators and traditional line officers. The most important distinguishing feature, which is revealed in several of the items, is the temporal frame of reference for action. Line officers traditionally focus on short-term problem solutions, seeking to satisfy the needs of a particular call for service and then moving on to the next call. Operators, however, are expected to always take into consideration the long-term or strategic implications of their actions. Closely tied to this is the expectation of mission integrity (discussed in the next section), where operators are expected to work within the long-term mission in the hot zone and to carry out operations or actions within command expectations. Both mission coherence and strategic vision are central to the operator concept, as well as to mission-based policing generally.

The Principle of Mission Integrity

The fourth principle of mission-based policing is mission integrity, which emphasizes that all elements of the chain of command working within a hot spot are responsible for carrying out that mission. Operators, under mission integrity, take orders from unit commanders, and on up the chain. The principle of *unity of effort* applies here. Unity of effort means *that all units of the department that are pertinent to the mission act together, and their actions flow from coherent and shared planning.*

	TRADITIONAL LINE OFFICER	OPERATOR
REFERENCE GROUP		
	Individual response with backup as needed	Squad, mutually assured backup
WORK DECISIONS		
	Self-needs of beat and citizens	Commander
COMMAND INTEGRITY		
	Limited: sergeant oversight	Required: Most recent command from a commander in supervisory chain
NATURE OF WORK		
	Order maintenance, crime suppression, RPP, calls for service	Crime suppression and prevention, directed patrol, POP. Legitimacy activities
ARRESTS: FUNCTION		
	Activity report: Work accomplished	Strategic: Arrests facilitate articulated goals
EXPECTED OUTCOMES		
	Speedy response to calls, create omnipresent effect though patrol, create pressure on crime areas, keep the lid on crime	Bring crime down, successfully deploy POP operations
RANGE OF PROBLEM SOLUTION		
	Resolution of immediate call	Resolution of underlying problem or criminal pattern/cluster
PREOPERATION INTELLIGENCE REVIEW		
	Limited: Roll call briefing	Open—intelligence, crime patterns, incidents, planning
AFTER-ACTION ASSESSMENT		
	No	Yes
ASSIGNMENT		
	District (fixed)	Hot zone (fluid)
EXPERIENCE		
	Not required	Required
ACTIVITY LEVEL		
	Misdemeanors, citizen interactions when responding to call, some serious crime	Serious crime, serious and repeat incidents, patterns, problems
DETERRENT INTENT		
	RPP, omnipresence	Directed patrol, omnipresence

Figure 4.1 Comparison of traditional officers to operators.

Unity of effort is structured by command. Commanders of hot zones fall under a single ranking officer (depending on department size and span of control) who occupies the rank equivalent to precinct commanders and is responsible for deployment and mission development. Midlevel command will take charge of task areas, with individual unit commanders assigned to shifts.

The overriding mission of operators assigned to a hot spot is the dissipation of crime. The strategy for carrying out this mission depends on the local structure of crime. That local structure is understood through (1) crime prevention and hot spot research, which operators are expected to know, (2) a detailed study of local areas, and (3) enforcement-initiated problem solving, according to which the police develop systematic and measured responses to crime.

Problem Solving, Not Incident Management,
Is the Task of the Police in Hot Zones

POP is widely studied but underdeveloped in US policing practices. Indeed, as Scott (2000) observed, in spite of a favorable track record of applications to complex crime problems, it has not taken hold in police practice. Our recommendation is the adaptation of Goldstein's (1977) model developed by Boba and Crank (2008). Goldstein argued that the police should focus on problems rather than incidents. Addressing problems, Goldstein argued, required not only the suppression of crime but also addressing the factors that caused the crime. Information Box 4-2 clarifies the distinction between POP and incident management.

Boba and Crank (2008) accepted the notion of problem solving "whole cloth" as a valued strategic response to crime. Its principle shortcoming, they argued, was that it invested problem identification and solution primarily in the line ranks. As the authors noted:

> The operational practice of problem oriented policing today is the conflation of problems and incidents. ... This conflation is a direct consequence of the tendency ... to make line officers the central actors in problem identification, problem analysis, and problem resolution accountability. Because of this, the scope of problems ... shifts to a more manageable incident-based size, simply conceived in terms of crime suppression and addressable within a short period of time, if at all.

INFORMATION BOX 4-2
POP VERSUS INCIDENT MANAGEMENT

The difference between POP and incident management is some-times difficult to identify. The *Center for Problem Oriented Policing* (2009) provides the following example to distinguish POP from traditional incident management.

Suppose police find themselves responding several times a day to calls about drug dealing and vandalism in a neighbor-hood park. The common approach of dispatching an officer to the scene and repeatedly arresting offenders may do little to resolve the long term crime and disorder problem. If, instead, police were to incorporate problem-oriented policing techniques into their approach, they would examine the conditions underly-ing the problem. This would likely include collecting additional information—perhaps by surveying neighborhood residents and park users, analyzing the time of day when incidents occur, determining who the offenders are and why they favor the park, and examining the particular areas of the park that are most con-ducive to the activity and evaluating their environmental design characteristics. The findings could form the basis of a response to the problem behaviors.

The problems with line level problem solving have been noted else-where in the literature. Skogan et al. (1999) noted that Chicago Police Department's efforts to decentralize problem solving were often inef-fective. Braga and Weisburd (2006: 148) described the central problems noted by Skogan as "inadequate management, poor leadership and vision, lack of training, and weak performance measures." They concluded:

> It is time for practitioners and policymakers to set aside the fantasy of street-level problem-oriented policing and embrace the reality of what they can expect from the beat officer in the development of crime pre-vention plans at the street level. (2006: 149)

Boba and Crank (2008) articulated a model (hereafter called the Boban model) that integrated problem solving to command authority and accountability. This model, consistent with Braga and Weisburd's recommendations, viewed line-level problem solving in terms of incident management and located increasingly sophisticated and costly problems up the chain of command. According to the model, level of problem complexity is directly tied to position in the chain of command. They identified six problem levels and associated commands:

Incidents, defined as "events to which typically an officer or civilian personnel responds to or discovers on patrol." These problems are addressed by first responders, usually line personnel.

Serious incidents, defined as "single events that are deemed more serious by laws and policies … they typically require additional investigation and/or a more extensive response." These problems are addressed by detectives or specially trained personnel.

Repeat incidents, defined as "two or more incidents that are similar in nature and have happened at the same place (typically) or have been carried out by the same person." First-line supervisors are responsible for problem solving at this level, most likely with the help of line officers.

Patterns, defined as "two or more crimes or serious incidents that seem to be related by victim, gender, location, or property." The goal of problem solving here is to provide in-depth analysis on serious crimes in order to link them together. Analysts with specific training perform problem analysis and scan for patterns, and first-line managers carry out the problem solution.

Problems, defined as a "set of related activity, both crime and disorder, that occurs over several months, seasons, or years that stems from systematic opportunities created by everyday behavior and environment." Problems will contain numerous crime activities and repeat incidents—problems suggest a structure of opportunity—and "crime and place" theory (Eck, 1993) becomes central to problem identification. Problem solving and analysis are carried out by a team of personnel, with a recommendation for the inclusion of nondepartment personnel who are experts in the criminology of places. The team should also include an analyst who provides data analysis and pattern analysis expertise, as well as line officers with experience in the area.

LEVEL OF ACTIVITY	PROBLEM SOLVING	ANALYSIS	ACCOUNTABILITY	MEETINGS
Incidents	Line Officers	Line Officers	First-Line Supervisors	Meeting on shift Daily briefings
Serious Incidents	Detectives	Detectives	First-Line Supervisors	Daily/weekly briefings
Repeat Incidents	Sergeants	Sergeants	Management	Weekly meetings
Patterns	Detective Sergeants Patrol Sergeants	Crime Analysts Sergeants Lieutenants	Crime Analyst Supervisor, Management	Weekly meetings Monthly meetings
Problems	Team of personnel	Team of personnel	Management	Monthly meetings

Figure 4.2   Activity level by problem complexity. *Source*: Boba and Gank, 2008: 386.

Social issues, defined as "an underlying cause of the routine behavior and opportunities for crime and disorder that have developed over long periods." Boba did not develop a command for social issues, viewing their solutions as beyond the statutory authority and financial capacity of the agency.

The Boban model (1) integrated problems across the chain of command, (2) identified chain of command accountability depending on the complexity of the problems, and (3) recognized the importance of using local government sources for large scale problems. Figure 4.2 presents the Boban model of problems, articulated within a graduated command structure.

Figure 4.2 shows how the complexity of problems is tied to the level of command responsible for problem solution and analysis, and the next higher command level is responsible for oversight and accountability. For example, we see that the responsibility for *repeat incidents* problem analysis fall to sergeants, and middle managers are responsible for accountability. Weekly meetings are held among sergeants for discussion and development of solutions and for assessment of current levels of success in addressing those problems. We view the Boban model as a structural advancement over the Goldsteinian model, in that it adapts problem complexity to command authority, experience, and resource access.

A second advantage of the Boban model is that, compared to COMPSTAT, it is a true command-driven, problem-solving model. As Weisburd and his colleagues noted, in COMPSTAT and other data-driven practices, middle managers tended to return to traditional crime suppression strategies under relentless pressures to produce, consequently innovative POP efforts were not developed. Because of this, Boba and Crank observed (2008; see Weisburd et al., 2003), COMPSTAT did not solve problems but instead focused crime suppression efforts on crime incident clustering. Incident clustering, Boba noted, was appropriate for an intermediate level of command, but did not achieve the level of actual problem solving.

However, the Boban model is still tied to an underlying geographic distribution of personnel at the line level who are accountable to calls for service. That is, problem solving is carried out by particular individuals or groups, while prevailing organizational practices are still tied to traditional notions of deployment according to RPP and calls for service. Efforts to blend the calls for service model and the POP model are problematic in that line officers face two contradictory masters: command officers within their department who may want to deploy officers for problem solving, and citizens who exert powerful claims on an officers' time, almost always for minor incidents. Boba and Crank attempt to address that issue by having calls for service viewed as a specific type of "problem" that can be integrated into higher or more complex problem solutions. We believe, however, that the best solution is to prioritize problem solving over calls for service, *altogether ceasing random preventive patrol.*

Boba and Crank's model of POP, to reach its maximum capability in the armament of crime solution strategies, needs to become *mission coherent.* The central problem with that model of POP is that it has not been tied in a logical way to a clear mission aimed at the long-term dissipation of crime in articulable areas. Hence, even when problems are solved, one cannot logically identify the solution's overall impact on crime or its ability to dissipate criminal opportunity across a hot zone. Problems tend to be organizationally treated as if they were isolated from each other; no effort that we know of knits problem solutions together to address crime strategically. *Mission coherence means that POP solutions should be logically and comprehensively organized to achieve a central mission—the dissipation of crime in hot zones.* The mechanisms for doing this are called logical lines of operation (LOO) (developed in Chapter 5), and problem-oriented solutions are strategically developed to accomplish each LOO.

The Boban model also needs to be tied more clearly to the hearts and minds of police officers. A significant shortcoming of POP, though not well developed in research, is that it does not seem, to line officers, to be tied in a meaningful way to doing something about crime. By creating a model of problem solving intended to redefine crime in noncriminal terms, this model inadvertently created the impression that it was not about crime solution. In the next section we will present a model, based on the Boban model, that is designed to be mission coherent and that is more clearly tied to crime suppression.

Hot Zone Problem Solving: Toward an Enforcement-Based Model

This section is intended to present a way to do problem solving that is adapted to a high crime environment. We recommend moving away from the Goldsteinian model, which is aptly scientific but too complex for routine operations. While acknowledging that Goldstein's model of POP is excellent in the abstract, it faces problems of complexity and analysis that are often beyond the practical constraints available for most routine police operations. Indeed, when one looks at the many POP experiments that have been carried out, they tend to be grant-associated or assisted by university-based researchers. This has been very good for research purposes, and has been excellent for advancing the understanding of what works for policing, but it rarely lends itself to day-to-day use.

Our model of problem solving builds on the problems of problem solving noted by Braga and Weisburd (2010). It is a focusing of that model around serious crime interventions. It also calibrates that model for routine police use in hot zones. It makes use of the Boban command-driven POP model to ensure adequate command involvement, command review, and resource allocation to problems. It also recognizes that formal problem solving is a special case of intelligence gathering, one that focuses on a particular kind of crime prevention outcome. We call this model *enforcement-initiated problem solving*.

POP and Shallow Problem Solving   POP, though widely acclaimed as a methodology for crime prevention, has faced a variety of hurdles. In addition to the critique of the problems of POP noted above by Boba and Crank (2008), Braga and Weisburd (2010) noted several problems with POP practices. Central was the tendency to relegate problem solving to line officers, resulting in underresourced and inadequately developed problem concepts. This is in contrast to the kinds of problems found in hot spots, which are often overlapping and complex. Information Box 4-3 presents a discussion of the "muddiness" of problem solving in hot spots.

In addition to the muddiness of problems, police rarely enter a problem-solving situation analytically. That is, they do not arrive at a crime scene and immediately focus their energies on a scientific investigation into the underlying causes of the crime prior to deciding on a course of action. Nor would citizens expect or want them to. For all of the long-term crime preventive advantages of problem solving—and there are many—the responsibility of the police is more immediate. That responsibility is to stop crime that is currently happening, try to remove an offender from the streets for crimes that have recently happened, and suppress further crimes by the same offender or from curious fence-sitters who wonder how they might similarly profit.

In other words, the police function in high crime areas is, in the face of an immediate or recent criminal event, to engage in suppression and high visibility presence. Such activity—at the center of police crime responses—cannot be abrogated. Moreover, it is expected by the public who, to paraphrase Bittner (1970), want the police to do something about crime *now*! The *now* component of police work cannot be wished away by any particular police strategy, however potentially viable or effective it is or how relatively ineffective a quick response tends to be.

Other issues with problem solving were noted by Braga and Weisburd (2010). They observed that, while problem solving was central to the police task in hot spots, the complex POP model developed

INFORMATION BOX 4-3.
THE "MUDDINESS" OF PROBLEMS IN HOT SPOTS

One can describe problems in hot spots as being "muddy." They do not bound well to specific characteristics of the environment, they tend to overlap, and they are complex, involving multiple features of places simultaneously. Braga and Weisburd (2010: 157) noted that "high-activity crime places tend to have multiple problems and the problems at crime places can be quite complex and involved." They provided three examples:

> Minneapolis study: Problem solutions encountered a heterogeneous mix of crime types rather than a concentration of one type of crime occurring.
>
> San Diego: Multiple problems overlapped, so that no *pure cases* were noted where a problem can be identified as a single type. Overlapping problems complicated prospects for individualized solutions.
>
> Oakland: Officers found it difficult to unravel "what had happened in a place and deciding how it should be addressed." (157).

Muddy problems do not lend themselves to simple identification or ready solution. One may encounter a mix of multiple environmental facilitators of crime, no clear way to increase guardianship or place management (see Braga and Weisburd, 2010: 169-172). Indeed, the opposite may characterize such places—potential guardians are intimidated or threatened and are highly unlikely to provide helpful areal oversight. Moreover, opportunistic criminals may share the space with hot shots, serious victimizers who tend to be present when crimes happen, and who will exploit the situation for personal gain or pleasure. In such circumstances, the ability to develop a formal problem solution based on the analytic and research-based Goldsteinian model is likely to give way—and reasonably so—to harsh enforcement focused on maximization of rapid suppression and enforcement tactics. It is this kind of "muddy problem" environment—characteristic of hot spots—that problem solving must adapt in order to prove its effectiveness.

by Goldstein might not be the best approach. Factors mitigating against it include:

1. The hierarchical structure of police work that tended to inhibit innovation.
2. An organizational culture that resists in-depth problem solving.
3. Lack of line empowerment for follow through.

For these reasons, they suggested that POP, as envisioned by Goldstein, was unlikely to catch on. Yet, they did not provide an alternative model beyond a discussion of shallow problem solving. This begs the question: How should police do police work in hot spots? What is it that the police do, if it is not problem solving? Braga and Weisburd (2010) suggest that, instead of full-blown problem solving, it might be adequate to simply focus police resources on hot spot risks: "Perhaps, simply focusing police resources on identifiable risks that come to the attention of problem-oriented policing projects, such as crime hot spots, may be enough to produce crime-control gains" (164). The focus on risks was similar to the notion of "shallow problem solving," discussed in Chapter 3, which they described as POP endeavors that tended to be small in scope, used only a rudimentary analysis, and were typically without any kind of formal assessments.

Enforcement-Initiated Problem Solving We propose a different way to think about problem solving, one that recognizes both the need for rapid response to serious crime incidents and that also aims more sharply at what Braga and Weisburd (2010) referred to as "risks" in hot zones. We call it enforcement-initiated problem solving. It stems from the recognition that, whatever an underlying problem is, what brings it to police attention and must be dealt with is a criminal event. Responding to that criminal event is the primary and irreducible responsibility of the police. The police response will have four components.

The first component of police response is *crime control and suppression*. Because police are deployed tactically as squads in hot zones, this response will always carry a suppressive or deterrent quality, in the sense that several officers will immediately make their presence known in the crime area, and a high number of contacts will be made rapidly after the crime event, both to residents in the immediate area and to individuals who might be implicated in or associated with the crime.

The second component is *problem solving*. Problem solving will occur simultaneously with crime suppression, can be thought of as critical follow-up for tactical dominance, and is essential for long-term strategic success. It represents the intelligence-gathering phase of problem solving: The deployed squad identifies and collects information from area residents, businesses, and other sources implicated in the particular instant event, with an eye toward the identification of underlying patterns, clusters, and problems. After-action reports and periodic command assessments provide the forum for problem so identified.

The third component is *squad deployment*. In the mission-based model, hot zone response is squad-based. This unit has the immediate advantage of providing five or six individuals, rather than one, to implement any particular problem solution. In split-squad situations, this would provide three officers for a response. The use of squad deployment has several advantages over single officer deployment for problem-solving purposes:

1. It permits a multioperational tactical response to particular problems and hence more likely to be tuned to the complex realities of the environment.
2. A deployed squad immediately provides a short-term deterrent. Importantly, because deployment in hot zones is permanent, it provides a police-based guardianship, discussed in Chapter 3, when citizen-based guardianship simply may be unavailable or unsustainable in such settings. That is, the squad deployment maximizes the deterrent effects that are achieved from both "being there" and "doing the right kinds of things."
3. A squad trained and engaged in problem-oriented techniques is more likely to provide a breadth of problem solution perspective that a single officer cannot.
4. A squad, permanently assigned, is not under the common pressures faced by officers to solve the problem and then get back into service.
5. Because the squad is tied structurally to crime prevention analysts in the department (see Chapter 9 example), the

ability to assess the results of ones work and make practical decisions about sustaining or changing a particular operation is facilitated.

6. Finally, and to be discussed extensively in Chapter 5, problem solutions are tied to the organizational mission in hot zones, which is the permanent dissipation of crime. The squad is the entity tasked with the street-based task of bringing crime down. Hence, problem solutions are never stand-alone projects but are always in the service of strategic efforts to achieve articulated goals. The criteria for success will always be crime preventive and realized as lower crime numbers for the specific crime signature that is tasked to the squad to solve.

Using the squad as the core unit for problem solving, but also recognizing the advantages of Boba and Crank's (2008) command-driven model of problem solving, we would adapt the Goldsteinian model as follows:

Crime engagement: This is the squad's initial response to a criminal event. This response will often be a dispatched call, though it may arise from other sources. The immediate goal is to exercise suppressive control over a particular area coupled with intelligence gathering. The presence of several officers facilitates a quick assessment of the situation and the rapid interviewing of witnesses and suspects. A squad-level "response blanket" provides immediate coverage of the crime and the larger area around it. A squad response is always a high contact operation, maximizing visibility, suppression through presence, and information gathering. A detective, assigned to work with the squad, is also deployed at this time. Problem solving is initiated at the time the crime is engaged.

Scanning and intelligence collection: This is the initial analysis of the criminal event and refers to data that are initiated by a criminal event and where initial data are collected during the response to the event. It should be emphasized that, unlike Goldstein, who emphasized that the problem should be made distinct from the criminal event, *we argue that crime and problems are inextricable, and that crime is the only reason for the police to respond at all.* Hence, scanning is a by-product of the response to the criminal event that triggered the original deployment. The high-contact activities of the squad, in which they seek immediate solutions to the crime and suppression of possibly linked crime, become data to be collected: To whom did they talk? What did they find out, what did local businesses or citizens say, etc.

Analysis: Analysis is initially embodied in the production of after-action reports. (It should be emphasized that all operations are strategically directed toward the broader goal of crime dissipations, so the squad is always acting based on planned information. Hence, analysis is not always reactive, but occurs during an ongoing intelligence assessment cycle.) After-action reports not only discuss the characteristics of the criminal event, but also any information that might suggest that underlying problems facilitated the crime and are likely to lead to future crime. These reports are produced by the squad during and after any crime action has been carried out. These reports will consequently contain two categories of information for all crime the squad responds to:

1. The specific crime dynamics, current information, and the self-perceptions of the squad's impact.
2. The presence of underlying problems and their characteristics, and providing an initial discussion of likely responses. This is the problem-solving component of the squad's actions.

After-action reports are reviewed up the chain of command, and all pertinent intelligence is recorded for processing. A weekly review, modeled after COMPSTAT meetings, will assess weekly activity and its impact on crime as well as the viability of ongoing problem solutions and consider the advancement of new problem solutions. This weekly review will also look at reports on intelligence received from detectives associated with the case and existing associated crime patterns as displayed through hot zone analyses.

Assessment: The assessment of the squad's operational activities and decisions about subsequent operations are made at weekly meetings of command staff responsible for coverage of the hot zone. The staff at this meeting may decide to move ahead on a new problem, to continue one already under-taken, to gather additional intelligence, or to withdraw from a problem-oriented operational activity that is not achieving its goals. Decisions from this staff meeting are made with the sergeants of the operator crews present and become the basis for continuance, addition, or ending existing problem solution responses. By making POP decisions at this level of command, the issues of accountability and breadth of operations, central to the Boban model of POP, are actualized. This means that commanders ensure that all operations are consistent with the mission, that any particular POP operation is adequately resourced, and that operations are achieving what they are intended to achieve.

The POP-intelligence loop. Because problem solutions are initiated by specific incidents, the police response to a crime will always be located somewhere in a problem-solving loop. This means, in practice, that while they are initiating an enforcement response in a particular instance, they may be developing or carrying out operations for another problem. This suggests that there will likely be more problems than problem solutions, and that operators must prioritize their responses. The POP-intelligence loop is designed to maximize the dispersion of information in a timely way to groups who need it.

The loop presented here is modeled after the intelligence cycle employed by the New Jersey State Police (NJSP) (Fuentes, 2006). It is redesigned from the NJSP model for simplification of presentation. The model is also consistent with the overall design of POP and is quite amenable to POP-focused operations that contain a significant enforcement and interrogation component. Figure 4.3 presents the NJSP intelligence cycle adapted to mission-based policing. It combines the strengths of the NJSP model with the POP structure of mission-based policing. The box on top (left) represents the first phase, *planning*, and recognizes that three kinds of planning groups are important to the production of intelligence: The squad, which plans specific details of operations; the hot zone command, where

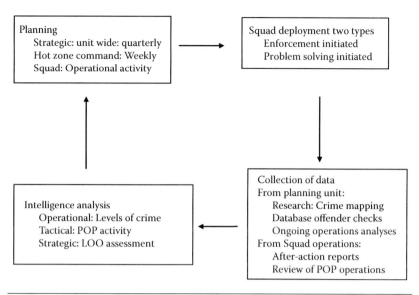

Figure 4.3   The POP intelligence loop.

decisions about new and ongoing POP operations are made, and the department, where the chief is responsible for the overall strategic mission. The second phase, deployment, is the actual activity of individual squads. It is either enforcement initiated or it is a specific POP operation. The third phase, the collection of data, recognizes that data are developed from both the department's planning unit and from squad operations. The fourth phase, intelligence analysis, is carried out by the squad in their after-action report, by the planning unit in their analysis of events, and by the detectives assigned to specific cases. Products of analysis are then returned to the primary entities that are responsible for carrying out the mission; the squad, the hot zone command unit, and the chief and department command staff.

It should be noted that the information reports provided as intelligence documents are fundamentally different from traditional investigative reports. Describing these reports, Fuentes (2006) noted:

> Unlike investigation reports, which are evidentiary in nature and must satisfy the elements of proof required for criminal prosecutions, the aim of intelligence reports is to provide lead information necessary for interpreting the environment, preventing crime, identifying and interdicting targets, influencing future operations and policy decisions, and guiding resource allocation. (14)

This intelligence expectation is transformative for a department's data analysis unit. Instead of being preoccupied with the preparation of reports for permanent record-keeping purposes, their role becomes *situational awareness*, which means that they provide rapid turnaround of data products so that operator squads and command staff can transition rapidly to changing circumstances in crime suppression and prevention activities. As we will describe in Chapter 9 when we diagram the hot zone command, the crime prevention planning specialists are structurally linked to the hot zone command so that they can work with and respond to the needs of the various squads for operational intelligence and to the command staff for tactical planning purposes.

Problem Solving and Hot Shots   The Goldstenian model focused heavily on crime places. That is, it looked at the criminogenic characteristics of particular locations and sought to identify what could be changed to alter their criminogenic aspect. We argue that the POP focus of hot zone policing should include "hot shots" as well. By hot shots we mean individuals who have substantial criminal histories who are currently associated with high levels of crime activity. Though person-based directed patrols have generally not met with much success, research has shown that, like places, a relatively small number of people account for most crimes.

We recommend the inclusion of hot shots into problem-solving activities. How any particular agency defines hot shots will vary, depending on the quantity of gang crime and particular serious crime signatures. We identify hot shots, for instance, by the symbolic number "66-100." This group was so named after the assignment of the term Code 66 to gang members who had one hundred local computer entries. Anyone who has that many entries, we have noted, is likely deeply involved in a criminal lifestyle, and it serves to separate out those deeply involved in crime from those with minimum involvement and investment. This tabulation also recognizes that criminals, in the current era, tend to be involved in a wide variety of activities, not a single crime type.

The one hundred entries might have been for combined traffic, criminal, warrant, and victim reports. The number 66-100 was selected because in the first seconds of getting a suspect's history, an officer can discern gang membership and his or her number of mainframe entries. It does not require a more time-consuming threat analysis, is amenable to rapid response and suppression, and provides information useful for the development of problem-oriented solutions. Contact with such individuals provides significant potential intelligence value.

Another advantage of the 66-100 code is that it recognizes that many individuals deeply involved in crime are frequently present at serious crime incidents, even if they are not directly involved. The issue of presence often indicates a "player": someone deeply involved in crime but with enough savvy not to be directly implicated in particular crime events. Importantly, this is just one of many different models for identifying hot shots. We believe that the problem-solving model provided here should not only look at changing the physical environment through decriminalization tactics, but also changing the cultural environment by addressing offenders with sustained records.

One issue is important to the focus on hot shots. As noted by Braga and Weisburd (2010), a focus on offenders is less likely to pay off in significant crime reductions than a focus on hot spots: offenders are mobile while places are static. Hence, any focus on offenders requires a much larger analysis of the crime-producing environment for success in any particular intervention or operation. Hence, focusing on offenders is more difficult and overall tends to be less productive work than hot spot work. Our recommendation, from this, is to be aware of this limitation of a hot shot focus. With that noted, some offenders are substantially involved in high levels of crime, and the department needs to think tactically about removing these high-risk offenders from the streets.

Whether hot spots or hot shots are the focus of any particular POP solution, the specific operation is always in the service of the underlying strategy—permanent and long-term reductions in crime. Hence, it is important to ensure that any POP activity focusing on hot shots does not inadvertently trigger goal displacement, by which we mean that making arrests becomes an end in itself. Any such tactical operation is always articulated within the broader purpose of crime dissipation.

Hot Spot Policing and Mission-Based Policing: A Comparison

In the discussion of this principle, we have provided a discussion and comparison of our concept of problem solving to the notion of problem solving discussed by Braga and Weisburd (2010).

Figure 4.4 provides a comparison of hot spots policing as articulated by Braga and Weisburd (2010) and mission-based policing. The two models should not be interpreted as alternative to each other but complementary. The hot spots model of policing primarily focuses on the nature of crime, particularly crime in hot spots, and builds a strong, research-based argument for focusing police resources in those areas. Its broad discussion and presentation of research findings regarding the value of a hot spot focus for police work is compelling. The mission-based model provides a model of policing that is designed specifically for hot spot areas. Both models focus on hot spots, have legitimacy as a central concern, recognize a need for some form of POP, and do not support a zero-tolerance focus for misdemeanor crime. Both models also perceive an important role for guardianship, though the two models operationalize guardianship in sharply different terms—hot spots policing in terms of place managers, and mission-based policing in terms of the police themselves.

Recognizing the extent to which the models complement each other, one can identify two general differences between hot spot policing and mission-based policing.

First, the hot spot model does not present a new concept of police practices, but generally emphasizes the tactical advantages of problem solving and problem-oriented policing. The mission-based model, on the other hand, identifies comparative differences with regard to deployment, mission structure, scope of activities, organizational design, strategic goal, and the police discretion.

Second, and perhaps the most far-reaching difference between the two models, is that the hot spots model does not articulate a long-term goal of crime dissipation or general "cooling" of hot spots, but is focused on the successful solution to crime problems. The mission-based policing strategically organizes police practices to achieve permanent reductions in crime. Put differently, hot spots policing is about specific tactical approaches to policing: What is the POP operation, that can solve a particular hot spot problem? Mission-based policing

MODE	HOT SPOT POLICING	MISSION BASED POLICING
DIFFERENCES		
DEPLOYMENT		
	Single officer with backup	Layered. Operator squad in hot zone over responder blanket
POP STRUCTURE		
	Flexible, recognizes limitations, concerns over shallow problem solving	Problem complexity tied to command level, POP planning component of intelligence collection
SCOPE OF ACTIVITIES		
	Problem solution-end in itself	Problem solution tied to strategic LOO
DEPLOYMENT STRATEGIC GOAL		
	Crime problem in hot spot	Dissipation of crime in hot zone
ORGANIZATIONAL CHANGE		
	Unspecified: reconsideration of traditional alignment	Precinct realignment and restructure, hot zone command, outreach positions
CRIME FOCUS IN HOT SPOTS		
	Driven by nature of problem, with a deemphasis on zero tolerance	Serious crime
LINE DISCRETION		
	Unchanged	Command Integrity
CAPABLE GUARDIANSHIP		
	Citizen based: place managers	Police based: Intensified presence and activity in hot zone
LEGITIMACY		
	Community-based police initiatives	Neighborhood Revitalization Committee, Strategic Information Officer
END GOAL		
	Police: Successful POP operations	Security-based community redevelopment
SIMILARITIES		
AREAL FOCUS ON HOT SPOTS		
	Yes	Yes
LEGITIMACY AS CENTRAL CONCERN		
	Yes	Yes
MODIFIED POP		
	Yes	Yes
ZERO TOLERANCE/PRIMARY FOCUS ON MISDEMEANORS		
	No	No

Figure 4.4   A comparison of hot spot policing and mission-based policing.

always takes the broader strategic approach: What is the contribution of a particular operation to broader strategic goals?

We will close this chapter by presenting Information Box 4-4, which refers to command orientation and represents a quick perspective on the aspect that officers and commanders should bring to mission-based policing. It encapsulates key elements of mission responsibilities as they apply to those who carry out the mission-based model of policing.

INFORMATION BOX 4-4
COMMAND ORIENTATION FOR
MISSION PERSONNEL

Command orientation refers to how mission personnel think about their work. The following statements and discussions provide this orientation.

1. **Mission Integrity** means that, from commanders down the chain of command, all personnel are fundamentally responsible for the mission. No arguing up the chain of command, *except and only* during operational planning and during after-action discussion where the focus should be on a truthful assessment of the actual success of the operation, including backfiring effects and mistakes.

2. **Unity of Command.** Commanders work together to achieve mission success. In the case of conflicts between command units, the responsibility of commanders is to find a solution rapidly, so as not to interfere with ongoing tactical operations.

3. **Act, don't React.** Acting is faster than reacting, and is superior for that reason. In interpersonal issues, the actor is the controller, while reacting puts the control in another's hands. Acting takes the initiative away from criminal elements. Acting, not reacting, lowers the likelihood of an overreaction that will end in failure. The point of this is to recognize that planning, acting on

that plan, and then assessing that plan will lead to success. This point also recognizes that the long term primary goal of the police mission is to reestablish a sense of security throughout hot spot areas, and that all units pull together for the mission.

4. **Tactical Planning for Mission Success.** This phrase means that operations that are adequately planned and carried out will lead to operational success. A string of operational successes will lead to strategic success. The combined strategic successes will ultimately lead to mission success. Hence, planning is the cornerstone of long term mission success.

5. **The Crime is More Important than the Criminal.** The ultimate goal is the lowering of crime. Often, an arrest will contribute toward that goal. But sometimes arrests backfire. For instance, an officer is out of service for the arrest, and that officer's presence may be essential for the success of that operation. The central point here is that all actions pull toward the success of each tactical operation, and the decision to arrest or not to arrest should not be independent of that consideration.

6. **Serious Crime is to be Stopped.** Every time a serious crime is stopped someone is not victimized. Whether it is through prevention or arrest, the central goal of mission based policing is to end the victimizations associated with serious crime.

Endnotes

1. The problem with routine preventive patrol is its tendency toward predictability. Criminals are adaptive, and they have adapted to the occasional presence of a patrol car driving through their areas of activity. Patrolling officers are in this sense a characteristic of a criminal's or gang's working environment, not a barrier to criminal activity in any true sense. For instance, research has shown that midlevel drug dealing criminals do not interact with drugs directly, but make youthful or "expendable" members carry out actual drug contacts and sales.

5

THE PRINCIPLE OF
MISSION'S END

Logical Lines of Operation

The principle of mission's end is straightforward. *The purpose of policing is to put into place a strategy whose purpose is to end crime as it is experienced in hot zones, permanently lowering it to levels of safe areas in the jurisdiction.* This is the central mission of a police department, to which all other purposes contribute. Yet, it is precisely this mission that is absent in US policing. In the mission-based model, all aspects of assignment, deployment, command integrity, and mission coherence are understood in terms of this principle.

At first glance, command structured problem-oriented policing (POP) looks like a means to achieve mission's end, in that by carrying out successful POP solutions, crimes related to problems should diminish or go away. However, herein is one of the central dilemmas of POP: Problems are treated as unique circumstances tied to specific articulable characteristics of the geography–crime interface. They are *not* seen as integrated elements of a broader articulated strategy of crime dissipation. *An additional step* needs to be added between problem solving and mission's end—*a structure that coordinates problem solutions into a logical plan for the permanent, long-term dissipation of crime.* The question here is: *What strategy enables a solved problem to be viewed as a systematic element in a broader, long-term mission of crime reduction?* Logical lines of operation, adapted from counterinsurgency practices, provide the strategic element tying problem solutions to permanent crime reductions.

Logical lines of operation (LOOs) are a contemporary counterinsurgency term developed in response to the characteristics of complex insurgencies. LOOs are an adaptation of the traditional military notion of physical lines of operation, modified to apply to conflicts in which descriptions of positional reference on a battlefield are not helpful. Contemporary insurgencies tend to be mosaic conflicts, in which an enemy adapts to an overpowering military threat through social and economic as well as terrorist means. They may be fought within a non-insurgent population so that efforts to target the enemy also result in civilian casualties. Bitterness about casualties provides ready recruits when combat efforts backfire, killing innocents. Moreover, insurgents may have lived in the resident population for extended periods and hence have become family members and religious actors, and as such valued members of the community (Kilcullen, 2008). Hence, a sophisticated strategy is needed to acquire long-term security. The strategic elements of that strategy, from initial engagement through resolution of conflict, are mapped out using logical lines of operation. This principle, the use of LOOs for the police, can similarly be used to connect independent problem solutions to long-term mission success. Chapters 5 through 7 discuss lines of operation and provide recommendations for staging them.

The Line of Operation Structure Applied to Police

LOOs are counterinsurgency efforts to think about a battlefield in a conflict where traditional approaches to military action do not work. The term traces its history to physical lines of operation, which embody the specific strategy used on a battlefield to plan and coordinate a military action. The term *logical* replaced *physical* in order to adapt to a conflict in which (1) the conflict was too complex—what we have called mosaic conflicts herein—for a single campaign to achieve victory, (2) where the enemy was integrated into the resident population, and (3) where military success was achieved, not by defeating an enemy, but by winning the hearts and minds of the local population.

LOOs represent a systematic strategy to visualize a conflict in the context of its physical and cultural environment and strategically plan for victory. Recognizing that counterinsurgencies require an immensely complex response, the LOO concept takes a mission—the underlying purpose of a military campaign—and organizes it into six separate strategies. These six strategies are (1) information operations, (2) security operations, (3) local security training and employment,

(4) establish and restore essential services, (5) security for economic development, and (6) establishment of governmental legitimacy. These strategies are roughly sequential, but all are the product of planning (LOO-1) and, given the unpredictability of conflict, several may be going on at the same time. The central value of LOOs is that they enable a way of thinking about crime based on a rational planning model, with the end point being long-term and significant crime reductions. They provide a way of thinking through the crime dissipation process that is citizen based, and that, in the end, local problems of long-term disinvestment will have to be addressed. They also recognize that, for an area to regain its vitality and its citizens adequate quality of life, security issues must first be addressed.

We adopt the LOO strategic model with modifications that recognize that, in a civilian setting different dynamics affect their utility.[1] Consequently, mission-based policing uses the following LOO structure:

LOO-1: Information Operations
LOO-2: Security Operations
LOO-3: Restoration of Essential Services
LOO-4: Security for Economic Development

An additional difference between our's and the counterinsurgency model lies in the staging of the LOOs. The counterinsurgency model views LOOs sequentially, with significant overlap. We view LOO-2 and -3 as simultaneous models. The reason for this is that LOO-3, restoration of essential services, is closely tied to the development of a strong police community platform we call the *neighborhood revitalization committee*. This committee is modeled after weed-and-seed steering committees, discussed extensively at the end of this chapter. We believe this committee needs to be established and fully functional at the beginning of security operations, and that without it, the police are unlikely to attain the legitimacy they need to achieve strategic success. The staging of LOOs is consequently presented in Figure 5.1.

The four lines of operation are discussed over this and the following chapter. This chapter discusses the first three LOOs, information, security, and service restoration. The first represents security planning, the second is the tactical deployment of security, and the third

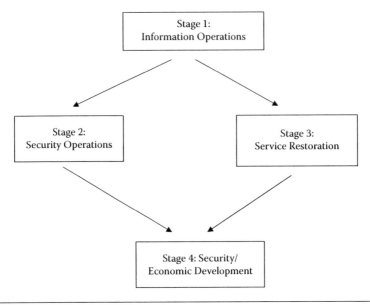

Figure 5.1   The staging of logical lines of operation.

is the facilitation and coordination of areal services under a security umbrella.[2]

LOO-1. Information Operations

The purpose of information operations is to develop an action plan, based on intelligence gained from a targeted area, to initiate and carry out the crime dissipation mission. Information operations are classified into two categories: crime intelligence and legitimacy. With regard to crime intelligence, we ask the question: *What information is needed to plan for comprehensive security operations, and how can we begin repointing police research units to effectively deliver this information?* With regard to legitimacy, we ask: *What information is needed to effectively reach out to the local population, to develop an understanding of them in their own terms, to win their hearts and minds?* "Winning their hearts" means that residents come to believe that the cause of security is the way that they are most likely to achieve the quality of life and safety they desire. "Winning their minds" means that residents come to believe that the police will provide greater safety than gangs, than other area intimidators or criminals who might seek an extortionate relationship, or than doing nothing.

We will first consider the crime intelligence function. What kind of information is needed? The first class of information is related to crime and the following data structures are needed:

1. *Crime maps of serious crimes, by type of crime.* The basic categories are violent crime, property crime, and business crime. This provides information for the designation of hot zones, to identify the areas of geographic deployment.

2. *Populations of areas, by district.* We recommend using beats, or districts, or whatever the organization designates its basic patrol coverage area. This provides information to calculate the number of officers in each hot zone.

3. *Ex-offender addresses in hot zones.* This information is increasingly difficult to acquire, as parole is no longer used in many states and a relatively large number of ex-offenders return to communities unsupervised. However, most states have juvenile probation and parole services that can provide tracking data. Also, some prisons are starting to track releasees through other measures, such as cell phone records. These tracking data will be helpful but muddy. Ex-offenders, for instance, are likely to have multiple relevant addresses: address of record, the address where he or she really lives, a work address (one hopes!), and an address where they play.

4. *Identities and locations of hot shots.* Hot shots refers to those individuals who are intensively associated with crime. These are the individuals who tend to be where crime and violence occur. Their signature characteristic is that, when bad things happen, they are present. They may be victim, actor, or instigator. Their presence tends to be crime generative. A police communism applies here: "Witness one day, suspect the next, victim on the third day." Hence, tracking witnesses will help identify hot shots. It is well worth the time spent to collate the appearance of witnesses at multiple crime scenes, as patterns will quickly emerge.

5. *Places with very high levels of crime.* These are specific places that are associated with very high crime levels. These might be particular businesses that are repeatedly robbed, apartment complexes where violent activities are routinely noted,

or shopping centers with inadequately supervised open parking. These data can sometimes be difficult to acquire because some businesses will not report crime for fear of losing their liquor license and where some landlords do not want their activities known to the police. Line level officer focus groups can help identify such places.

6. *Gangs and membership, with associated criminal activity.* This information is routinely collected by police departments and should be reviewed for its specific impact on crime.

The second class of intelligence is information about community resources to deal with crime. Needed data include:

1. *Interdiction and prevention groups.* Location, purpose, and activities of all organizations and organizational heads responsible for dealing with gang members, ex-felons and the recently released, victims of shootings and other forms of violence, and at-risk youth. This particularly involves training and education programs such as the Urban League.

2. *Identification of groups who have knowledge or skills that might contribute to anticrime efforts.* The faith community, schools, area hospitals, humane society, boys and girls clubs, private security contractors.

3. *Locals who are invested in the community.* Local and state politicians who live in the area, city council members, mayor's office, local business representatives, neighborhood association or alliance leaders.

Legitimacy

The second component of LOO-1 is legitimacy. We separate legitimacy into two components: community outreach and grievances.

Legitimacy 1: Community Outreach   The local community needs to know why the police are present and what they are doing. This outreach principle is consistent with the security maxim that the most effective security does not lie in secrecy, but in security operations or structures that potential lawbreakers know about but cannot do anything about. That maxim, applied here, means that the police can likely be more open about tactical deployment for operations than the level to which they are accustomed. We encourage openness of tactical information, though we believe that departments may want to be more discretionary about operational specifics. The community outreach function of this LOO has the following elements:

1. *Audience identification.* Several audiences need to know about police purposes and tactics. These include other professional organizations working with at-risk individuals and local news outlets. The public needs to be informed of police tactics and the broader strategies those tactics serve. The police will have to encourage businesses to report crimes, a challenging task in that few municipalities have ordinances requiring businesses to report crime.

2. *Community leadership.* Community leaders in hot zones have a voice, and the police should recognize and acknowledge that voice. When important voices in the community are unfavorable to police activity, the police must establish dialogues with community leaders to resolve situations, within the broader goals of long-term security for the hot zone.

3. *Communicate accomplishments.* Let the public know about violence carried out against community members. It must always be emphasized that the purpose of local police activity and operations is tied to victimization, and the end state is a sharp reduction of victimization. Hold press conferences to announce accomplishments.

4. *Commitment to citizens.* Let the public know the police are there for the long haul. If someone testifies or provides evidence against someone else, they must be comfortable knowing that the police will remain in the area to provide protection.

5. *Engagement.* Stay engaged with the population. The most important guardianship effects derive from being seen frequently by local citizens.

6. *Narrative and culture.* Learn local narratives that are critical to the police and develop counter responses. Some of these narratives will be political and will argue against police presence. Importantly, do not retrench. Acknowledge these

and provide counter narratives in terms of victimization protection.

7. *Involve city politicians.* Political officials should periodically meet with community leaders to show support for police activities.

Legitimacy 2: Grievances   Central to planning should be the development of strategic ways to deal with grievances. The role of police in governance is complex and politically perilous. Chiefs serve at the pleasure of the mayor and, should problems emerge, can be fired on little more than a whim. Indeed, the firing of chiefs stemming from problems beyond their control is characteristic of US urban policing (Crank and Langworthy, 1992). Many Americans, moreover, distrust police as a strong-arm agent of central governance.[3] We have the following recommendations:

1. *Reduce the spread of grievances by openly acknowledging them.* Some individuals or groups in the community may be hostile to the police. The department needs to put in place a system in the hot zone for addressing hostility and resolving grievances. Do not ask individuals to go to headquarters to resolve grievances, since the environment there will be intimidating. What is important here is to stop grievances from spreading, unaddressed, thus amplifying their effect. This leads to the next point.

2. *Address grievances as rapidly as possible.* It should be noted that true grievances will be difficult to separate from false ones. While it is important to separate true from false grievances against the police, it is far more important to openly acknowledge and discuss them.

3. *Establish positive relations with citizens as well.* Work will be facilitated as two-way communication between street officers and citizens is expanded.

4. *Work with the business or economic development groups.* As discussed in the next section, develop recreational, historical, and cultural resources. Participate in events that display the area's local culture, history, and valued traditions (even if parts of that history are associated with police repression). This activity will

serve to bolster a positive community identity and protect key community assets that may form the basis for reinvestment.

5. *Encourage and support community leaders.* There is a counterinsurgency aphorism that is widely used that applies here: It is far more important that the locals do their own governance half right than having outsiders do it very well. The lesson of this aphorism is that local community leaders take pride in their own identity and sense of purpose. There is no particular reason to believe its identity will be the same as other zones, or that it will mirror the police worldview.

6. *Develop a position of strategic information officer.* The role of this officer will be developed through the media, but its primary purpose is to serve as the face of the department to the public. However, we want to emphasize at this point that the officer is not only a public relations person. This person will be responsible for assisting the various hot zone squads with the development of strategic information, both before operations and after, developing operational tactics, and then reviewing outcomes, assessing what information can be used both to guide the department to its tactical goals and in how to present operational plans and outcomes to the public. The strategic information officer will nurture relationships with the members of the neighborhood revitalization committee, providing them information and, in effect, making them insiders to the process. These individuals can be used to speak with greater authority than police on issues of appropriateness. When the "politics of grievance" complaints are voiced, these defenders will provide critical legitimacy, recognizing that it is far more believable for a third party to defend the police actions than for the police to defend themselves. In those cases where it will be helpful, the strategic information officer can facilitate the interview process by connecting the media to the right community members. Certainly, there will be differences of opinion at times, but if these community defenders are appropriately independent of police, the occasional tension this may create will be more than rewarded by the increased legitimacy the police will enjoy.

Hence, LOO planning at this stage should focus on development of (1) a security framework, (2) legitimacy-grievance response mechanisms, and (3) local community identity.

LOO-2. Security Operations

In this LOO we will first discuss the elements of the LOO strategy. Next we will provide an example of security operations regarding serious inner city crime. The former is intended to show the potentially positive effects of suppression, and the latter the beneficial effects from changing the built environment. The examples represent the twin aspects of enforcement-initiated problem solving: some hot zone squad activity will aim directly at crime patterns and will be suppressive in nature, and some will be more subtle, aimed at problem solutions that are the result of intelligence analysis.

Our first concern is the element of LOO strategy for security. Security operations are the specific actions taken by the police to establish security for citizens in a hot zone. The key activity is to assert control over crime through persistent presence. Operations require the development of block-level detailed information about the crime signatures and their causes in hot zones, such as:

1. *Operations are enforcement initiated POP.* Operations are guided by the demands of enforcement coupled with intelligence collection, organized around the logic of problem-oriented policing. Hence, they are aimed at the reduction of crime through specific operations carried out by officers assigned inside the hot zone. All operations are tied logically to the end state of security. The specific methodology of police strategic interdiction is wholly contingent on the local crime signature, which will vary.

2. *Mission integrity.* All police actions are accountable to the mission and to the specific operations that are intended to further the mission. Operators are assigned for the explicit purpose of carrying out the strategic goals of the mission. Chain of command will be respected.

3. *POP preoperation analysis.* A strategic information operator, working with the crime prevention specialists and with the operator units themselves, will evaluate inbound and outbound information for its supporting value to the mission.

Inbound information will be mined for actionable intelligence and unanswered questions. Actionable intelligence will be forwarded quickly to field operations. Unanswered questions can be formulated as intelligence-gathering directives, meaning that in a particular instance an operation may be designed primarily to gather information as opposed to being primarily a crime suppression tactic.

4. *Intelligence debriefing (after-action reports).* All operations are followed by postoperation debriefing that identifies what actions were taken, what did not work or went wrong, what went right, and what was unexpected. The debriefing of an operation becomes part of the information base for future POP operations.

5. *Dissemination of operations.* The strategic information officer will utilize outbound information as a tool to achieve the mission goals. Information can be released, privately or through the media, in order to prompt a particular action from a mission partner or the community. Information will also be used to market (sell) the tactics, strategies, and department legitimacy. The strategic information officer will work in cooperation with the department's regular public information unit, but reports to the operation commander and is primarily focused on gaining, using, and disseminating information as an operational tool.

6. *Multiple operations.* Several operations may be carried out at the same time. What is important is that after-operation briefings enable the reformulation of crime problems, and that each reformulation focuses strategically on the logic of lowering crime in the zone.

7. *Deterrence and guardianship.* Police actions have both moral and practical limitations. It is important to recognize that the elements of guardianship, which are legitimacy and deterrence, may act at cross-purposes. For instance, a deterrent effort to control a rough street through a curfew or street sweep may net a local person who is highly regarded. Also, actions not perceived by the public as justifiable, or that appear to be an overuse of force, will undercut legitimacy. On the other hand, an overconcern with legitimacy may undercut effectiveness.

The police must constantly balance these two goals, recognizing that both are important to long-term security.

8. *Community information.* The department should keep the community informed through two mechanisms:

   a. First, postoperation briefings should be held with community members, and this is a part of the purpose of the neighborhood revitalization committee. This committee is discussed at length in Information Box 5-3 later in this chapter. It is important that community representatives do not find themselves surprised by police actions. Such a result could (1) undermine the legitimacy of representatives for their own communities, and (2) undermine any good will the police may have built with those representatives.

   b. A strategic information officer, assigned to the hot zone command, should carry out a briefing every morning, and the press and citizens should be invited. This post is discussed extensively in Chapter 9. The strategic information officer provides a daily briefing to provide knowledge about operations and can answer broader questions about the purposes of operations. This person is the face of the hot zone command to the community and to the city and must have public speaking skills.

9. *Detectives.* A squad of special detectives will also be assigned to hot zones. The work of detectives will be (1) interrogation in support of real-time police response and (2) active participation in the development of POP solutions. These squads are tied to the mission through unity of command.

In Chapter 4, we developed the notion that security operations were intelligence-led and were organized specifically around intelligence that facilitated problem solving. This means that items 3 and 4 above, preoperational analysis and after-action reporting, always occur within an already existing intelligence environment. One can develop the following model in Figure 5.2 to capture this layered intelligence cycle.

Figure 5.2 shows that the intelligence debriefing for the squad is conducted during a weekly intelligence review by the hot zone command, and that both are in turn located inside the quarterly intelligence

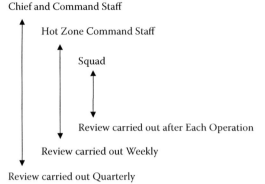

Figure 5.2   The layered intelligence cycle.

review, with progress assessment carried out by the department chief and command staff. Figure 5.2 is related to Figure 4.3, the POP intelligence loop. Specifically, Figure 5.2 refers to the Planning box in Figure 4.3 and shows how planning is layered in an increasingly wide intelligence timeline.

POP and Violent Crime

The notion that violent crime can be dealt with through POP is central to the notion that police can do something about serious crime. Central for most cities is the importance of doing something about violent crime. Successful problem-solving interventions for such crimes are relatively infrequent. Two important examples are presented below. The first deals with a focused deterrence intervention into violent street crime, and the second is an example of the use of environmental design to affect crime.

Our first example, Operation Cease-Fire, is discussed in Information Box 5-1. It provides an example of an intervention into gang activity, an area historically highly resistant to police deterrence.

Operation Cease-Fire provided what David Kennedy (2008) referred to as "focused deterrence," clearly aimed at a specific criminogenic identity. These were the relatively small numbers of individuals involved in serious gang crime. A deliberate attempt was made to avoid what might be called the "crack-down" effect—arrest indiscriminantly—thus undercutting police legitimacy and losing neighborhood support.

INFORMATION BOX 5-1: OPERATION CEASE-FIRE AN EXAMPLE OF POP FOR VIOLENT CRIME

Boston's [Cease-Fire] strategy grew from an unusual partnership: in-the-trenches cops from the gang unit, black clergy from the worst-hit neighborhoods and Harvard University professors. The Boston Gun Project, as the research effort was dubbed, began by dissecting the problem of gang homicides.

Its aha! moment, the lead professor, David Kennedy, later wrote, was the discovery of what's since become a common principle of criminology: how relatively few offenders were involved. Sixty percent of the youth homicides could be traced to vendetta-style, must-get-respect hostility among about five dozen gangs. Their core membership was just 1,300 individuals, about 1 percent of the city's youths hardly enough to populate two average American high schools. Armed with that insight, researchers drew other players into the working group—federal, state and local prosecutors, city departments, community groups and social workers who dealt with gangs on the street.

From those odd bedfellows evolved the new strategy, which the city dubbed Operation Cease-Fire and launched in 1996.

Its essentials:

A laser-like focus on understanding one specific problem, gun homicides among youths: They set aside worries about root causes— poverty, racism, education, broken families and drugs—instead concentrating on the here and now. Intense research into why people were shooting one another produced a list of the "worst of the worst" gang members, replete with detailed personal information.

Focused deterrence: All the gang members on the list who could be summoned—most were on probation or parole—were called to a giant meeting. Police gave them a message: We know who you are and what you've been doing, and from now on an entire gang will be punished if one of its members kills.

A second message came from clerics, ex-gang members and the parents of victims: Your neighborhood loves you and needs you, but not if you're dead. You are better than this.

The social workers added a third message: If you want out of gang life, we'll help you find jobs, addiction treatment, education, whatever.

The three messages—group punishment awaits, do right, not wrong, and here's a way out of thug life—became the strategy's hallmarks, Kennedy told The *World-Herald*.

Making it stick: When killings happened, police carried out their threats against the offending gang, using the personal data gathered earlier to pressure members, through unusual tactics called "pulling levers." They impounded the unregistered cars of gang members, for instance, and visited their homes unannounced to talk to parents. The cops shut down favorite gang hangouts, busted members for public drinking, enforced probation curfews in "bed check" style and turned any legal screw they could—all while repeating the message: The crackdown continues until the shooting stops.

Just as important, Kennedy said, was what police *didn't* do. They avoided indiscriminate tactics of the past—such as neighborhood sweeps and traffic checkpoints—to encourage now-budding cooperation between residents and police.

The city's homicides among people 24 and younger fell from an average of 44 a year in the first half of the decade to 26 in 1996, the first year of Ceasefire. In 1997, the number dropped to 15. Total homicides, of all ages, fell from an annual average of 100 during the decade's first half to 31 in the second.

Source: Buddenberg, Roger (2010) "A Fresh Grip on Gangs, Gun Crimes." *Omaha World-Herald*. June 27. http://www.omaha. com/article/20100627/NEWS01/706279917

Members of the community, particularly the faith community, were engaged to assist in the effort to get the most serious offenders under routine police contact or off the streets altogether.

Importantly, the program is not only a security-based effort. Box 5-1 discusses how one of the individuals of interest to the police received employment through the program, providing an alternative to violent crime. This program in microcosm provides a glimpse of the broader possibilities under a focused, mission-based police approach to hot zone crime.

The second example is an example that modifies the environment to address inner city serious crime. Welsh and Farrington (2009: 105) reviewed several programs related to the use of street closures and barricades in dealing with inner city crime and concluded that "there is fairly strong and consistent evidence that the defensible space technique of street closures or barricades is effective" in preventing crime in inner city neighborhoods. While cautioning against a blanket "it works" conclusion, the authors noted with regard to four of the five studies:

> The other four evaluations of defensible space represent a largely uniform subset of this surveillance measure. Each implemented street closures or barriocades, three of the four were carried out in high crime inner city neighborhoods (the other was implemented across a city) and each produced desirable effects on overall crime or a specific crime type (violence on one case and property in the other). (105)

Welsh and Farrington cited a study carried out by Lasley (1998) in Los Angeles. It was called Operation Cul de Sac, because the use of barriers turned many roads into cul-de-sacs. These barriers were inserted into a ten-block inner city area. Comparing changes in crime rates to a control group after two years, Lasley found significant reductions in assault and homicide. Lasley did not find significant changes in property crime rates. However, a study carried out by Donnelly and Kimble (1997), also assessing the effects of street closures on crime, found substantial reductions in both violent and property crimes. These findings are evidence that planned interventions can have a significant effect on violent crime.

There is an important condition on the discussion of successful operations above. Decker's (2003) work on police interventions in youth gangs shows that many interventions do not work and that some backfire. Nor is there a clear pattern to whether problem-solving interventions work better than suppression interventions (Greene, 2003). We believe the lessons for hot zone operations are twofold:

1. It is critical to constantly assess the consequences of operations. After action reports must be carried out with the

recognition that tactical operations are sometimes not going to be successful and must adapt to changing circumstances.

2. One of the important characteristics of operators is that they familiarize themselves with what other police departments are doing. Part of this is reviewing research that has been carried out, with an eye toward what does not work in other settings. To an extent, operations will have the "spaghetti on the wall" quality—one throws spaghetti against the wall, hoping that at some point it sticks. As we have emphasized, operations are always in the service of strategy, and strategy is in service to the mission. Hence, the best operators are those with a wide knowledge of what works in the field of police research, who can best envision the consequences of their activities, and who are flexible enough to change practices when current practices fail.

LOO-3: Establish/Restore Essential Services

The establishment of essential services, to include an adequate electrical grid and running water, is integral to counterinsurgency. The central role of security operations in LOO-3 is to provide safety for these services. This element recognizes that governmental legitimacy cannot be obtained if core services, essential for a minimal quality of life, are inadequate.

US communities rarely deal with problems such as the absence of fresh water or the destruction of an electrical grid, problems more associated with interstate conflicts. However, community disinvestment conditions can mimic the absence of essential services. These conditions can act as accelerants to serious crime. They are "mimicking conditions" and they stem from the unaffordability of utilities for heating and cooling, a large number of impoverished households, a significant population of resident homeless, medically infirm residents who cannot afford medical care, the unemployed and unemployable, and the mentally ill. For example, elderly residents and the impoverished may be unable to afford electricity in the summer to cool their houses or provide adequate heating in the winter. Large homeless populations, particularly those who are mentally ill, have service needs that most communities find difficult to afford, even with federal supports, grants, and investment. Even financial services cost much more for the poor than for the rich. Higher rates of interest, payday lenders, and a cash economy that precludes shopping for the best deals all have an abrasive effect on a community's ability to direct its own economy and resources in the best ways. The indebted poor, moreover, are subject to victimization from a grab bag of predatory lenders, pawns, and loan sharks.

The police are frequently the only point of contact to needed services for the poor and disenfranchised. That these problems occur in impoverished neighborhoods means that each problem is an additional financial burden on neighborhoods that cannot afford it, further contributing to loss of resident control and security problems.

Comprehensive urban programs that bring together security and the provision of basic services can be found in two strategic endeavors. In the Department of Defense literature, one finds US military investment in economic development and infrastructure issues, in part because counterinsurgency is tied intimately with nation state development, and in part because the US government has "very deep pockets." Internally in the United States, Weed and Seed, a National Institute of Justice grant program, represents the only integrated model that brings together security and development.

The mission-based policing strategy, to be effective, adapts what we consider to be the central strengths of the Weed and Seed police–citizen model. Those strengths are (1) its effort to be comprehensive—it locates crime control throughout the neighborhood security and reinvestment regimen, and (2) its recognition that effective crime prevention and suppression require the cooperation of neighborhood residents with the police critical for legitimacy. Local residents bring to the table a central feature of crime prevention—the understanding of neighborhood dynamics, players, and causal factors in the production of crime. Hence, we view the Weed and Seed steering committee as the model to be used for the "police-community bridge" central to this LOO. We expand on its base, which is the use of the steering committee as a communicative forum, to develop this LOO. This LOO, consequently, reviews and critiques the Weed and Seed model and emplaces the police-neighborhood work group at the center of the police-community partnership.

Weed and Seed programs provide a model for structuring crime control–community activist–local agency interaction. Weed and Seed steering committees are empowerment entities, with 50 percent of the members being local residents, that try to facilitate local agencies with small grants and assist those in their area who are in need of help. By empowerment we mean that the committee gains its credibility from local or grassroots support and builds on local agency support to improve Weed and Seed designated areas. However, it is a notion of empowerment tied to the provision of security; it is, after all, a Department of Justice program.

The Weed and Seed model is a desirable one in that it provides a forum for communication across a diversity of work groups in the resident community as well as with city crime control agencies. Its goals are self-determining, not imposed from the outside. Hence, when it is done right, Weed and Seed steering committees tend to have more legitimacy than outside groups, however helpful those outside groups may desire to be. The next section discusses weed and seed in detail.

Weed and Seed

Weed and Seed (W&S) is a widely applied and one of the most popular Department of Justice programs. Its web page describes W&S as "a community-based multi-agency approach to law enforcement, crime prevention, and neighborhood restoration." The national database lists 184 current W&S sites in 2009 and 98 graduated W&S sites in 2010.[4] The metaphor *weed* refers to the work carried out by police and prosecutors, who focus on "weeding" activities: crime suppression and enforcement. The metaphor *seed* refers to community interventions, individual treatments, and neighborhood revitalization. The seed component is intended to

> revitalize distressed neighborhoods and improve the quality of life of designated communities through economic development and a revitalization of the community's health and wellness. Neighborhood restoration programs help to improve living conditions; enhance home security; allow for low cost physical improvements; develop long-term efforts to renovate and maintain housing; and provide educational, economic, social, recreational, and other opportunities. (U.S. Department of Justice, 2004)

W&S addresses issues through a spectrum of areal interventions that can be described as *community security, prevention and intervention,* and *economic revitalization.* It has an areal focus: W&S areas are geographically demarcated, and programs focus on activities whose purpose is to address problems, especially crime problems, within those areas. It recognizes that community restoration and reinvestment require security as well as rebuilding and reinvestment in the community.

Particularly important in the current era is the development of sustainable W&S programs. By *sustainability* we mean that program goals aim at preserving the steering committee and continue community restoration beyond the life of the W&S granting period.

Reviews of W&S programs have been, for the most part, favorable. In a national evaluation of eight W&S programs, Dunworth and Mills (1999: 2) found "significant favorable effects of Weed and Seed in key outcome measures for some sites and time periods. The evidence is modest in terms of its statistical significance, but the indicators consistently point in favorable directions."

W&S Barriers to Success   Though the goals of W&S are lofty, we believe that W&S faces three areas of conflict that interfere with its ability to achieve the larger goal of neighborhood reinvestment and long-term viability. We discuss below three such conflicts, recognizing that (1) W&S was never intended to be a stand-alone community rebuilding resource, but rather is better thought of as a coordinated empowerment effort toward that important goal, and that (2) these barriers represent difficult issues that tend to be intractable, but can be surmounted with creative and steadfast leadership, together with adequate municipal support.[5]

Conflicts between Weeders and Seeders   Central to W&S is its efforts to bring together crime control (weeder) with prevention/intervention (seeder) organizations. These organizations have historically not communicated effectively with each other. Police and prosecutors focus on crime suppression through arrest and prosecution. They favor criminal sanctions. Police have tended to "weed" aggressively, seeking out law breakers, enforcing quality-of-life misdemeanor crime, and cracking down on gangs and drug sellers in the designated W&S areas. They also tend to tightly control their data—often for good reasons—limiting the extent to which outsiders can actually see what the police are doing and who they are doing it to.

Prevention and intervention agencies, on the other hand, are oriented toward rehabilitative ends. These include, for instance, intercepting likely offenders and at-risk individuals prior to criminal involvement, interceding in gang activities, providing education and summer jobs for area youth, or facilitating reentry into society. Many of the intervention and prevention agencies in the designated areas establish their credibility with local youth with their knowledge of street life and willingness to help. They often work with youth who are at risk or already involved in gangs and criminal activity. They are disinclined to work with the police because it would undercut their legitimacy and trust with local troubled youth. The police, consequently, do not fully trust these organizations and sometimes view them as obstacles to enforcement.

Conflicts between Weeders and Community Members   Dunworth and Mills (1999) observed conflicts that emerged between the "weed" agencies and local community residents. They observed that residents in designated areas resisted W&S because of its emphasis on enforcement and out of fears of police harassment. Sciarabba (2009), in a study of W&S in New York City, found high levels of dissatisfaction with policing in the W&S area, with 68 percent of the respondents reporting dissatisfaction. Moreover, most neighborhood residents perceived that serious crime had increased. For instance, Sciarabba found that "84% of the residents reported that they believe that violent crime in 2008 is 'worse' or 'much worse' than in 2007" (2009: 37). Fear of crime had also risen substantially in the W&S areas.

Conflicts with residents were also apparent in differing perceptions of crime levels. Eterno identified what he called a "substantial disconnect" between the perceptions of citizens in the W&S areas and the official New York police statistics. The police, Eterno observed, reported substantial improvements in crime statistics, while the citizens perceived substantial increases in serious crime. He concluded that W&S, in this instance, was not accomplishing one of its primary missions—constructing positive relations between the community and the police. To the contrary, he argued that community policing, as envisioned in the W&S model, had been supplanted by aggressive, zero-tolerance policing practices carried out under compare statistics (COMPSTAT) programs.

Sciarabba (2009) addressed an issue critical to W&S—the viability of its community policing component. W&S was initiated in 1991, during the peak of the community policing movement. Community policing, with its emphasis on police–community relations, was the unifying segment that bridged the differences between the weeders and the seeders. Since the mid-1990s, however, police departments have become more aggressive and law enforcement focused, transitioning into what might be called the era of COMPSTAT, or what Crank, Kadleck, and Koski (2010) called a "police neo-professionalism movement." In the contemporary era, we find police agencies carrying out highly focused suppression strategies at all levels of law breaking. Community policing has appeared to lose momentum as a police reform movement.

Limited Investment Base of W&S   Community restoration is an important part of the W&S model. Yet, it suffers from its design as an "empowerment" model of community development. A W&S steering committee, of which at least 50 percent are local residents, is responsible for directing neighborhood activities and for deciding on funding and evaluation programs. The nonempowerment component of the steering committee—those brought in from outside the W&S area—is typically comprised of the mayor's office, local police officials, and the prosecutors' office. This model, however, lacks the capital resources needed to sustain viable community development and to actually restore and rebuild communities.

We want to emphasize that W&S was never intended to fulfill the function of community redevelopment. However, that function needs to be fulfilled if long-term crime dissipation is to be achieved. Community development is a wide-ranging and complex enterprise, requiring professional skills, substantial infrastructural analysis and support, an understanding of federal and local tax structures, and detailed analysis of property development and sustenance opportunities. In a word, successful community restoration requires that those factors that have brought about neighborhood disinvestment over the past fifty years be stabilized and then reversed. Local neighborhood groups, coordinated by a steering committee along the empowerment model of W&S, rarely have the skills or economic base for that level of community planning and investment. Hence, the seeming central strength of Weed and Seed—its comprehensive approach to neighborhood development—is also its primary weakness; local groups lack the resources to fully accomplish long-term successes in either the weed or the seed component of the program.

W&S consequently looks like a comprehensive program, but it isn't. It operates on the good faith and sustained efforts of its steering committee members. The steering committee provides local grants to a small number of organizations, typically with a limited and short-term (annual) scope. Because individual grants to local agencies are relatively small, agencies tend to use them to bolster existing services, not create new ones. Those who have participated in W&S programs have faced the difficulties of maintaining the interest and involvement of community organizations in their steering committees once their funding has ended. W&S consequently offers both strengths and weaknesses, as listed in Information Box 5-2.

INFORMATION BOX 5-2: WEED AND SEED: STRENGTHS AND WEAKNESSES

The strengths of W&S are summarized as follows.

1. Comprehensive, tying security to community redevelopment. And it recognizes that security is a central component of community reform and reinvestment.
2. Recognizes that community members are integral to program success.
3. Recognizes that community principals are central to program success and need to be on any development board from the beginning.
4. Recognizes that community agencies and the police deed to work together to develop constructive dialogue, and that this is always a difficult task for both partners.
5. Recognizes that crime is place specific, and seeks strategies that address those places. It does so by reaching out

to various groups involved with people in those places to more effectively address crime.

6. Has produced a large and accessible body of research on community partnerships in crime prevention and suppression in high crime areas. The importance of this body of information cannot be overstated.

Shortcomings of W&S can be summarized as follows:

1. Lack of adequate investment in community problems. The relatively small grants are not adequate to actually change communities.

2. Uneasy relationships between the weeders and the seeders.

3. Changes in the nature of policing since 1990, which has become more aggressive and crime control focused. The community policing role appears to be diminishing in police organizations.

4. Reliance on a community empowerment model. The problem with this is that community members rarely have adequate expertise for urban planning or of the pertinent municipal laws, city codes, and local governmental practices.

5. Lack of partnerships with the private sector. Such relationships are part of W&S's sustainability plan, but not part of its operating structure. Consequently, such partnerships are neglected.

The LOO structure adapted from counterinsurgency practice is similar to W&S in many ways. Most important, both share a recognition that security and development are interrelated and inseparable. However, the LOO model we present here is adaptable to a more comprehensive and thorough strategic realignment of planning and for thinking through the resources needed for development.

W&S and the Problem of Disinvestment   In this section we discuss W&S and the central problem most of the W&S neighborhoods face—long-term disinvestment processes. The purpose of this is to lay the groundwork for the kind of committee that we think can serve this function and to which the W&S model contributes. This discussion will also begin the process of developing a broader economic-security response, which will be the final LOO discussed in the next chapter.

Long-term problems of neighborhood disinvestment typically have clear historical roots. Public housing in the United States, for instance, was widely built as a response to the great migration of the 1930s through the 1960s and was designed to deal with large migrant populations arriving from the southern states throughout that period (Lemann, 1992). The flight of migrants from the South to northern urban centers, itself encouraged by open resistance to settlement by the northern rural population (Piven and Cloward, 1997), set the stage for long-term neighborhood disinvestment processes of white flight to the suburbs from the 1950s forward, the redlining and the collapse of property values, the widespread property destruction from the riots of the 1960s, the destructive impact of the interstate highway system on African American urban communities in the 1960s, and the steady erosion of business investment in these areas for the past 70 years. The story of local and national failures to meet the needs of displaced African Americans—and widespread resistance in many cities—is widely chronicled. Virtually all of the problems faced in impoverished communities today can be traced to this sad history. Design features of public housing today, the last and often only choice for the truly disadvantaged, have made it a source of continuing crime problems in many communities.

The central problems associated with long-term neighborhood disinvestment—crime and poverty—have devolved to the police. For instance, business complaints against the homeless may result in the arrest of mentally ill individuals loitering and frightening customers. The incarceration of the mentally ill contributes to prison instability, violence, and lack of adequate medical care. Similarly, releasees from prison often return to these communities lacking skills for employment. A large number of these releasees went into prison as youth and now face a lifetime of bleak prospects.

W&S is simply not on a scale to address these problems, even with its contemporary emphasis on sustainability. However, the core concept of the steering committee, and the research conducted on committee problems and viability, set the stage for our recommendations for a structure for police community relations. Further, the W&S empowerment model is based on a notion of decentralized democracy that is highly institutionalized in US society. It needs to be tuned to the larger picture of disinvestment, which we will present in the next chapter. The following are recommendations derived from the discussion of W&S for LOO-3. The mission recommendation is presented in Information Box 5-3.

INFORMATION BOX 5-3

NEIGHBORHOOD REVITALIZATION COMMITTEES

Neighborhood Revitalization groups, modeled after the W&S steering committee model, are recommended. This model should be formed at the beginning of the mission. The identification of the group's membership is a product of the first LOO, information operations, and should meet prior to the first mission assignments in the area. The primary purpose of this group is the maintenance of open communications between all actors in the neighborhood. It also serves the legitimacy function, insuring that police have a forum to describe their actions and the reasons for them, while also permitting residents an opportunity to respond.

Committee Membership: Participants should include the precinct and hot zone commanders, strategic information officer, prosecutors office, juvenile parole and probations services, neighborhood institutional representatives such as faith groups and schools, city council representatives, local neighborhood activists, mayors office, neighborhood groups members, service agencies such as boys and girls clubs, Urban League, and reentry groups, local entrepreneurs and chamber of commerce representatives.

Meeting information: The identification of key community services—a needs assessment—is integral to the planning stage, and police involvement in services have to be clearly tied through the LOO to the end state of crime dissipation across the hot zone. A comprehensive list of the target populations and activities of neighborhood organizations should be the first task of the group, and strategies for converting that into a contact list for neighborhood members should be carried out.

Action plan: It should be emphasized that this is an action group whose purpose is twofold:

a. Open discussion about security issues, outreach strategy, and local community problems. The committee seeks ways to reach out to citizens in the area (always a difficult task), provides information to residents on current federal supports and grant opportunities, discusses recent business ventures in the area, reports on crime and gang activity.

b. As an action group, acts as a task force for business development, assists families of crime victims, carries out community surveys of important issues, and works closely with the mayor's office to develop funding opportunities.

Endnotes

1. First, LOO-3, security training and employment, is inapplicable in that municipal areas already have security forces in place: municipal police. LOO-6, governmental legitimacy, does not apply in the same way; local police do not face a coherent quasi-military challenger vying for legitimacy, but rather a fragmented threat from violent crime activity, property crime activity, and from a garden variety of quasi-organized gangs that operate independently and are often in conflict with one another. However, due to long-term disinvestment and deep traditions of segregation, minority communities in the United States tend not to trust the police. Consequently, LOO-6 is redesigned and relocated as a component of the first line of operation—information operations. In our model, it enables the other LOOs to achieve success, in that both legitimacy and information need to be addressed from the onset of mission strategy.

2. LOO-3 looks like economic development, but is not truly developmental. It is about how existing service organizations in a hot zone can be maximized both in a security setting and to set the stage for economic development.

3. An exception to this principle is that police unions are frequently involved in local politics, especially at the mayoral level.
4. http://www.weedandseed.info/docs/site-list.pdf
5. We might be accused of setting up a "straw dog," critiquing W&S for something it was not intended to do. Our purpose here is not to diminish the accomplishments of the program, which have been widely noted, but instead to use it as a basis for our effort, which is broader in scope, to develop a model for broad community reinvestment and redevelopment. Hence, the critiques should be understood as ways to modify the program to our specific purposes.

6

THE INTEGRATION OF URBAN PLANNING, ECONOMIC DEVELOPMENT, AND SECURITY

The applicant for chief continues the interview. She asks the mayor *What's your plan for reinvesting in the concentrated poverty areas in your city?* The mayor is agitated, pensive. He thinks "Why is this woman bugging me with these planning questions? She's police." He is dismissive. *You have a community policing unit for that.* She responds without hesitation. *I need that commitment from you. Otherwise we are all wasting our time.* The mayor hesitates and takes a deep breath. Maybe it's time for boldness. *Why don't you come back tomorrow at this time? I'll set up a meeting with my chief of staff and the regional planning director.*

Thinking Big: The Development of Viable Urban Centers

This final logical line of operation—LOO-4—represents the merger of security and long-term reinvestment in root-cause problems. This can be thought of as stabilization, and its purpose is to minimize the likelihood that the profound urban problems that exist in a vicious reciprocal relationship with high levels of crime do not return. We assert that the historical, political, and strategic failure to include these elements in US police strategy is a significant part of the inability to sustain crime reduction efforts in hot zones. This failure stems from the historical strategic separation of urban redevelopment and public security.

The end game of the security effort has to be neighborhood well-being, which means that neighborhoods have to be desirable places to live. This end goal is in itself enormously complex, requiring a dedicated mayor supported by professional and committed urban development personnel working closely with the police chief's office. Successful crime prevention and economic well-being are inseparable phenomena. In hot zones this has two meanings. The first, and widely noted, is that root causes—poverty and local disinvestment processes—are cyclically integrated with crime; that is, disinvestment accelerates crime just as crime accelerates disinvestment. The second, and integral throughout this book, is that security is fundamental to economic development. Root causes cannot be addressed without adequate and highly focused security planning, mission carry through, assessment, and operational redeployment.

Boba and Crank (2008) recognized the importance of rebuilding LOOs in their command-driven model of problem-oriented policing (POP). They located root-cause problems in a category called "social problems," requiring senior command intercession. Their model locates the police as *primary agents* for urban redevelopment problems, though this role is not articulated therein.

Root-cause problems, obviously, cannot be solved by the police alone; they require levels of investment and expertise that are located in the offices of the mayor and urban planners, and they need funding from private sector and foundation sources. Police provide the security so that root problems can be addressed, but there also must be a conscious and intentional supporter and promoter of these efforts.

That economic success is at the core of the police mission is suggested by parallel counterinsurgency policy. As Petraeus, Amos, and Nagl (2007: 173) noted, "In the long run, (mission) success depends on supporting people's livelihoods." Without a viable economy, investment structure, and employment opportunities, the security gains achieved by the police in hot zone are unlikely to endure, leaving in their wake disappointment, frustration, and a resurgence of criminal activity. This also decreases the likelihood that citizens in these areas will view the police as legitimate mechanisms of social control, seeking long-term solutions. Gangs and organized crime may foster the conditions that keep the economy in a hot zone stagnant, to the extent that such actions are favorable to their own interests. The entrepreneurial role is consequently tied to the crime dissipation mission. This means that processes of neighborhood disinvestment are seen as a series of POP problems, and those problem solutions are clearly linked to crime dissipation.

LOO-4 commences with the development of a comprehensive plan, organized around economic development that directly addresses disinvestment processes in hot zones. The heart of the plan aims at central issues of urban financial health and well-being: increasing property values, building permanent (not temporary government financed) business opportunities, urban enrichment, construction of entertainment districts, and attracting clientele for shopping and entertainment. The plan takes into consideration residents' goals and desires and is clearly focused on revitalization through economic development and growth beyond a secure area.

This sort of urban revitalization is typically carried out through the city planning office, the mayor's office, and local investors. This group contacts specialists who are skilled in neighborhood assessment and business development. These groups develop plans, meet with locals, modify and refine plans, meet again, and then begin the work of reinvestment and redevelopment. This chapter discusses this process as a partnership with security, a partnership surprisingly often absent from both police and city objectives.

Neighborhood Reinvestment and Recovery in the Current Era

The question for LOO-4 is *What is the strategy that ends urban blight in these high-crime areas?* The answer is to work within the existing framework of federal and municipal funding mandates and constraints, and within the municipal tax base and codes, to develop problem-oriented practices to achieve this desired outcome, assess the outcomes of those practices, and then to move forward strategically.

What types of practices can be used to achieve this LOO? In the remainder of this chapter we review contemporary urban revitalization practices, and then we suggest ways in which security—particularly problem-oriented policing—can facilitate these revitalization practices.

In Information Box 6-1, Kromer (2000) identifies central areas that need to be addressed for neighborhood recovery to occur. As Kromer notes, the process of neighborhood recovery is complex and involves many different elements of the community working together. One can see in his model that the core concept of empowerment is a necessary condition for recovery. However, it is not a sufficient condition; also needed are "buy-in" from business owners, political knowledge at the

INFORMATION BOX 6-1: NEIGHBORHOOD
RECOVERY, BY JOHN KROMER (2000).

Neighborhood recovery is about investing in areas suffering from long term disinvestment processes. In the current era, these areas have several items in common. They have suffered substantial decline in urban quality of life, in loss of property value, significant loss in job sites, and in processes of poverty and racial concentration.

Urban investment can be, and often is, done badly. Kromer cautions against two strategic frameworks that tend to result in failure and frustration. A "Marshall Plan" approach, in which a central agency, run by a czar with a deep resource base simply won't happen in the current era. The federal funding for large scale urban development—comparable to the model cities programs of the 1960s—simply is not there. Moreover, central planning tends, for a lot of uncontrollable reasons, to concentrate both poverty and race.

A "community empowerment" approach, where programs are run by enlightened residents who bring local sensitivity to government programs, won't work either. The skills to run government programs and sophisticated investment strategies are not present. Moreover, public appeals for more money do not work, to the dismay of both strategies. Private, profit-minded investment, with sophisticated and savvy use of government resources is what is needed.

Recovery requires government–community collaboration. By working together, both can produce what Kromer calls "neighborhood strategic plans," whose purpose is to organize resources to address problems systematically and rationally. It should address three areas: vacant housing and property, neighborhood commercial corridors, and publicly owned property.

The work of urban reinvestment requires dedication and commitment from local community members. Such people bring to the table a deep and practical understanding of neighborhood dynamics. Urban reinvestment also requires sophisticated

> analysis of programmatic features of available programs and related tax structures, including Community Development Block Grants, Housing and Urban Development programs and requirements, and community development corporations. This is brought to the table by the mayor's office. This collaboration is essential to successfully develop neighborhood strategy for the long term.

municipal level, collaboration with the mayor's office, knowledge of the tax base of the area together with attractive tax opportunities for investors, and detailed understandings of the retail marketplace. These conditions are found within Business Improvement Districts (BIDs), which we discuss in the next section. These are presented as examples of the kinds of partnerships that can spur community development.

BIDs: Private/Public Partnerships for Funding Neighborhood Recovery

In the current era, BIDs are widely used investment mechanisms for urban renewal and development. BIDs, which first emerged in the 1990s as a private-public strategy for reinvestment, are today widely used and are increasingly the primary urban strategy in many areas that seek development. BIDs are fully described in Information Box 6-2.

BIDs sought to change neighborhood environments through a variety of strategies that aimed at beautification, marketing, and improved security. These variables were described in terms of improvements in social and physical disorder, variables that tap social disorganization theory (Bursik and Grasmick, 1993; Sampson and Groves, 1989). BIDs, consistent with disorganization theory, should lower crime by improving the overall quality of life in these communities. Findings, however, did not provide support for a BID effect for crime overall, though in BID areas, household burglary declined significantly. Analysis comparing BID areas with matching comparison neighborhoods found that, while violent crime went down 8 percent in BID areas, comparison areas also had a reduction of 7.2 percent, so that the difference for BID areas was not statistically significant.

INFORMATION BOX 6-2.
CONTEMPORARY URBAN DEVELOPMENT STRATEGY: BUSINESS IMPROVEMENT DISTRICTS

Emerging scarcely 20 years ago, BID's increasingly drive urban development both nationally and internationally. It is estimated that there are approximately 1000 BIDs in the US, with the largest number, 65, in New York City. They have received supportive legislation in Canada, Germany, and the United Kingdom.

BIDs are defined as "self-organizing, local public-private organizations that collect assessments and invest in local area service provisions and activities, such as place promotion, street cleaning, and public safety" (McDonald, Ricky Blumenthal, Golinelli, Kofner, Stokes, Sehgal, and Beletsky, 2009: xiii). This development model relies on special assessments of commercial properties, tends to be focused in economically distressed areas, and may include a wide range of services such as homeless outreach, youth and employment opportunities and training, and school-based activities. BIDs consequently are characteristic of the model of public–private development discussed previously by Kromer (2007) while recognizing a role for local government, they rely heavily on private interests for operation and for funding.

BIDs have emerged in a milieu in which large scale, publicly funded models failed to achieve desired neighborhood and community changes. They represent the "general trend away from publically controlled redevelopment efforts..." (McDonald et al., 2009: 6). They surged in popularity through the 1990s in part, because, as a public–private partnership model, services themselves are wholly provided through the private sector, while government provides an oversight role. Hence, businesses can directly control their interests rather than rely on the grace of government for efficient use of tax revenues. BIDs can be consequently described as grass roots organizations, based in local community development boards and retail interests.

The 30 BIDs studied in Los Angeles by McDonald (2009) were created by a majority vote of property owners and merchants, with reauthorization required after 5 years. The city required the use of outside consultants in the initial organization of the district and in the development of the member database for assessments. The city provided oversight by requiring public meetings and an enabling vote by the city council. BID managers also provide the city with financial reports that track the use of assessment monies. The city is authorized to audit the books and may stop BID operations if compliance or audit problems emerge. In this research, BIDs ranged in value from $55,000 to $3,414,000.

One might ask whether contemporary private–public efforts aimed at neighborhood reinvestment, in and of themselves, can reduce crime and violence. By changing the nature of the built environment to lower the likelihood of crime, by beautification of areas, or through increasing the economic opportunity structure within neighborhoods, BIDs might lower crime independent of changes in police activity. To assess this possibility, the Rand Corporation assessed 30 BIDS in Los Angeles. BIDs, they suggested, might affect violent crime in several ways: They can contribute to community level attributes that might reduce crime and youth violence by increasing informal social control, reducing visible signs of disorder and blight, improving order maintenance, and providing enriched employment opportunities by facilitating overall improvements in the local business environment. (McDonald et al., 2009: xiii)

BIDs serve as an increasingly popular contemporary way to address neighborhood reinvestment and rehabilitation. However, as shown by the research above, they are not in themselves enough to bring down violent crime. Although they show serious promise, they are but one piece of the puzzle in solving crime. A broader integrative effort is needed for BIDs to successfully address underlying crime dynamics. That integrative effort involves the use of the police to specifically address articulated crime problems in a strategic way, adapted to the characteristics of crime in BID areas.

Below, by way of a hypothetical example, we discuss the North Omaha Village concept as an urban plan that takes the larger vision of a BID for urban reinvigoration of North Omaha, but this effort is specifically tied to a security platform.

Reinvestment Planning in North Omaha

North Omaha is a primarily African American area with high levels of poverty that is endeavoring to redevelop and modernize economically. It has the highest level of African American child poverty in the United States (Cordes, Gonzales, and Grace, 2007). It has a history of disinvestment, racial tension, weak property values, and high levels of serious crime. Like many other areas in northern cities, North Omaha emerged as a black area from the Great Migration in the 1930s and was polarized in political and racial conflict in the 1960s. It was fractured by the interstate system and outmigration of those who could afford to escape, and today suffers intense disinvestment consequences. In the current high-incarceration era in the United States, its problems are compounded by the financial, medical, and crime burden of a substantial and growing postprison reentry population.

In spite of its once vital urban life, today it has no theater or sit-down restaurant. Many residents who would seek employment are handicapped by a lack of adequate personal or public transportation. One of North Omaha's potential attractions, the home of Malcolm X, was bulldozed several years ago and today sits as an empty lot. There have been many attempts to bring in economic development and revitalization, with varying rates of success. Below we will review an economic endeavor for this area: The North Omaha Village Zone Action Plan, which is an affiliated component of the North Omaha Development Project (NODP). We will use this project to describe what we believe the corresponding mission-based role for the police should be.

North Omaha Development Project   NODP is a BID encompassing North Omaha. It is comprised of four "development opportunity" areas, each of which has several components. A review of those elements shows that the BID is aimed at improving quality of life through areal enhancement of North Omaha, the expansion of business investment, development of cultural opportunities, the improvement of public areas, provision of residential development, and expansion of educational offerings tailored to local needs. Together, these items seek to reverse the long-term disinvestment that has characterized North Omaha.

The North Omaha Village Zone Action Plan   The North Omaha Village Zone Plan is a specific coordinated effort to redevelop a section of the NODP BID described above. The Village Zone plan is a broad coalition effort to reverse the cycle of decay, poverty, and loss of business and investment in North Omaha. A map of the plan is presented in Figure 6.1.

The North Omaha Village Zone Action Plan began as an idea in 2007, when the North Omaha 360 Empowerment Network (hereafter called the 360) carried out an assessment of community interest in rebuilding the zones and began the process of developing an action plan. That initial assessment showed a great deal of interest

Figure 6.1   Map of North Omaha Village zone plan.

in development. The 360 then contacted the Nebraska Investment Finance Authority (NIFA) and worked with it to contract with two consultants to develop a digitalized model of the East and West Village Zones, and identify both their strengths and problem areas. The West Zone was assessed by Shemmer Consultancy, and the East by Mortgensen Associates.[1] The combined size of the zones is about six square miles. The specific goals of the plan were:

1. Comprehensive, Coordinated Plan for Redevelopment
2. Connected, Sustainable, Thriving Community
3. Focus on Targeted Areas with the Greatest Potential
4. Identify "Iconic" Catalyst Projects
5. Develop Real, Tangible Proposals
6. Create Detailed Budgets and Implementation Plans
7. Establish Partners and Raise Funds
8. Implement Sustainable Projects, Models, and Plans

The consultants then met with community members and leaders in early 2010 to present their findings and discuss specific proposals for the economic development of both areas. The meeting was conducted by the consultants and moderated by the 360. Consultants described their work and distributed digitalized maps of their respective areas. Community members and leaders worked with the maps to suggest areas that needed specific improvement, to provide local insight into possible obstructions, and to give feedback to the overall process. The product of this meeting was an action plan for the implementation of broad-based economic revitalization of the village zones, which included recommendations for an entertainment district, an expansion of practical educational opportunities, the rebuilding of municipal infrastructure such as connective plumbing and problematic road grid system, and a variety of other ends.

In April 2010 the consultants again met with community members to take the action plan to the next phase. During this meeting, community members and stakeholders discussed options for development and prioritized developmental stages. After this meeting, the 360 intends to meet consistently with foundations and business leaders, prepared to provide concrete estimates of financial opportunities within the matrix of information provided through the two consultancies.

The Role of Hot Zone Security for Village Zone Complex Investment and Development   One can see in the development of the Village Zone an elaborate, thoughtful, and well-designed plan that carries great potential to attract business investment. It is not a unique design or practice, but characteristic of many urban recovery areas. Our position is that this type of development, as comprehensive as it is, still needs to be married to long-term security that is planned and organized in conjunction with development. What, one would ask, is the specific contribution of security to the Village Zone complex? We can describe two phases to the development: the first phase, where there is vacant housing that requires security protection, and the second phase, where new construction requires a new set of security measures.

Phase 1: The Protection of Existing Housing   City planning carries a variety of responsibilities with regard to vacant housing. The ones listed here were suggested by Kromer (2007):

1. Prevent future vacancy by promoting the local real estate market.
2. Preserve existing owned housing with city funded repair programs.
3. Plan for neighborhood's future with strategic decisions about rehabilitation of houses.
4. Repair recently abandoned houses in relatively good condition.
5. Mothball good houses that are abandoned by low-cost "encapsulation."
6. Use the local agriculture extension to plant grass and trees on vacant lots.
7. Develop low income housing through the Low Income Housing Tax Credit program.
8. Collaborate with local public housing authority for improvement of public housing.
9. Spread new housing, through large lots with generous yard space.
10. Demolish vacant houses too expensive to fix, with planning toward reconstruction.

A review of these ten vacant housing plan principles suggests several additional security dimensions to facilitate the recovery effort:

1. The houses to be rehabilitated may have extra materials lying about and require a close watch to ensure they are not stolen.
2. In addition, recently abandoned houses must also be closely watched. Police should have a way to enter these units and track any undesired attention.
3. "Encapsulated" houses should be adequately visible from the street. Ensure that they do not have exterior criminogenic features such as large bushes near the front door that could hide potential offenders.
4. Track housing-related stolen goods sales points. Where is copper, for instance, most likely to be sold? Who is buying it?
5. Ensure that any new low income housing has adequate security protections. What is the plan for securing any built areas? This means that a police officer, trained in Crime Prevention through Environmental Design (CPTED) (Jeffery, 1971), sits on boards responsible for the development or rehabilitation of public housing.
6. Facilitate the development of citizen patrols in the areas where housing activity is occurring.

Phase 2: The Construction of New Housing   The specific mission-based role of the police to the village complex is described below.

1. Information operations should:
    a. Provide and disseminate crime statistics to lessen fear of crime. This includes frequent media contacts to discuss the nature of police activities and the success of crime dissipation efforts. What are the police actually doing in the village complex? What crimes have been solved?
    b. Ensure that the steering committee recognizes and builds into the BID a recognition of the importance of security both in terms of design (see number 2) and in terms of police presence.
    c. Review existing literature on pertinent POP research. For instance, the POP document on police strategies for dealing with vacant housing discussed in Information Box 6-1.

2. Incorporate CPTED decision making into the village zone. That is, make sure that all developments and activities recognize that opportunities to "build crime out" should be used. This work would make the police an integral element of the revitalization effort.

3. Continued focus and problem solving by police on hot crime areas and serious crime in the village complex area.

4. Maintain a high police visibility. The significant presence of police in these areas, if marketed correctly as an investment of the city into the well-being of the village complex, should contribute positively to efforts to attract investors.

5. Focus on graffiti. Graffiti, though not widely seen as a victim-based crime, has an immediate and chilling effect on business interests in an area. Contemporary software is increasingly efficacious at identifying styles of graffiti and identities of graffiti artists. The police should:

   a. Get graffiti immediately cleaned up.
   b. Engage in rapid identification and suppression of graffiti taggers.

Problem-Oriented Policing for Single Family Construction Home Theft   The problems described above apply to existing vacant lots and vacated properties. Once rebuilding has begun, a new set of crime problems arise, requiring an adaptive set of POP responses to provide adequate protection in a changed security environment. Boba and Santos (2007), working with the Port Saint Lucie (Florida) Police Department, have developed a concrete set of problem-oriented solutions for construction site theft. Their model involves four stages: scanning, analysis, response, and assessment (SARA). Each are considered below.

Scanning   The authors first developed a check sheet for officers to be filled out for every construction site theft. This sheet contained the following information:

Builder information: Builders had the broadest perspective of the construction operations and often tied thefts to subcontractors.

Subcontractor information: Subcontractors, present at different stages of the building process, might have information about suspects or themselves be suspects.

Property delivered by: Who delivered the property to the site that was stolen? How did they have access to inside the property?

Stage of building: Different stages offered different opportunities for theft. The house was most accessible in its early stages, yet the most valuable goods were not available until the later stages when the house was "sealed in."

Tools needed: What kind of tools were needed to take the property, and how sophisticated did the thieves need to be? Were the necessary tools characteristic of the tools of the trade of any of the subcontractors?

The authors held builder focus groups whose purpose was to identify crime characteristics. These focus groups were particularly valuable because they provided the authors with a great deal of practical information about the construction trades and about homebuilding processes. The authors also met with the city building department, and obtained an overall picture of building practices across the city. For instance, they found that nearly 6,300 single family dwellings were under construction at the time of the research. Importantly, they found that houses were considered securable about three weeks prior to closing, when the electricity inspection was carried out.

Analysis An assessment of property taken showed that particular contractors were more likely than others to have property taken. Seventy percent of the crimes happened with 20 percent of the builders, suggesting that individual practices strongly contributed to theft. An assessment of repeat victimization did not, however, show a large number of repeats. This was attributed to the constantly changing nature of the work site; the stage of completion tended to change the crime dynamics needed to carry out the theft. Interestingly, an analysis of the frequency of theft by stage of completion showed that most theft—just over 50 percent—occurred after the building was securable. These findings strongly supported the position that individuals with knowledge about and access to the site were carrying out the crimes. The authors also identified and listed property by the difficulty in carrying out the crime. Interestingly, they found that most crimes required the greatest amount of skill. This finding suggested that offenders in Port Saint Lucie "may have more a high degree of knowledge about construction materials and equipment, since the highest level of skill was required in nearly half of the crimes" (2007: 225).

Response   Several different responses were implemented:

A pattern analysis, using crime mapping, enabled traditional responses aimed at apprehending offenders. For instance, a pattern showing cement mixer thefts indicated they were located near a freeway. By locating a cement mixer with a "no trespassing" sign on it in that area, the police were able to make an arrest within two days.

A media campaign was carried out.

Meetings with builders enabled the delivery of crime prevention advice. These meetings improved communications between builders and the police.

Addresses identified as the highest risk were prioritized for crime prevention checks.

The authors worked with specific builders. The builder with the highest theft rate also had the fewest supervisors per house. By adding more supervisors, crime was sharply curtailed. Also, builders were encouraged not to provide subcontractors with keys to houses, but to ensure that supervisors maintained control of the keys at all times.

Assessment   The assessment of the findings was carried out for overall crimes and for crimes by particular builders. A linear presentation of findings showed that, both overall and for builders individually, crimes had been increasing steadily prior to the implementation of the program. However, after implementation, crimes immediately dropped and thereafter continued decreasing. The POP project was a success.

This is only one example of a circumstance where development is paired with security where the two are tied strategically through problem-oriented practices. Information Box 6-3 lists a broad array of problem-oriented categories potentially useful for a variety of development-security partnerships.

INFORMATION BOX 6-3:
PROBLEM-SPECIFIC GUIDES FROM THE
CENTER FOR PROBLEM ORIENTED POLICING

Below is a partial list of problem oriented guides that provide direction for POP solutions to common problems. This list was taken from the web site for the center for problem oriented policing (http://www.popcenter.org). The site also lists specific examples, various application ideas, and concrete research projects that carry out problem oriented policing.

Alcohol and Drug Problems
    Drug Dealing in Privately Owned Apartment Complexes
    Assaults in and around Bars
Burglary and Theft
    Thefts of and from Cars in Parking Facilities
    Burglary of Retail Establishments
    Crimes against Tourists
    Thefts of and from Cars on Residential Streets and
        Driveways
Business Related Problems
    Disorder at Day Laborer Sites
    Burglary at Single Family House Construction Sites
    Robbery of Convenience Stores
Disorder and Nuisance Problems
    Speeding in Residential Areas
    Graffiti
    Street Prostitution
    Abandoned Vehicles
Gang Problems
    Gun Violence among Serious Young Offenders
    Drug Dealing in Open Air Markets
    Witness Intimidation
    Drive-By Shootings
Vehicle-Related Problems

Traffic Congestion around Schools
Robbery of Taxi Drivers
Youth-Juvenile Problems
Gun Violence from Serious Young Offenders
Underage Drinking
Child Abuse and Neglect in the Home

An inspection of Information Box 6-3 shows that problem-oriented guides cover a wide range of problems faced by businesses and citizens alike. *The importance of these guides is that they enable a police agency to strategically develop a plan to anticipate problems in hot zones prior to the actual start of urban development, and tailor their crime prevention and suppression activities to specific characteristics of development.* A guide on burglary of single home construction, for instance, enables police to anticipate the types of crime-related problems that emerge when contractors are encouraged to develop or redevelop largely empty or nonusable areas that typify some parts of most hot zones. Guides on convenience store robbery, burglary of retail establishments, crimes against tourists, and thefts of and from cars in retail areas all can help guide police strategy during business development.

These guides, moreover, tap only the surface of problem-oriented research on crimes related to business or that can be useful in developing an integrated strategy to fight crime once a hot zone's crime signature has been fully elaborated. What's more, while focusing on business and property crime is the most feasible way police can become involved in economic rejuvenation, it can also lead to an increased sense of legitimacy and trust between residents and police, which might further inhibit violent crime as well.

The partnership of business and crime prevention is certainly not a new concept. Importantly, in spite of substantial progress in crime prevention for businesses in the academic setting, one finds precious little at the level of practice, by which we mean the systematic integration of urban planning and development and crime suppression and

prevention.[2] Our advocacy here, and central to long-term crime dissipation in hot zones, is that of level of planning, as suggested in the
hypothetical conversation between a mayor and applicant for police
chief, presented at the beginning of this chapter. However, the private sector, with public oversight, is beginning to see some of this
integration. The next section will present the contemporary form of
urban reinvestment, business improvement districts, and discuss links
to crime prevention or suppression activities.

The goals of NODP and its vision of the potential for development
for the village complex are hopeful. Its aim is the revitalization of an
area economically ravaged through the many factors discussed at the
beginning of this chapter. Leaders today in the area take the same bold
stand we take with regard to crime. Just as we believe that crime can
be ended, they believe that poverty can be ended. And they are taking
the concrete steps needed to achieve that goal. Their goal, and ours,
is not a pie-in-the-sky hope; the goals will come about through the
hard work, thoughtful planning, and comprehensive activity needed
to achieve permanent and lasting change.

Two Seeming Contradictions of Mission

The discussion of LOO-4 seems to create two contradictions. The
first is that we have asserted that the police, in and of themselves, can
reduce serious crime to levels that are not significantly different from
those of the overall level within the city. In this chapter, however, we
intimate that they cannot, because such an outcome is primarily a
municipal and political function residing in the mayor's office. Second,
we have advocated throughout that the role of operators in hot zones
is to end serious crime. Yet, some of the problem-oriented practices
that facilitate business and residential development will involve misdemeanor crimes such as vandalism and code violations.

With regard to the former, we believe that the police, in and of themselves and following the principles in this book, can bring serious crime
down to city-wide levels. The issue salient to LOO-4 is that without
real reform (meaning economic and social reform) those levels will not
stay down. It should be recalled that the structure for addressing crime,
on a permanent basis, was adapted from the strategic counterterrorism
model developed by Petraeus. He recognized, and we similarly assert,

that long-term success requires economic revitalization, governmental legitimacy, infrastructure redevelopment, and employment. Security enables these to happen. It can bring the levels of violence down, but it alone cannot keep them down indefinitely. The central point of a population-centric model is to provide for the well-being of the population. Otherwise, at the end of the mission, we have only the enemy-centric model. It will enjoy short-term success, but in the end will fail, and may inadvertently exacerbate precisely those problems we seek to address.

With regard to the latter—a refocusing on nonserious crime—the general answer is that the security needs of the LOO strategy change over time. The LOO strategy is a staged strategy, with a complex task structure needed to integrate the LOOs into a coherent and focused mission. For the police, we have conceived of that task structure in terms of POP solutions within each LOO, according to its particular needs. For the first three LOOs, that task structure was serious crime. For the fourth LOO, the focus is on serious crime *and* the specific kind of security operation that facilitates development and neighborhood recovery. To understand the different stages and their relationship, we turn to the next chapter, on model integration, to describe the "large picture" of mission-based policing.

Endnotes

1. These consultants were provided by the Planning Consultants and Housing Developers section of the Affordable Housing Resources Inventory. A list at their website serves as a Directory of Consultants that communities and organizations across the state of Nebraska can use to assist them in selecting a consultant. The web page states that "These consultants have been of service to our clients in the past and are honored to be part of this directory." They are located online at http://www.neded.org/content/view/458/676/.
2. A very promising crime-prevention/rebuilding strategy is provided by Geller and Belsky (2009). The authors note that coalitions of police and community developers can have a substantial impact on crime. This important work should be noted and studied by developers and police alike who wish to make a long-term impact on crime and, at the same time, improve the quality of the lives of citizens who live in poverty areas.

7

MODEL INTEGRATION AND STAGING LINES OF OPERATION

We end Part I with a summary look at the mission-based model. The first part of this chapter looks at the relationship among the lines of operation (LOOs) and focuses on the progressive stages of the strategy and mission. The contribution of each LOO to mission goals shifts according to the stage the mission is in. This chapter begins with a presentation of the staging process for LOOs. The second part of the chapter summarizes the overall model of hot zone deployment.

Staging Logical Lines of Operation

As with previous strategic modeling, the staging process adapts counterinsurgency logic to municipal police practices. Staging means that the *groundwork is set for particular kinds of tactics and practices to be put into place at the beginning of the stage.* As the stage moves into an action plan, tactics are implemented and the success of those tactics is assessed. Tactics may then be modified as the "reality on the ground" changes, but should stay within the overall strategic model of the LOO.

The model developed by Petraeus, Amos, and Nagl (2007) is characterized by three stages, to which we add a fourth stage to emphasize the importance of the planning component of the mission.

Stage 1: Identify the Injury

This stage is sometimes referred to as prestaging, which refers to the period prior to the deployment of officers into hot zones. In our model, stage 1 represents the first LOO, information operations. This stage is characterized by the development of information operations and ends at (1) the deployment of officers to the hot zone and (2) the formal empowerment of the neighborhood revitalization committee.

This stage, though not treated as a separate stage in the counterinsurgency literature, is the most important because wrong decisions made here, about the nature of crime, deployment, community relations, and tactics, may well stymie any future successes the mission will have. Moreover, in the current era a tremendous quantity of knowledge is available about crime analysis, environmental crime characteristics, and problem-oriented solutions to get a sense of what works in crime suppression and prevention. Failing to capitalize adequately on that knowledge and experience would be a tragedy.

This stage organizes crime interventions as well as for police–community development. The numbered items below are similar to those presented in Chapter 5, particularly with regard to the first LOO. The difference here is that the *LOO discussion presents general categories of information and is intended to orient the reader to the strategic purpose of the element. The staging process here is intended to locate that information into an action plan.* This first stage includes the following eight elements:

1. *Identify the block addresses that constitute the hot zone.* Build the computer models that will allow one to track crime by type, known offenders, gang members, released prisoners, and traffic accidents within that zone. Include in the model adjacent zones to look for crime spillover, hotels, and residents associated with repeat criminal activity. All crime maps should overlay a detailed geographic map of the hot zone.

2. *Identify the crime signature.* Measure how many crimes and what kinds of crimes as well as who (or what organization) is committing them. Develop a theory of crime for each crime type, identify all types within the zone, and build those theories of crime into the mission plan. This theory should be concrete and practical: What are the characteristics of the crime and how are they related to hot shots, gangs, or to the immediate structure of opportunities or inhibitors? This "practical theory" is central to the mission; it will direct all of the initial problem-oriented policing responses.

3. *Carry out analyses that identify the hot, at-risk, and safe zones* (see Chapter 8). Adapt the hot zones to existing beats or districts for reassignment purposes (see Chapter 8). Realign the organizational chart to maximize presence and response capacity in the hot zones (see Chapter 9). Build units that are responsive to at-risk zones that are not under the hot zone command (see Chapter 9).

4. *Develop initial problem-oriented policing (POP) suppressive and tactical crime prevention responses.* Keep in mind factors such as:
   a. Hot crime patterns and tactical responses. What is the most effective way to immediately suppress hot activity? Plan deployment for operations, but retain a high contact presence even postoperation. Plan simultaneously around traditional POP elements associated with crime prevention; this will suppress future recurrence of the same crime pattern.
   b. The presence or absence of managers.
   c. Population flows conducive to crime.
   d. Routine crime patterns.
   e. Crime target presentation.
   Keep in mind a paradox: Suppression and patrol activities should maximize visibility. Prevention strategies should minimize police visibility.[1]

5. *Develop an after-action protocol designed to rapidly assess the outcome.* It should be emphasized that after-action review will likely serve as the only detailed record of the POP suppressive and crime preventive operations. Protocol includes:
   a. Forms used. A summary is distributed to all squad members and a more detailed report to commanders.
   b. Meeting times for after-action participants.
   c. Distribution of forms—when and to whom?
   d. Library of after-action reports for periodic review.

6. *Identify road systems that are thought to be used by individuals with criminal intent.* These are also likely to be the arterials with the greatest number of accidents per mileage unit. Designate these for high levels of data-driven approaches to crime and traffic safety (DDACTS) traffic enforcement activity. Also, work with the county sheriff and state police to the extent that

they also can be deployed in these areas. The state police, for instance, have an interest in lowering deaths per one hundred million miles and will provide patrol assistance to those areas.

7. *Identify crime hot shots in the hot zone.* These are known offenders who have criminal histories. Hot shots can be identified by their consistent presence at crime-related incidents, whether or not they are known to have actively played a role in the crimes. Develop a model to contact them regularly.

8. *Develop an inventory of local businesses, with a focus on illicit businesses.* Some businesses are considered gray zones—pawn shops, for instance, vary in the degree to which they work with the legal and black markets. Hotel managers may charge extortionate rents for illegal immigrants who need to find a room to bed large numbers of family and friends. Businesses that contribute to crime markets—some hotels and pawn shops, for example—will be problem-oriented policed to increase accountability or control over their activities. Third-party policing tactics should be developed and employed here, with an eye toward pressure techniques to bring business properties and users in compliance with the law. As security is fully extended across the zones, businesses may have to be encouraged to expand. One of the roles of police here is the maintenance of a visible presence and ongoing contact for local businesses so that their owners and investors will perceive them to be located in a favorable security setting.

The items listed below are related to police-community relations and economic development:

1. Set up the neighborhood revitalization committee. This committee has been extensively described in Chapter 5. Actions here include:
   a. Develop a functional list of community leaders. The mayor's office and the police department should work together to establish the membership of this group. Some of these individuals will willingly participate and some may be reluctant. Persevere.
   b. Develop a list of support agencies and their contact information across the hot zone or that works with hot zone

residents. These are, for instance, boys and girls clubs, faith groups, and the like. One of the first tasks of the neighborhood revitalization committee will be to develop a brochure and website to bring this information to citizens in the hot zone.

    c. Identify and develop contact information for all citizen groups, particularly neighborhood associations, collectives, and citizen patrols in the area. One of the first tasks of the neighborhood revitalization committee will be to invigorate these neighborhood-based alliances.

2. Plan for a publicity operation. This includes:

    a. The announcement of the beginning of operations.

    b. Identification of mass media, public meetings, and other media strategies that can be used by the police to communicate with the citizens in the area.

    c. A specific plan for commanders to meet periodically with citizen groups.

    d. Identification and invitation of local reporters who are invited to participate with the police within the zone.

    e. Introduction of the strategic information officer, responsible for press contacts and for general liaison duties.

Stage 2: Stop the Bleeding

A great deal of work during this stage is in shaping the information environment and establishing expectations for citizens in the hot zone.[2] In US urban settings, it is commonly perceived that this stage had already been addressed, with hot zones characterized by calls for service, random preventive patrol, and with the widespread presence of specialized operations aimed at particular crime producers or kinds of crime activities. Citizens know what to expect; they have likely been around their police departments for many years.

What is needed is to change citizen expectations, because many citizens in poor urban areas expect almost nothing positive from the police. The rise of gangs in US urban life is evidence for the failure of formal social control. This feature of the information environment is not positive toward the police and needs to be changed.

One might best describe many of the hot zones in urban areas as "perpetually falling off a cliff." These areas have not hit bottom—exactly—yet seem incapable of improvement or even of finding their way back to the edge of the precipice. Moreover, when one looks at the full panoply of problems many hot zones face that have been reiterated herein—crime and victimization, economic disinvestment, high unemployment, lack of jobs, poor property values, underfunded schools with relatively high absentee rates among both students and teachers, relatively low levels of education and a broad lack of professional skills, inadequate medical treatment, high alcohol sales density, rampant drugs, a significant and active gang presence, high levels of absentee landlordism, and large, growing, and mostly unemployable ex offender populations—one recognizes that crime is part and parcel of a broad array of institutional failures at all levels.

"Stopping the bleeding" is a significant and difficult task. The security task, established at the outset, is the permanent presence of a hot zone command layered on top of existing calls for service activity carried out by the department. Its first task is the management of the information environment. A variety of efforts are important at this stage:

1. *Get the message out.* It is important for everyone to know that the police are there and what they are doing. To encourage witness participation, citizens need to know that the police are assigned for extended periods, and not simply present for a brief operation. Criminals and fence-sitters need to know that the police presence is permanent.

   The "message maker" is the strategic information officer who works with the public relations officer or officers in the department. This individual needs to be highly visible during the initial days of the campaign to put into place the command, operator and patrol units, and the initial POP operations.

   Information deployment should be citywide. Some residents will believe that they are not receiving comparable or adequate police services. The police must emphasize the central issue—they are repressing the areas of highest crime, and that by addressing crime in those areas it will benefit the broader community. Crime prevention and suppression are characterized by a diffusion of benefits—when crime in one area is repressed, it tends to go down in adjacent areas as well.

2. *Deploy the hot zone command.* Publicly announce the deployment; the department should be able to enjoy a brief "announcement effect" that will dampen crime. But this will just as quickly disappear.

   a. Ensure that deployed officers actually go to their new assignments.
   b. In the precincts, review the current assignments.
   c. Anticipate immediate problems with complaints against the department. Grievances will happen almost immediately. The tone set by the department in responding to them here will set the stage for later public relations and establish the legitimacy of the police actions in the hot zones.

3. *Begin regular meetings for the neighborhood revitalization committee.* A rule for the crime control partners in these groups is that no police action should take other committee members by surprise. This is critical for police legitimacy and ultimately for mission success.

4. *Transparency and legitimacy in all actions.* Record all interrogations and vehicular interdictions. Act professionally at all times. Provide proof and emphasize to the citizens in the hot zone that the department is committed to acting on their behalf. Mistakes are acknowledged.

5. *Control the message.* This means that if a police tactic, practice, or individual is challenged, police immediately challenge the message across the community if the challenger is mistaken, but acknowledge the importance of the concern. It cannot be overemphasized: A community concern or grievance that is technically wrong is nevertheless an issue that should be heartfully addressed. Citizens' hearts and minds cannot be otherwise won. The delicate balance here is to be open to criticism but at the same time to control the message in the face of untruths or distortions. The important, commonly shared item in both is that the police exert a strong, positive public image that conveys openness for dialogue.

6. *Identify and develop a media campaign against antisnitch advocates and groups.* Carry out a public relations campaign aimed at encouraging individuals to talk to the police. If witnesses come forward, provide security and protection. Encourage crime stoppers and other citizen support groups.

Stage 3: Inpatient Care and Treatment

This stage refers to the actions that are set in motion when crime is beginning to be contained and reduced. The primary goal here is to keep focused on the mission and to neither become complacent nor frustrated. The important issue here is focus—stay within the strategic model and adapt to changes in the territory and characteristics of crime. Many in the community will begin to challenge the continued role of the police. Changes in city council makeup may lead to sustained political opposition. Pressure will emerge to redeploy to safe zones in the low crime precincts. Occasional crime spikes or instances of crime with high media coverage will create pressure to shift to a traditional model, or alternatively, to pay less attention to legitimacy issues in an effort to crack down on particular felons or suspects. These responses will not "heal the patient." The following elements characterize this stage:

1. High levels of security are continued, and surveys carried out by the neighborhood revitalization committee should address whether residents feel more secure in their neighborhoods.
2. It should be anticipated during this stage that crime will change in tenor and type as criminals seek to creatively adapt to police tactics. Consequently, constant monitoring of crime and revision of tactical operations should be sustained throughout this stage.
3. Operational successes and crime prevention programs become central to the information campaign. It is critical during this stage that both the hot zone resident perceptions of crime and their fear of crime are gradually reduced.
4. It is also critical during this stage that police become accepted as a legitimate security presence, not as an outside occupying force. This means that information operations continue to be

central to the police task and that transparency and accountability to local residents are institutionalized.

5. The mayor's office, as a representative of legitimate governance, is taking an active role in activities inside the hot
zone. Any grants work or programs that pass through the
mayor's office should be publicly discussed in town meetings
inside the hot zone.

6. All parties—police, mayor's office, and local groups—need to
bring to the neighborhood revitalization committee economic
opportunities during this period. These include grant opportunities, training for youth as well as for ex-offenders, local
scholarship programs, active development of job opportunities, and succoring of businesses to the area. These are central
to long-term mission success.

It needs to be emphasized that each of the above infrastructural
and economic items are structured within the LOOs. This means that
the social or economic problem is clearly tied to a security element,
and that the end result is clearly articulated in terms of how it contributes to stability. For instance, jobs development is not simply seen
as an end in itself, but rather, a specific "jobs development" goal is
established, the goal is clearly associated with the end state "residential stability," and success in achieving that goal is measured.

Stage 4: Recovery

This stage begins when security is established and is measured by
the lowering of serious crime to nonsignificant differences with safe
zones. The primary emphasis in this period is the development of local
economic opportunity and infrastructure supports. During this stage
all of the nonsecurity elements described in stage 3 should continue,
with concrete measures identifying their success. Just as crime markers are used to measure the success of security, so too are economic
markers—employment statistics, housing values, and the like—used
to assess hot zone stability. Security begins the work of progressive
redeployment of the command force out of the hot zone, ensuring
that crime does not reappear with successive drops in deployment
presence.

State and National Recommendations

Finally, we present recommendations that are broad in scope and refer to the state and federal fiscal and political environment. These represent areas where local hot zone missions could be supplemented by state and federal aid.

1. *Retool federal Weed and Seed programs* to fit into the economic reconstruction efforts of hot zones. This recommendation is to make areas designated at risk, those with a fully developed "prestage" program, first priority for Weed and Seed program funding.
2. The *state should provide earmarks* for hot zones. Earmarks would have a security component to them, but would primarily be aimed at development of economic infrastructure. These earmarks would include consulting for infrastructure development.
3. The development of *tax incentive programs* for the succoring of business opportunities inside hot zones. These need to be developed by the mayor's office and will need to be approved by the planning board and the city council.
4. The provision of *no interest mortgage loans* for police officers who establish primary residences inside hot zones.
5. In addition to the *National Institute of Justice, the Housing and Urban Development, National Institute of Mental Health, and National Institute of Health* should all develop specialized granting programs that provide funding for hot zone development. These can provide critical supports to the zone's residents as the area undergoes economic revitalization.

The Hot Zone Model: Population-Centric Crime Suppression Control

This section gives a graphic presentation of the overall model of deployment of hot zones, with the model designed around the command level of strategic responsibility. The model presented in Figure 7.1 shows the structure of the hot zone, with an overlay of the security model for crime dissipation. Figure 7.1 presents the following elements:

Top level of pyramid: Mission. This is the articulated mission of the hot zone. Its central element is the dissipation of crime. It is articulated in LOO-1, information operations. It includes an analysis of the zone's threat environment, the hot zone's crime signature, the theory of the crime signature, the block-level physical geography of the zone, the flow of populations through the zone by time of day, multiyear resource estimates for police expenditures for the zone, estimates of force levels for addressing crime, and the identification and forging of alliances with community groups that can facilitate security as well as economic and social development.

Second level: Logical lines of operation. These LOOs are command responsibility levels, and they represent the four population-centric fronts of the overall mission. They are information operations, security operations, restoration of essential services, and economic development. Note that the social and economic elements are located inside the overall security plan for the hot zone. This enables the police to retain a critical role through all of these elements, though that role

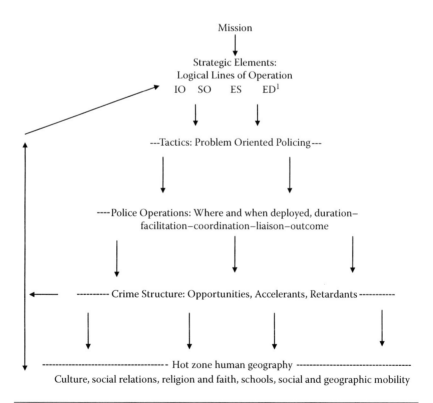

Figure 7.1   Security model for a hot zone.

changes to adapt both to the particular LOO and to changes
in the hot zone environment as needed.

Third level: Tactical POP deployment. This refers to POP tactics used to achieve LOOs. This line is intended to address
the question: What POP operations are employed to achieve
success according to the logical line of operation? It invokes
The Boba model of tying problem complexity to command
level and also extends POP tactics to each of the LOOs. The
model above views the core logic of problem solving—identification of the underlying problems, development of a plan,
application of the plan, and assessment of the success of the
plan—as integral across the LOO spectrum.

   The initial security POP operations may be developed during
information operations; however, POP solutions will be developed in accordance with the situation as it is faced at each stage
of the mission. That is, POP not only can provide for concrete
planning and implementation of specific projects, but it has the
flexibility to adapt to changes in the hot zone environment.

Fourth level: Police operations. This level identifies the specific
activities of the police across the hot zones and is the interface between the POP solutions and the crime characteristics of the hot zone. The hot zone command is constructed
so that it can carry out several operations simultaneously. The
police will provide a permanent presence in the hot zone,
which is designed to have both a background deterrent for
their presence and a legitimating effect for their actions. They
will carry out POP tactical operations with that presence, in
which all operations are developed based on POP assessments
and after-action reports. The role of the hot zone command
throughout is population centric, in terms of hot zone crime
prevention and dissipation, not criminal centric, in terms of
maximizing opportunities to arrest offenders. The assigned
strategic information officer will liaison and direct ongoing
media operations and relations.

Fifth level: Crime structure and accelerants. "Crime structure"
refers to the structure of opportunity for crime and is defined
in terms of Felson's (2002) tripartite crime facilitation model,
comprised of a likely offender, the absence of guardians, and

target attractiveness. The structure usually occurs in a micro location and is assessed as the specific elements of the crime or crime pattern as it happened in a specific place. "Accelerants" facilitate crime in a particular area, but are more broad than the immediate crime structure. Accelerants include poverty, gang presence, residential decay, ex-felon population, and the like, all of which represent potential problems that may extend across a hot spot and that intensify the likelihood that a micro location will produce a criminal event.

Sixth level: Hot zone human geography. This is the most important element of the population-centric model. It recognizes that the ultimate goal of the police is the reinvigoration of economic life and civil society for the citizenry of the hot zone, and that all police actions ultimately have to be addressed in ways that further the legitimacy of the police for this population.

Note that there are two feedback arrows. The lowest arrow is extended from the bottom of the figure to the level of the LOOs. The purpose of this arrow is to indicate that the LOOs are responsive to changing conditions in the hot zone. The population-centric model "works" to the extent that mission commanders have constructed administrative mechanisms for obtaining systematic feedback from the population about the consequences of their operations. The other arrow is from the next lowest level—crime structure and accelerants—to the LOOs. This is included to emphasize that the LOOs will have to be continually adaptable to changes in criminal behavior and crime opportunities.

Endnotes

1. Suppression and other deterrent activities are based on presence, so any activity that amplifies presence will increase the overall impact of deterrence. Crime prevention, on the other hand, is guided by the notion that, at some point, crime will dissipate to normal levels and the hot zone command can step down. These crime prevention activities, consequently, need to be empowered without the actual presence of the police.
2. In counterinsurgency, this refers to initial efforts to protect the population, stopping the momentum of the insurgents, and establishing the conditions for further engagement.

PART 2
HOT ZONE REDEPLOYMENT AND COMMAND RESTRUCTURING
A Practical Example

Part II of this book provides a concrete example of the deployment of mission-based policing based on crime. This is not a demonstration project, in the sense that it represents an actual instance of mission-based policing in action. It is instead an effort to show, using real-world data, how a police department's existing resources, particularly existing manpower levels, can be used to redeploy according to crime intensity. This is carried out for the following reasons:

First, and perhaps most importantly, police departments, like all government agencies, are currently in a severe financial crisis and are unable to staff additional units, particularly those that seem "experimental."

Second, and closely related to the first, is the idea that mission-based policing is *smarter* policing, not *larger* policing. One of the lessons learned from initiatives such as the US Department of Justice's Community Oriented Policing Services (COPS) program was its draining effect on federal and local resources without, by most accounts, significantly changing the basic functions of policing (Zhao, Lovrich, and Robinson, 2001).

Third, any police innovation needs to work within existing resources and capabilities. Consequently, our concerns here are to provide practical recommendations for estimation of hot spots and apply those recommendations to existing patrol geographies. By tying hot spots to the geography of districts, we enable a realistic estimation of police assignments.

Fourth, redeployment and redesign of command structures should be minimally intrusive to existing command structures. The question that arises through this process is: How does one redesign a police department to fight serious crime without a wholesale remodeling of command? The model developed here provides an example, using real data, for the addition of hierarchical command units at levels equivalent existing command.

Because of this smarter-not-bigger underlying theme, the specifics with regard to how this type of policing might work are crucial. Chapter 8 will discuss the first challenge—identification of hot spots and location in proximity to existing patrol districts. It will first provide a historical assessment of how spatial data have historically driven policing theory and police practices. Chapter 9 will discuss the specifics of command redesign, particularly focusing on the changing command expectations associated with modifications of command responsibilities. It will use the Omaha Police Department as an example of current deployment, presenting their manpower estimates. That will be followed by the presentation of an alternative command structure based on the redesign for mission-based policing. Chapter 10 will conclude with a discussion of important issues facing mission-based policing.

8

HOT SPOTS AND POLICE DISTRICTS

Place and Crime in Historical Perspective

A Brief History of Place

The importance of place has always been a part of both criminal justice practice and theoretical understandings of crime. Although criminal events tend to have many different aspects, every event is in some way hindered or facilitated by the characteristics of the place where it occurs. Indeed, the location of crimes has been of interest to social scientists throughout the history of criminology. Before the work of Lombroso (1911) and his focus on individual criminal traits, a handful of social scientists noted that crimes seemed to be consistently higher in some places and lower in other places (Voss and Petersen, 1971). Morris (1957), for instance, pointed out that several early French and English researchers, predating Lombroso, surmised that ecological factors might have played a part in crimes that were distinct from criminal motivation (see also Vold, Bernard, and Snipes, 2002). These early researchers, while recognizing the importance of criminal motivation, held that place-bound factors related to poverty, education, and population density were also important in explaining crime.

France was the first country to keep official statistics of crime. A. M. Guerry, with assistance from geographer Adriano Balbi, published a map that compared crime with education in 1829 (Morris, 1957). Significantly, Guerry's decision to map crime levels was used by ecologists of the time and was also used later by the Chicago school, a term identifying a group of researchers from various universities in Chicago who gave rise to urban sociology (Morris, 1957). Guerry identified the variations in rates of crimes against persons as well as property crimes among the different regions of France. Guerry was the first to provide evidence that criminal acts involved the characteristics of places where people lived.

Adolphe Quetelet utilized many of Guerry's ideas about the geographic patterns of crime in France and noted the regularity of the spatial distributions of social data such as age, gender, and climate (Morris, 1957). He postulated the idea of "social physics" that gave rise to the notion that habitats may have had an influence on social relations and actions. He, like Guerry, utilized maps to draw attention to the visual distribution of crime across the country.

The work of English researchers between 1830 and 1860 also assessed the role of place in crime. Henry Mayhew and Joseph Fletcher both focused on official statistics in their examinations of crime and social deterioration (Levin and Lindesmith, 1937/1971). Mayhew included a detailed description of crime in London in terms of its ecology and included maps presenting the "intensity" of various crimes in different parts of the city. He observed that the rates of juvenile delinquency were highest in counties that had large cities in them, and perhaps more importantly, that crime was not evenly distributed within cities but varied even by units as small as police districts (Levin and Lindesmith, 1937/1971).

Fletcher's work, also discussed by Levin and Lindesmith (1971: 60), centered on connecting areas with "indices to moral influences and moral results." Fletcher sought to develop an index of crime for the districts of England that would not be affected by the migration of individuals. Unfortunately, a limited knowledge of statistical techniques precluded these researchers from carrying out sophisticated analyses of the connection between the characteristics of areas and crime. Their work, nevertheless, showed that their observations and general knowledge about crime directed them toward ecological explanations, which were concerned with the effects of the spatial distributions of people and their living conditions.

Contemporary Research on Place

The twentieth century has produced more conceptually detailed and statistically elaborate examinations of the *effects* of the characteristics of places on crime (see the works of Brantingham and Brantingham, 1981, 1984; Cohen and Felson, 1979; Felson, 2002; Meier, Kennedy, and Sacco, 2001; Murray, 2002; Murray and Roncek, 2008; Park, Burgess and McKenzie, 1925; Roncek and Bell, 1981; Roncek and Faggiani, 1985; Roncek and Maier, 1991; Shaw and McKay, 1942; Sherman et al., 1989; Skogan, 1990; Taylor and Harrell, 1996; and Wilson and Kelling, 1982). The concern with place, which has come to be known as environmental criminology, has increased substantially in a historically short period of time (Brantingham and Brantingham, 1995; Lipton and Gruenewald, 2002; Meier et al., 2001). Police emphasis on place, focusing on data mapping, has also become important for crime suppression and prevention (Boba, 2005). Nowhere has this been more evident than with the advent of recognition of hot spots and their use in police work.

Sherman, Gartin, and Buerger (1989) drew particular attention to locations of crime with their use of Spring and Block's (1989) idea of criminal hot spots. They argued that certain areas of a city were characterized by more crime than others. They examined calls for service from specific addresses or intersections and noted that a small number of addresses were responsible for a majority of calls for service, an indicator that crime was concentrated rather than randomly distributed. Studies of the surroundings or environment of criminal activities has since become a focus of criminal research (Skogan, 1990; Taylor and Harrell, 1996; Wilson and Kelling, 1982).

One of the strengths of hot spot analysis was that it facilitated the joining of crime research and police practice. It enabled a real-time visualization of high-density crime areas that could benefit from increased police presence, and facilitated the tailoring of police patrol and operations to those areas. Indeed, this type of visual analysis has been used by police departments in some form or another (beginning with stick pins on a map) for decades. In its current form, hot spot analysis, because it can reproduce crime by characteristic on a map, provides actionable information. That is, its particular strength in police organizations is its ability to join statistical and tactical analysis. However, although many departments use hot spot analysis as a diagnostic tool, especially for tactical purposes, very few departments have successfully used hot spot analysis as a consistent tool for long-term patrol strategies (Boba, 2005; Boba and Crank, 2008). Its utility as a problem-solving tool, incorporated into long-term strategic analysis, is underdeveloped.

The inability of police departments to potentiate spatial analysis likely stems from several issues.

First, hot spot (or any) spatial analysis has historically been somewhat complex. Spatial analysis that utilized complex logarithms and expensive software was typically done outside of police departments and often took place in other offices such as in city planning (Block, 1995). Even when accessible mapping software and small computers that were easily able to handle the software became commonplace in departments, the crime analysis unit, while housed centrally, was still run by individuals who were not trained in patrol or policing. The result was that complex mapping techniques evolved separately from the rest of the police department.

Second, even in departments where mapping is routine, the more robust analytical mapping tools and products are not available for field analysis. This is a particularly important shortcoming. Departments, though producing crime mapping products for *comparative statistics* (COMPSTAT) meetings and for public consumption, often do not have a ready mechanism for relaying that information to street-engaged commanders.

Third, even where available at the local command level, the type of analysis utilized by most computer-generated software has not lent itself to on-the-ground operations. For example, the typical shape of a hot spot tends to be spherical or elliptical, which differs from patrol zones or even discernible blocks in a city (Murray and Roncek, 2008). On the other hand, efforts to fit a statistically determined hot spot boundary line to a geographically based police patrol unit may produce practical complications, for example, a hot spot may spill over into several patrol areas, each area containing only a small portion of the hot spot.

Fourth, it is difficult for police agencies to focus patrol or to develop specialized strategies on hot spot areas of crime when their time and resources are consistently being called upon for faster response times to calls for service, which, while geography-dependent, does not concentrate on areas that are consistently high-crime.

Fifth, departments tend to focus on characteristics of individuals with criminal intent, not on places. Hence, one sees a specialized gang unit, or a robbery unit, aimed at the suppression of those crimes, typically by identifying individuals associated with those crimes. While they may have a crime analysis unit that tells us where crimes are, departments often don't have a hot spot unit, which looks at criminogenic characteristics of places.

Research indicates that so-called hot spot policing can substantially reduce crime (Clarke and Weisburd, 1994; Eck, 1993; Skogan and Frydl, 2004). The capacity to identify hot spots can increase the capacity of the police to focus and distinguish among crime types. Because hot spots lay the crucial groundwork to mission-based policing, a more specific discussion on how the hot spots are practically determined and how they may be used in mission-based policing is in order.

What Is a Hot Spot and How Is It Measured?

Hot spots, in their most general sense, refer to specific locations that host a number of crimes (Spring and Block, 1989). Visually, the idea of hot spots simply means that an area of high concentration of crime can be identified on a map. This concentration can be of particular crimes such as a cluster of gang shootings or a more general grouping of crimes such as violent hot spots. But beyond this, there is little consensus regarding the make-up of a hot spot.

One of the reasons that the classification of hot spots has been difficult to use is because they don't conform to other standard units of measurement, such as blocks, police districts, or census tracts. One way that this has been addressed is to try to force the points to conform to other measures. Usually this occurs by "aggregating up," a process by which the individual points are counted within these other units. For instance, rather than just noting the concentrated points of crime themselves, this process would identify the number of points in a block or a police district. So rather than looking at hot spots one would have hot districts or hot blocks. This technique is beneficial in that it allows agencies to work with a space that is already known. However, this technique also has many drawbacks. One of these issues is called the modifiable aerial unit problem (MAUP). This complex term means that if data are inappropriately aggregated—for instance, if the hot spot area is made to be too large—the findings can be misleading or incorrect (Openshaw, 1984).

Figure 8.1 displays a pair of thematic maps that use the police district as the unit of measure for the hot or warm area (red indicates hot, green indicates warm). This figure, developed using 2009 Omaha crime data, gives a closeup of several police districts (the numbered units) and demonstrates the problem of district-level aggregation—crime

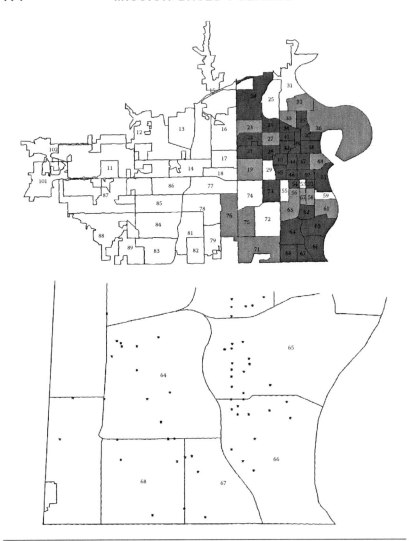

Figure 8.1   A comparison of "crime cluster" districts and the actual locations of crime clusters.

incidents are not evenly spread throughout the districts. The top half of Figure 8.1 shows the hot districts, or districts where crime clusters are located. The bottom half shows the actual location of the crime clusters. Note that the actual location of the crime clusters is concentrations near one side of the districts. Consequently, the use of police districts as an indicator of hot spots needs to be carefully considered on a unit-to-unit basis. Most of the incidents in Districts 65 and 66 shown in shown the bottom half of Figure 8.1 are concentrated in the western portion of the district, and allocations of personnel elsewhere in the district would actually relocate them away from the hot spot.

The concrete implication of this is that a hot spot map-determined basis for police activity is in itself inadequate for tactical deployment. The alignment of hot spots with districts is at best an approximation, but tactical success will be tied to concrete knowledge about the *specific* nature of crime patterns, clusters, and their relationship to specific addresses and places (together with an analysis of place characteristics).

A more accurate technique for identifying hot spots involves drawing ellipses, or ovals, around the places of concentrated areas of crime. There are various software packages that do this, but the most common technique used by police agencies involves an analysis tool called STAC (spatial and temporal analysis of crime). This tool uses an algorithm, which is a set of mathematical instructions, to determine how many "points" of crime need to be counted and how close they need to be to each other to be called a hot spot. First, the program places a grid, which looks like a table, over a mapped surface, then circles or rings are drawn around each node, or the intersection, of the cells of the table.

In Figure 8.2, a grid is placed over the city of Omaha. The size of the rings (see the upper left hand corner of Figure 8.2) is determined by the user.[1] The number of events in each ring is counted, and the density of the events is measured (Bates, 1987; Spring and Block, 1989). After the density of all the events is measured, an ellipse, or oval, is used to bind them together, creating the crime map. This technique can be done through statistical packages such as SpaceStat or directly through geographic information system (GIS) applications such as ArcGIS.[2]

This technique provides the flexibility of defining the radius of measurement (and thus the hot spot) based on user specifications. Consequently, departments can tailor hot spots to specific needs. For instance, an inspection of burglaries might lead to a more inclusive zone, with crimes connected by approximate time of occurrence. This also means that the number of hot spots can change based on who specifies the measurement. In other words, the sizes and shapes of hot spots are highly user dependent. There are no hard and fast rules.

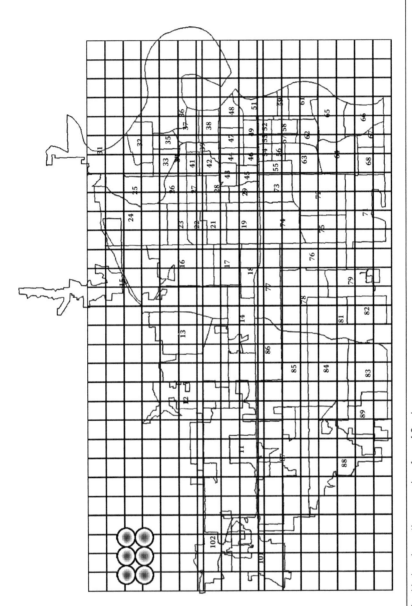

Figure 8.2 A grid placed over the mapped surface of Omaha.

Buffer regions, which are the *areas that border* the hot spots, can be created around the hot spots. They can vary in size according to user preference and intent. Such regions have a long history in criminology dating back to Shaw and McKay (1942) and their attempted application of the Burgess zonal hypothesis (Park, Burgess, and McKenzie, 1925) to juvenile delinquency. More recently, buffers have been used to measure displacement of crime (Buckley, 1996; Clark and Lab, 2000) and have become entrenched in policy implications, such as the incorporation of buffers into drug-free zone legislation (Kleiman and Smith, 1990) and more recently into sex-offender legislation (Sample and Bray, 2003). However, buffers developed in hot spot analysis are mathematical rather than theoretical creations, and do not always fit the topography of the city itself, creating potential complications for using them for patrol. This is the opposite of the previous problem where the use of the district did not match the actual location of the hot spot. Here, the hot spot and its buffer zone may not fit well into existing patrol areas or natural geographies.

Hypothetical Operational Example: Omaha, Nebraska

Omaha is a medium-sized midwestern city whose demographics typify middle-sized cities in the United States. In 2009, estimates for Omaha's population were at 454,731, the fortieth most populous city in the United States (U.S. Bureau of the Census, 2010). Omaha has approximately 5,659 residential city blocks out of 6,947 total city blocks. The average population of the blocks from the 2000 US Census was 62 people.

Omaha is primarily a white, middle-class city, with an ethnic composition as follows: 76.7 percent white, 12.8 percent black, 11.4 percent Hispanic origin, and 1.7 percent other ethnicities (U.S. Bureau of the Census, 2010). The median age for Omaha in 2009 was 34.1 years, which was lower than the national median age of 37.1; and the median household effective buying income of Omaha's metro area was $59,130 at the beginning of 2009, compared to the national median of $53,684 (Greater Omaha Chamber of Commerce, 2010).

Geographically, Omaha is approximately 119 square miles (U.S. Bureau of the Census, 2010) and is bordered by the Missouri River on the east. The Metropolitan Statistical Area of Omaha consists of

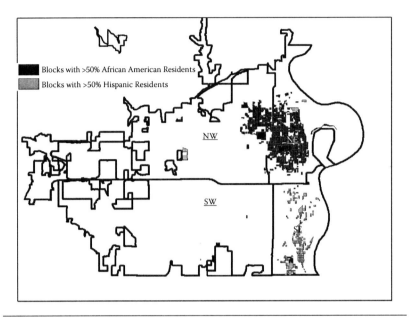

Blocks with >50% African American Residents
Blocks with >50% Hispanic Residents

NW

SW

Figure 8.3   Blocks with more than 50 percent African American/Hispanic residences.

eight counties; five in Nebraska and three in Iowa, and boasts a population of over 800,000 (U.S. Bureau of the Census, 2010). Omaha is generally divided into four regions: downtown, North Omaha, South Omaha, and West Omaha. Much of Omaha is sharply segregated, with blocks in North Omaha between 70 and 98 percent African American, in South Omaha between 50 and 80 percent Hispanic, and in West Omaha between 85 and 100 percent white/Anglo. Figure 8.3 shows blocks whose residents are either primarily African American or Hispanic and the location (and clustering) of these blocks in Omaha.

Omaha Police Department (OPD) provides the primary policing services in Omaha. According to Law Enforcement Management and Administrative Statistics (LEMAS) data for 2009, OPD had 750 full-time sworn officers, of which 80.3 percent were male and 19.7 percent were female; 81.9 percent were white/Anglo, 11.1 percent were African American, and 5.5 percent were Hispanic. OPD employs foot, bicycle, motorcycle, and horse patrols, and 64 percent of their officers are assigned to patrol (U.S. Bureau of Justice Statistics, 2010).

Figure 8.4 outlines the area of patrol, which is identified by four large precincts (NE, NW, SE, and SW) and then divided again

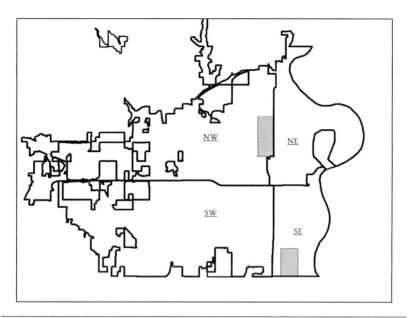

Figure 8.4   Precinct and district patrol boundaries.

into the much smaller districts, which dictate traditional patrol for the police department. It is organized into four precincts, each with twenty districts. The east-west axis of the precincts is Dodge Street, and the north-south axis is 42nd Street. The districts with numbers between 10-20 are in the NW precinct, between 30-40 are in the NE precinct, between 50-60 are located in the SE precinct, and between 70-80 are in the SW precinct. All districts are assigned a single officer to provide "omnipresent" coverage—random preventive patrol (RPP) and calls for service response. The figure also includes both north and south Weed and Seed areas, (shown as gray boxes) to give an idea of other groups working in the areas.

In terms of crime, Omaha had a total of 21,440 part I crimes which include the 8 serious crimes of aggrauated assault, forcible rape, murder, robbery, arson, burglary, larceny-theft and motor-vehicle theft in 2008, or a rate of 24.52 crimes per 1,000 people. These can be broken down further into rates of 6.06 violent crimes per 1,000 people and 42.98 property crimes per 1,000 people. This overall part I rate is comparable though somewhat lower than most other cities where the population is between 250,000 and 500,000. The average rate of part I crimes during 2008 for all middle-sized cities was 27.5 (U.S. Bureau of Justice Statistics, 2010). Like most comparison cities, crime hot spots are geographically disproportionate, occurring in areas where poverty, minority population, and unemployment are high.

Hot Spots in Omaha

In this section, hot spot analyses of property crime, violent crime, and business crime are presented and discussed, using the mapping technique described at the opening of this chapter. Two levels of aggregation were used, a hot spot and a warm spot, and were calculated based on one-third and two-thirds of the range of standard deviation for the relative frequency of crimes inside the level. For property crimes (with thefts from motor vehicles) the mean per unit (referring to the overlying grid as discussed in Figure 8.2) is 1.18 crimes, while the standard deviation is 2.22.[3] The top range of 17.32 is 7.8, a standard deviation above the mean. Dividing this by 3 means that the warm and hot spots are 2.6 and 5.2 SD above the mean, respectively (giving the warm spot lower boundary of property crime density at 6.95) and the hot spot lower boundary of property crime density at 12.72). These calculations allow a standard version of warm and hot spots based on the differing ranges of data. For purposes of patrol, we decided that identifying two levels for hot spots was best for setting up our deployment model of hot zones and at-risk zones. The specific range for hot and warm spots is shown on the lower left corner of each of the figures discussed below.

Figure 8.5 shows the hot and warm spots of property crimes, including thefts from motor vehicles, while Figures 8.6 and 8.7 show hot and warm spots for violent crimes and business crimes, respectively. It should be emphasized that these spots are not bound to city units such as blocks, nor are they confined to radii or ellipses, but instead are a product simply of the concentration of crimes. Hence, these spots are the primary data for the development of at-risk and hot zones that we will use to model deployment, but they are not the same. For purposes of mission-based assignments, these "raw" hot spots allow for a more tailored patrol response and should maximize resource efficiency.

Figure 8.5 shows that, for property crimes, there appears to be one substantial hot spot across the downtown area (laying across the

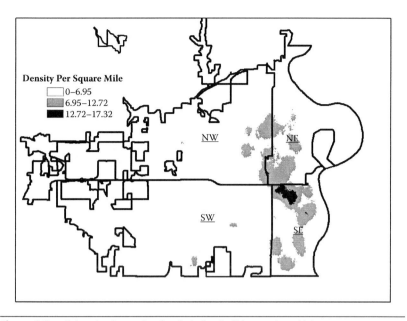

Figure 8.5   Hot spots of property crime including theft from motor vehicles.

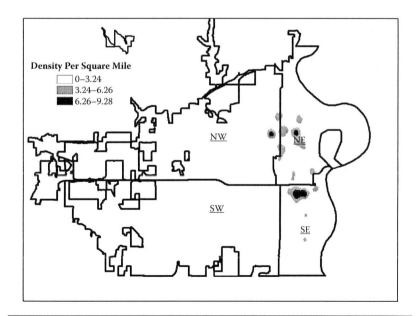

Figure 8.6   Hot spots of violent crime.

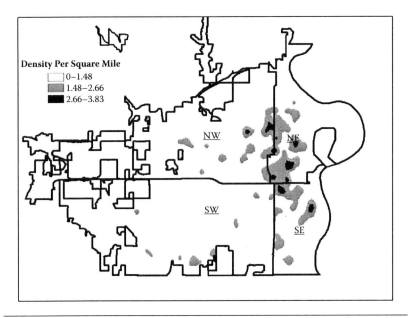

Figure 8.7   Hot spots of business crime.

east–west precinct axis), along with several warm spots in both North and South Omaha. This significant hot spot area is associated with a large public housing area and a nearby cluster of apartment complexes in this area. It is on the edge of midtown, which is located just south of Dodge Street (the central east–west corridor noted on the map in Figure 8.5). The location of the hot spot is in an area generally referred to as midtown. This assessment fits well with the geographic reality of the city. A large number of businesses (such as bars and restaurants) exist in close proximity to the large hot spot, many of which attract crowds, especially at night, and provide a number of suitable offenders and victims who might leave vehicles and property unguarded (Cohen and Felson, 1979; Felson, 2002). Only two smaller warm spots, where the crime is associated with apartment complexes, are in SW Omaha, and some warm spots are similarly noted in NW Omaha along the north-south precinct divide noted on the map, which is 42nd Street.

Figure 8.6 shows that the hot spots for violent crime are much more concentrated, with the largest cluster on the south side of Dodge Street. However, two hot and several warm spots exist in NE Omaha, consistent with the demographic information indicating that poverty areas with higher percentages of minority residences tend to also be at increased economic disadvantage and accelerants of serious violent crime. Note that one hot spot is also noted in NW Omaha. The SW precinct is entirely "cool" with regard to violent crime.

Figure 8.7 shows that there are several small hot and warm pockets of business crimes, but the general pattern of density extends from SE Omaha, through the downtown business area, and into North Omaha. All three of these areas have business districts in which businesses exist in higher concentrations than in West Omaha, or where many businesses exist in strip malls that are within residential areas.

Hot Spots and Police Districts

Although the shapes of the hot and warm spots above are not bound by anything but the density of the crimes themselves, using these for patrol allocation requires an assessment of current patrol design. Figures 8.8 to 8.10 show the same hot spot analysis, bound by the police districts noted in Figure 8.4. This visual assessment identifies four potential levels of crime activity by district: districts that are largely covered by dense concentrations of crime (hot spots); districts

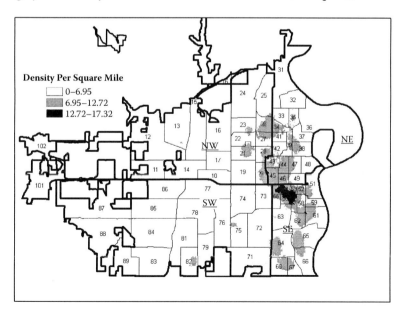

Figure 8.8 Hot spots of property crimes (with thefts from motor vehicles) bounded by police districts.

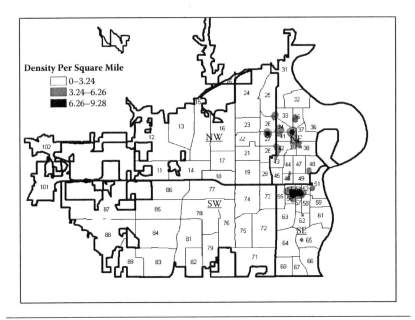

Figure 8.9   Hot spots of violent crimes bound by police districts.

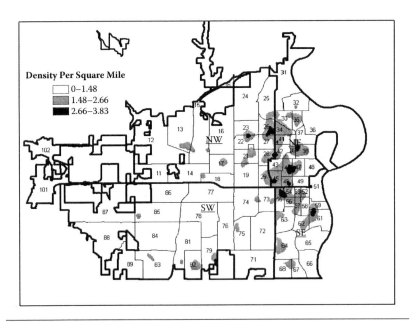

Figure 8.10   Hot spots of business crimes bound by police districts.

that are largely covered by moderately dense concentrations of crime (warm spots); districts that are only partially or minimally covered by dense or moderately dense concentrations; and districts that do not cover dense or moderate density of crime. District differences in crime are important in mission-based policing, where on-the-ground decisions depend on concrete knowledge of where hot and warm spots exist—both within and across district boundaries.

In Figure 8.8, it is clear that there are two districts (54 and 56) that contain high levels of property crime. One can also see the effects of areas of concentration that exist only in part of a district (such as District 65) or splits evenly between districts (such as 64 and 68) or even across precinct lines (such as 26, 27, and 34), where the one hot spot overlaps two precincts.

Figure 8.9 shows a similar though more concentrated geography for violent crime. The issue of overlapping districts for hot spots is again visible, for Districts 34 and 41, and for Districts 52, 53, 54, 56, 57, and 58.

Violent crime also clearly shows one hot spot in the NE precinct and one in the NW precinct, located mostly within District 27 and then splitting Districts 34 and 41, with six hot and warm spots generally clustering around District 41. Note that this pattern is sharply different from that of property crime, which showed only a single gray spot in the vicinity of District 41, and that one was located almost wholly in District 26. This shows that different areas, even when adjacent, can have quite different crime signatures and cannot be treated through the same crime suppression or prevention modalities.

Figure 8.10 presents business crime clusters by district. Business crimes tend to exist in a broken conglomerate on the east portion of the city (again crossing both district and precinct lines). A cluster of at-risk and hot zones can also be noted in the NW precinct, and most of this near the NE precinct boundary. Strategically, business crimes are fragmented across nine hot spots. However, the gray spots provide a certain degree of unity to the overall pattern, showing the greatest concentration just north of the Omaha downtown area and radiating east and west. Complicating this assessment is that the majority of business crimes tend to be reported during the day, though many of these crimes have taken place during evening and night hours. This suggests that a mission-based policing deployment

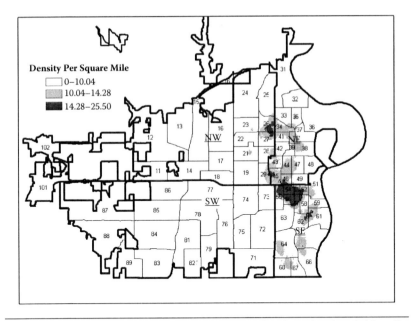

Figure 8.11   Hot spots in the All Crimes Map: Aggregated serious crime bounded by police districts.

strategy should have a time-sensitive strategy in addressing these crime hot spots.

Figure 8.11 presents a summary hot spot map of all serious crime in Omaha. It shows that hot spots are located primarily just within and south of the downtown area, in police Districts 53, 54, 55, 56, and 57. (Note that the downtown area corresponds to Districts 46, 49, 51, 52, 53, and 54.) Three smaller hot spots are noted, one connecting Districts 61 and 62, a second located about two miles north of downtown, connecting Districts 26, 27, and 34, and a third just north of the downtown area, connecting Districts 29 and 45.

It is instructive to compare this map to the different crime maps displayed in the previous figures. The northernmost hot spot is noted both for business and violent crime, but is warm for property crime. The small hot spot just north of downtown is also in business crime, and it is also warm (an at-risk zone) for property crime. The large hot spot in downtown is also a hot spot for business, violent, and property crime. The smaller hot spot about a mile south of downtown (Districts 61 and 62) is similarly noted for business and property crimes.

We also see that several business hot spots (Figure 8.10) are not noted as hot spots in the all crimes map in Figure 8.11. However, they are all noted as at-risk zones on the all crimes map. The exceptions to this are several at-risk property zones that are isolated from one another and from hot spots in the western part of the city. The violent crime hot spot in District 37 is a warm area in the all crimes map. Property crime hot spots match those noted in the all crimes map.

These comparisons suggest that an analyst can acquire a good sense of the combined hot and at-risk geography of each of the three crime categories, when taking into consideration both hot and at-risk zones, by looking only at the *all crimes map*, Figure 8.11. (It should be emphasized that the all crimes map represents all *serious* crime.) This is important for deployment. It means that separate deployments do not have to be made depending on crime type. The all crimes map provides virtually all the information needed for deployment, with the individual crime-type maps (Figures 8.8 to 8.10) suggestive of the different kinds of police response, the nature of the intelligence needed, and the problem-oriented tactics for those locations.

The all crimes map leads us to suggest that the boundaries for the deployment of the operator units are a trapezoid, what we call the central crime zone, as follows:

A western perimeter: NW to SW (26, 27, 28, 29, 73).
A middle high intensity band: NW to SW (34, 41, 42, 44, 46, 54, 53, 56, 57, 62, 65).
An eastern perimeter: NE to SE (37, 38, 47, 52, 59, 61, 62, 65).

There are several points that can be drawn from this:

1. The central crime zone is roughly the size of a precinct and is wholly contained within two of the existing precincts.
2. All of the identified districts are contiguous with each other. This means that deployment in the central crime zone can be focused across this zone, without being fragmented into a series of unrelated areas. This will enable areal unity of command.
3. An area that is a hot zone in one map is almost always a hot zone or an at-risk zone in another.
4. There are only a few at-risk zones, on the individual crime type maps, outside the all crimes map. The model needs to

pay attention to these areas while concentrating operator units inside the central crime zone.

In Chapter 9, we will identify the traditional deployment of the Omaha Police Department and then discuss how this might change to better address the concentrations of crime exhibited here.

Endnotes

1. This makes a surface that gives a standard measure for determining how concentrated crime incidents are.
2. The website for SpaceStat is www.terraseer.com; the website for ArcGIS is www.esri.com.
3. The maximum number of property crime concentration per unit is 27.88, which is 8.14 standard deviations above the mean.

9

TOWARD A MISSION-BASED COMMAND AND DEPLOYMENT STRUCTURE

The purpose of this chapter is to present an actual deployment and command structure, and from that provide a suggestive model for restructuring and redeployment around the mission-based concept.

The Omaha Police Department (OPD) will be the example used to develop the hypothetical redeployment model. We want to emphasize that the mission recommendations are not in any way a critique of the current model used in the OPD. Indeed, the OPD is currently engaged with its many audiences in ways that are quite favorable to what we consider to be good police work. Theirs is a traditional model. This means that it is constructed around random preventive patrol and calls for services, in which calls are prioritized for response. The police districts—characteristic of virtually all cities in the United States—enable the omnipresence of police officers across the city while facilitating the response time for calls for service. Omnipresence is further enhanced through selective patrol, a large command that is responsible for vehicular traffic control. A variety of specialty units focus on more serious crime. These units tend to operate in hot zones, and they respond to exigent crime dynamics. These crime units are backed up by a significant detective squad who (1) carry a caseload of existing crimes, or (2) facilitate the work of crime suppression units. Finally, the various crime prevention programs—the neighborhood services unit, the watches, the school resource officers, and the prevention programs squad—are under the direct command of the executive officer, who is one of OPD's deputy chiefs.

The data for this model were adapted from OPD's allocation of personnel document for September 2008 through March 2009. It is not intended to be a precise model of the department, and it is likely that these numbers will change depending on grants' availability, changes in operations, and level of staffing shortfall. They are presented here as a model for a police department for a middle-size city, solely to provide insight into the issues and nature of any effort to redesign and redeploy a department based on a mission model.

Current Commands, Deployments, and Assignments

The basic structure of the organizational model for geographic deployment is carried out by the Uniform Patrol Bureau and is presented in Figure 9.1. When uniform patrol is examined, we note that each precinct has 14 command staff and about 82 officers, with minor variation on that average. The SW precinct commander is also responsible for selective enforcement, which has about 34 patrol officers and sergeants, including accident investigation and the canine units. The motor squad is also referred to as the "solo" squad, a title that harkens to the early days of patrol in Omaha when the motorized patrol made use of motorbikes with side cars.

The riverfront and mounted patrol cover an area called the entertainment district, which refers to an area generally from midtown east to the Missouri River. This is an area associated with a venue of restaurants, outdoor activities, and outdoor festivals. These two patrols are

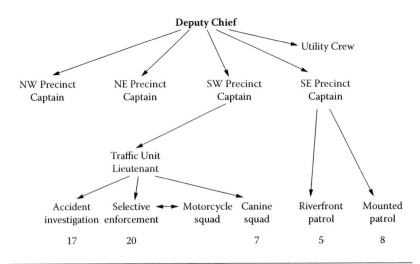

Figure 9.1 Command structure: The Uniform Patrol Bureau.

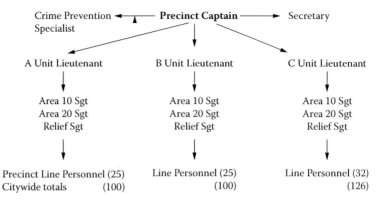

Figure 9.2   Command structure for precincts: NW Precinct.

specifically adapted to this area, with the riverfront patrol primarily covering the Omaha side of the river and its various associated parks, and the mounted patrol providing access to areas not quickly accessible by car.

The SE precinct, in addition to uniform patrol, is responsible for eight mounted patrol and five riverfront patrol officers. The structure of the precinct commands is presented in Figure 9.2. This figure shows that the title "Area 10 Sgt" not only indicates rank but span of control; the Area 10 Sgt for the A shift is responsible for all districts between 10 and 19, and the Area 20 Sgt for the districts from 20 to 29. The relief sergeant is responsible for duty during periods when the area sergeants are on vacation or otherwise out of duty.

Each precinct commander has a crime prevention specialist (CPS) assigned to the precinct. The role of the CPS is not well defined, and for this reason the duties of the position are largely a product of the energies of the specialist. A specialist can take a largely ceremonial role, with little impact on crime in the precinct, or can take a proactive role, working with commanders to alert officers to specific problems and individuals.

One can see from this map that, across the city, during the A and B shift about one hundred officers are on patrol across the city. However, for the C shift about 126 officers are on patrol across the city.

The other organizational component of crime suppression is the criminal investigations unit. Figure 9.3 displays the command structure

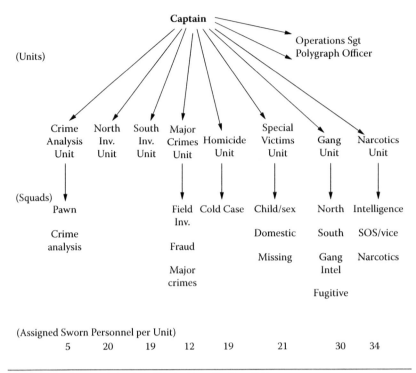

(Units)

Captain

Operations Sgt
Polygraph Officer

Crime Analysis Unit	North Inv. Unit	South Inv. Unit	Major Crimes Unit	Homicide Unit	Special Victims Unit	Gang Unit	Narcotics Unit

(Squads)

Pawn			Field Inv.	Cold Case	Child/sex	North	Intelligence
Crime analysis			Fraud		Domestic	South	SOS/vice
			Major crimes		Missing	Gang Intel	Narcotics
						Fugitive	

(Assigned Sworn Personnel per Unit)

5	20	19	12	19	21	30	34

Figure 9.3　Command structure: Criminal Investigations Unit.

for this unit. Figure 9.3 requires some elaboration. First, the figure does not include civilian personnel. This is particularly important in the presentation of the crime analysis unit, all of which (except for its commander) are civilian personnel. The five officers are all associated with pawn. (The pawn unit is a part of the detective bureau that traces pawned items and works to recover stolen property.)

Second, the unit and squad design is replicated in all the units. All units are commanded by a lieutenant. Almost all of them (excluding crime analysis) also have a B shift and a C shift (sergeant in command), with the B shift larger than the C shift. Third, all units also have civilian secretarial support staff.

The graphic presented in Figure 9.4 depicts the professional standards section. This section houses the crime prevention and community-oriented components of the department.

It should be noted that in Figure 9.4, the human resources department is staffed entirely by civilians and consequently has no sworn officers assigned to it. Also, the school resource officers (SROs) comprise

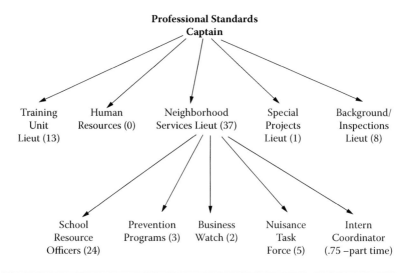

Figure 9.4   Command structure: Professional Standards Section.

four assignments or posts: truancy officers (two), high school SROs (twelve including one sergeant), middle school SROs (seven including one sergeant), and twelve part-time SROs.

In sum, any redeployment is most likely to be reassigned from the OPD units listed in Figure 9.5, with their commands and numbers of patrol officers.

Deputy Chief, Uniform Patrol Bureau
    Precinct Commanders
        Four Precincts: A and B shifts: 25 per shift. C shift: 32 per shift.
    SW Precinct Commander
        Selective enforcement: 20 + 17 for accident investigation.
    Utility Crew: 14
    Crime Prevention Specialists: 4
Deputy Chief, Criminal Investigations Bureau:
    Investigative Operations Section Captain
        Criminal Investigations Unit: 30
        Narcotics Unit: 34
        Major Crimes Unit: 12
        North and South Investigations Unit: 39
Executive Officer and Deputy Chief
    Professional Standards Captain
        SROs: 24
        Prevention Programs: 3

Figure 9.5   Potentially redeployable units.

Reorganization toward a Mission Structure

In this section we will present two areas of organizational redesign and reorganization. The first, called *precinct integrity*, aims at moving officers assigned to specific districts to broader precinct responsibilities according to command assessments of crime effectiveness. The second presents the creation of a new command responsible for hot spot deployment, organized under the title *strategic operations unit*.

The Precinct Integrity Model: From Fixed District
Assignments to Command-Driven Deployment

The precincts will be redesigned for a command-driven model, with a reformulated strategy for responding to calls for service and with an emphasis on crime intervention in at-risk areas within the precincts. The model will alter the precinct command structure of the Uniform Patrol Bureau. There are three components to this realignment of the command structure:

1. One unit will be comprised of five officers, taken from the districts that show the lowest overall crime pressures. The determination of which district assignments will be converted to this unit is made, precinct by precinct, through intelligence planning. This unit will be called the crime precinct mobile squad. Their primary work will be to develop crime responses for at-risk zones inside their precincts and will be staffed by supporters (see Chapter 4). This unit may also work with the operator units in strategic operations, in that information operations may show that crime in these precincts is associated with crime or criminal activity in the central crime hot zone.

2. Other assignments across the precinct will not be fixed, but will depend on the precinct commander's perceptions of the best way to balance calls for service and active crime suppression. Hence, multiple districts may be staffed by a single officer. However, if there is any indication that crime is increasing or that crime patterns in the area seem to suggest the need for an urgent response, the commander will have the authority to immediately shift other officers to that area, or shift the precinct mobile squad to focus on problems in that area.

3. All patrol officers assigned to precinct commands are transitioned to twelve-hour shifts. The basic model for this is three days on, four days off, followed by four days on, three days off. This totals to four hours a week above forty. Given the availability and based on seniority, officers can choose which of those four hours they want off. This serves two functions:

   a. Quality of life—the concentration of time off, together with the four-hour flex time addition, provides officers with more time off for outside pursuits.

   b. Refocusing of patrol on most active police times. Officers will transition to an A shift (2 p.m. to 2 a.m.) and a B shift (2 a.m. to 2 p.m.). This provides the A shift with the greatest overall workload, covering the time immediately after school to one hour after bars close. B-shift officers, facing a lower calls for service expectation, will take on an assignment of four districts each. An inspection of the at-risk and hot zones reveals that twenty-seven districts are affected, fifty-five districts are not. Dividing fifty-five by four (four officers per district for B shift) frees up fourteen B-shift officers. Note that fourteen officers are moved from uniform crime to strategic operations. This is 3.5 shifts per precinct. However, the shift model has transitioned to a twelve-hour model. Figure 9.6 presents the modified NW precinct command structure as a model for all the precincts.

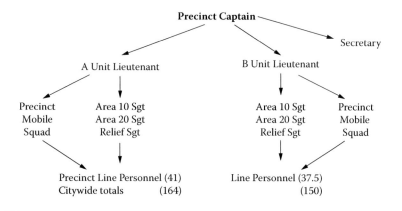

Figure 9.6 Command structure for precincts in the *Precinct Integrity* model: NW Precinct.

Note that all precincts would take the model in Figure 9.6, not only the NW precinct. This model enables a much more proactive response to crime as it develops across the precincts and will facilitate the precinct captain's capacity to respond to any intensification of crime in her or his precinct.

The move to the precinct integrity model will be facilitated by three additional practices:

1. Expansion of online reporting. The department should encourage more online reporting, particularly for minor crimes. The central advantage of online reporting is that citizens who so report will be able to immediately visualize their report on publicly available crime maps. This will be particularly useful for neighborhoods that have active neighborhood associations or neighborhood patrol units. They will be able to identify any crime clusters in their neighborhood, by address. This is a substantial improvement for citizens who are active in neighborhood self-defense.

2. Call prioritization needs to be operationally enforced. Call prioritization is typically a five-category process, with priority 1 being emergency calls and priority 5 being in-house calls. Typically, most calls are responded upward as priority 2 calls—urgent calls. Many of these are category 3, which are "as soon as possible" calls and refer to routine nonserious calls. Category 3 downward should be treated at its priority level, with call stacking carried out on an as available need, with callers urged to use online crime reporting.

3. Selective enforcement can supplement precinct commands in responding to calls for service.

The Strategic Operations Unit

The mission command is a second captaincy, a strategic operations unit organized under the Criminal Investigations Bureau (see Figure 9.3). The reason for this selection is that all elements of this bureau already deal extensively with crime in the hot and at-risk zones. Also, a second captaincy in this unit facilitates overall command integrity because both are serious crime control units under the deputy chief of the Criminal Investigations Bureau. Finally, this helps address concerns that the Criminal Investigations Bureau has been "cannibalized," in that the core services provided under that unit remain under the same overall command.

Elements to be assigned to the new command will be as follows:

1. **The gang unit, both North and South, and the narcotics unit:** Both of these units are combined into a unit called the dangerous offense unit. This is based on the following logic:

   a. First, with regard to the former gang unit, the operator position is intended to be more general than a gang-only focus. We justify moving away from a gang unit per se on the following principle: the gang designation lacks adequate generality. By focusing on a narrow or technical definition of a gang member, the unit may miss false positives, those individuals who are in fact dangerous, but for whatever reason do not show up on the radar as gang members.

   b. With regard to the former narcotics unit, it is to be split, with B and C shifts transitioned to the hot zone command and the remaining B shift in its current assignment. Narcotics crimes are present across the city, and a significant presence—in this instance, a squad—needs to be retained to address problems outside the hot zones.

   c. The newly constituted dangerous offense units, consequently, will tend to focus on narcotics, gangs, and firearms. This will provide two units per shift, capable of taking simultaneous operations in different hot zone areas.

   d. This unit is called offense rather than offender to emphasize that it is focused on the crime, not the person. This is not to say that the unit will never focus on particular individuals. That focus will be determined according to the specific needs of any problem solution carried out by the unit. However, the title of the unit reflects the strategic goal, which prioritizes serious crime.

2. **Patrol reassignments from the Uniform Patrol Bureau, and utility crew:** Two squads, developed from positions discussed previously from the Uniform Patrol Bureau, will be moved into

the strategic operations unit (SOU). In addition, the utility crew, which is also two squads, will be moved into the SOU. Both of these will be reclassified as selective operations specialists. This will provide two A-shift squads and two B-shift squads, for simultaneous operations. These units focus on complex missions involving specific problem-oriented policing (POP) problems. These units should, working with the unit captain and the crime prevention specialists, be capable of taking the specific mission, developing a design, carrying it out, and then assessing it in an after-action report.

3. **Crime prevention specialists:** Reassigned from their current positions across the professional standards section and the four precincts. The area of crime prevention will play a central role across the lines of operation (LOO) strategy. This entity will be retained in whole, but will extensively develop its skills in the area of crime prevention. This unit will carry out two main functions: (1) crime mapping of the hot zone, and (2) development of specialized crime prevention skills and knowledge.

4. **Strategic information officer:** This is a new post. The strategic information officer is directly responsible for providing information to the public about past and current operations. The core task of the strategic information officer is to provide a daily briefing to news agencies and other interested parties about the specific activities planned by the strategic operations unit. The person who fills this task recognizes that information can be tactically deployed to both provide knowledge about forthcoming operations and to ensure that the public is adequately informed about all the actions of the SOU. This role consequently *anticipates* mission activity and *incorporates* the community into that foreknowledge.

   The role of the strategic information officer, however, is much more than public relations. Central to the mission model is the recognition that, to win the hearts and minds of citizens to the long-term goals of the mission, constant reminder is required about its purpose—the virtual ending of serious crime in strife-ridden town neighborhoods. The role of this officer is to serve as the voice of the department, reminding citizens of this goal. This officer is the conscience of the operations, reminding citizens and officers alike of the strategic goals and reaffirming the ends served by the operations.

This post, consequently, requires someone who is not afraid to take on broader responsibilities in talking about police practices with the public. It requires an incumbent who is committed to the goals and is willing to take chances in the release of information, within command protocols. And it requires that commanders recognize the importance of the free exchange of information between the police and the public, and work with this officer to further such a dialogue.

5. **North and South investigations unit:** Much of the work of this unit deals with existing cases, and detectives carry a caseload. However, six members are to be reassigned to the mission command, three for A and B shifts (see reassigned shift times below). The role of investigation changes to the gathering of real-time intelligence, through interrogation and witness interviewing. Their role is always in "real time" in the sense that their primary responsibility is to gather actionable intelligence that can be immediately fed back into an operator unit for action. This is a quasi-military notion of intelligence gathering in real time aimed at intercepting criminal activity.

6. **SROs:** The SRO assignments will be split. All SROs in schools in the hot and at-risk zones will be assigned to the mission. This is a somewhat problematic reassignment in that the schools maintain tight control over the SROs. Consequently, it is important that the schools are reassured that the unit reassignment does not change their task, but serves the purpose of providing information about potential gang and criminal activity more rapidly to the appropriate commander. SROs should work closely with the gang units in the hot and at-risk zones for the following reasons:

    a. Schools sometimes assign students who are gang members from different gangs to the same school. This has high violence potential and can increase the presence of guns on campus.

    b. Gang members may enter schools from off campus.

    c. After-school bussing often drops youth off in areas that facilitate gang activity, especially where parents are not present.

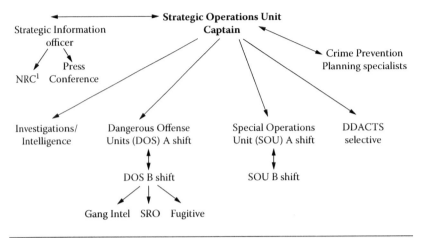

Figure 9.7   Command structure: Hot zone command.

The suggested command structure for the hot zone command con-sequently is presented in Figure 9.7. The command is titled strategic operations. First, Figure 9.7 shows that the A- and B-shift designa-tion is based on the notion that the department shifts to the twelve-hour design, as recommended above. The A shift is from 2 p.m. to 2 a.m., and B shift is from 2 a.m. to 2 p.m.

Note the features of the hot zone command. The *investigation func-tion* takes on an intelligence function, in which investigators view their work primarily in terms of actionable intelligence and in which inves-tigation is only a component. The Crime Prevention Planning squad shows a two-way arrow because of its intelligence planning function, which feeds back into the captain's tactical deployment as needed to develop, provide recommendations, or alter operations.

The *dangerous offense units* are expanded so that they deal with youth generally, with particular skills associated with gangs, drugs, and weapons, all significant problems in hot zones. *Gang intel* is also relocated since intelligence about gangs will be integral to any long-term crime solution.

The *special operations units*, derived from the former utility crew and from the Uniform Patrol Bureau, focus on POP problems and solutions. This provides four units that are integrated into the spe-cific problem-solving and security activities identified in the hot zones.

The assignments for both the dangerous offender units and the special operations units are intended to be flexible. Generally, the assignments are intended to represent a flattening operational structure that provides, in the hot zones, four squads during A shift and four during B shift. The advantage of this flat structure is that units can carry out several operations simultaneously, focusing different tactical responses on the same problem. In other words, the unit will be able to sharply increase pressure on specific problems, assess the merits of each, and then adapt to bring a different solution into play.

Data-driven approaches to crime and traffic safety (*DDACTS*) *selective* represents one squad of officers reassigned from the traffic patrol. Recent applied research has found a high geographic correlation between traffic accident and crime data. This unit will be employed for operations specifically for creating an additional visible presence on major roads and will also carry out high contact activities. Otherwise they will be on patrol across the hot zone or as needed by the unit captain.

The work of all units will shift to a problem-oriented basis, within the mission phase determined by the logical line of operation. For instance, we may find that a dangerous offenders squad might be working on a tactical problem involving gang members identified as active in drug sales in a particular location, while at the same time the DDACTS selective is making a lot of contacts in the immediate area of the operation, increasing the pressure on potential buyers. Additionally the crime prevention unit seeks ways to restructure the physical environment to prevent the reoccurrence of this activity at this location. If an individual involved in drugs is arrested, detectives immediately interrogate to find if a unit needs to be deployed or refocused on another individual or location where drugs are believed to be. Hence, multiple units are immediately active on the same problem case, using real-time data to increase their focus on specific crime problems.

Finally, note the work associated with the *strategic information officer*. This person is responsible as a formal liaison with the neighborhood revitalization committees. This person will also carry out a daily press briefing. This part of the structure, consequently, also represents the formal ties to the community living in the hot zone.

Finally, the role of data-driven assessment cannot be overestimated. Three categories of data are required: (1) geographic data on crime type that has emerged in the tradition of compare statistics (COMPSTAT), (2) after-action reports, aimed at identifying specifically what worked and what did not, and (3) real-time intelligence collected by investigators during operations.

The Five Principles of Mission-Based Policing: Local Applications

The redeployment and restructuring of command in Omaha toward a mission-based model is not intended to be the definitive model for every police department. Every department will face its own particular issues, and it will have its particular ways of organizing to satisfy its population base and address criminal activity. The point in the exercise carried out in this chapter and the previous one is to show how crime mapping, combined with a reconsideration of organizational structure and deployment, can be used to develop a mission-based model. Importantly, the hypothetical model developed for Omaha is faithful to the five principles of mission-based policing developed in Chapters 3 through 5. We will briefly discuss their application to the Omaha example.

The Principle of Focus

If you want to do something about serious crime, then do something about serious crime. Integral to the first principle is that the police mission is organized around serious crime.

The principle of focus was constructed into the organizational chart reconstruction: (1) The existing Criminal Investigation Bureau was expanded with a captaincy over the new strategic operations unit and complemented the existing investigative operations section (IOS). While some of the SOU personnel were taken directly from the IOS, some elements were also derived from other areas of the organization, substantially increasing the organizational complement dealing with serious crime. (2) Each precinct under the Uniform Crime Bureau was reorganized to contain a precinct mobile squad, whose primary purposes were to deal with serious crime in the precincts themselves and to focus particularly on at-risk zones in the precincts.

The Principle of Police Effectiveness

The police can have a significant and long-lasting impact on crime. Effectiveness flows from guardianship, which is grounded in background deterrence, focused deterrence, and legitimacy.

The principle of effectiveness is evinced by the permanent assignment of the various squads to the hot zones. The "center of mass" of these assignments is the four A-shift and four B-shift squads taken from strategic operations, dangerous offense, and special operations squads. That these units are permanently assigned to the hot zones satisfies the definition of background deterrence. And that they carry out POP operations satisfies the definition of focused deterrence. This effect is substantially enhanced by the presence of the DDACTS select squad, which will provide heightened vehicle coverage across the hot zone both routinely and as part of special operations as needed.

The Principle of Layered Deployment

This principle is that the police should not neglect their other missions, but should prioritize efforts to combat serious crime by being where serious crime is.

The precincts have redesigned their underlying calls for service model for flexibility. Consequently, most officers assigned to the precincts will continue to patrol in the traditional way, responding primarily to calls for service while serving an omnipresent function in their districts. They may, however, be reassigned according to need. This applies to districts within hot zones as well as others. However, where a hot or at-risk zone is present, the other layer—the strategic operations section for hot zones and the precinct mobile squads for at-risk zones—will also be active at the same time.

The Principle of Mission Integrity

Integrity means that all elements of the chain of command working within a hot spot are responsible for carrying out that mission. Operators, under mission integrity, take orders from unit commanders, and on up the chain.

This principle is active in the remodeled precinct commands, according to which district assignments are based on the commander's perceptions of need and on decisions about where to deploy the precinct mobile squads. It is also the reason for the location of the strategic operations section under the deputy chief of the investigative operations section. The purpose of that construction is to ensure that a single deputy chief has final responsibility for strategic deployment, specific assignments, and coordination with the other serious crime unit, the IOS.

The Principle of Mission's End

The purpose of police is to put into place a strategy whose purpose is to end crime. This principle recognizes that long-term success lies not only on security efforts but also on economic development, and these two goals require the integration of urban planning and security.

The model presented here represents the kind of organizational work that should be carried out in the planning stages. The application of the fifth principle, mission's end, depends on two items: (1) the correct initial application of the first four principles, and (2) the full application of the LOO strategic structure. Mission's end—the goal of crime dissipation and the focusing of all police practices on tactical decisions to bring about that end—needs to be part of the planning and training for all the squads who are involved in hot zone interdictions and for all commanders who may carry precinct-level responsibilities and will be in charge of units who interdict crime in at-risk zones in their precincts. In other words, units deployed to deal with serious crime need to have the vision to see the larger purpose, the tactical expertise to develop POP tactics to combat crime, the intelligence to work directly with commanders to weigh among different courses of action and see which is likely the most effective, and the command support to provide them protection so that they can critically evaluate their own work—without fear of reprisal—in after-action reports.

We strongly believe that the application of this model will have an immediate impact on crime, and its continued application will both bring crime down to safe zone levels and will resolve many crime problems. Yet, we believe as strongly that the application of all LOO strategic elements are needed to keep crime down. If LOO-3 and -4 are not part of the mission plan, then we have grave concerns that the crime suppression momentum gained through LOO-1 and -2 will stall, and that the local resident communities where the heaviest use of force tactics is carried out will lose faith. Ultimately the gains that the model offers will be lost as a continued police presence comes to be seen as one more example of an ineffectual heavy handed police practice.

10

ANTICIPATED PROBLEMS

This final chapter looks at some of the anticipated problems with the mission-based policing model. We attempt to respond to some concerns that readers may have. Some problems will be substantial and will not have perfect answers. However, it is our hope that this chapter will help to clarify some of the issues raised by the proposed model of policing.

> **How do we maintain a perception of legitimacy when in fact we are sharply increasing police proactive involvement within a particular community's geography? And how do we avoid accusations of racism and other bias charges?**

Legitimacy problems can occur in several different ways, all of which can undermine police effectiveness and community support.

Legitimacy will be immediately challenged by some in the community when the police first deploy to hot zones. This challenge will likely be echoed in local media. The police need to anticipate this, and they need to react to it. This challenge is anticipated through the organization of effective community organizations modeled after Weed and Seed, as discussed in the first lines of operation (LOO). This organization can contribute to the police by providing a sensibility of community expectations, a recognition of sensitive police-community issues, and a buffer against charges that the police do not "represent" the community.

Second, legitimate grievances will occur, and the police will have to respond to those grievances. The identification and addressing of grievances will inevitably occur during security operations and should be carried out immediately by the police, working with community members.

News media will inevitably find challengers to police security operations in high crime areas. A local city councilperson, for instance, may see political opportunity in charges that the police are an "invading and occupying force" without the support of the community. In these circumstances, the openness of the police to discussion with community members is important. The political adage "do not let a shot across the bow go unanswered" comes into play here. The police, both within the local community and to other media sources, should vigorously challenge any such political gamesmanship.

Importantly, the model developed here is a victimization model. The model is about the identification and resolution of crime, and only has a secondary—though substantive—focus on criminals. The end result, that should be constantly emphasized, is that the model seeks lower levels of victimization and the protection of citizens. Indeed, the underlying basis for the construction of the victim-based model— serious crime hot spot analysis—is aimed at reducing levels of community victimization in precisely those areas where it is the highest. This model increases safety by increasing the speed and effectiveness of tactical deployment in all parts of the municipality. The police tactics incubated in the hot spots will translate well and perhaps be even more effective in warm and cool crime areas.

> **What about the possibility that citizens who live in other parts of town will face increases in victimization when police services are reallocated to hot zones? How do we justify the reallocation of officers away from areas where crime is lowest, but where the property values may be the highest? Those who pay the most taxes will face lower levels of police coverage.**

There are several dimensions to this problem. One is that individuals will fear that, with lower levels of random preventive patrol and a de-emphasis on calls for service, their risk for victimization will increase.

A component of the answer lies in emphasizing that routine police patrols will continue in an area. Prioritization of 911 calls will increase; however, departments are increasingly prioritizing 911 calls in any case. Serious calls will receive the level of attention that they historically have in an area.

Just as serious crimes tend to be located in identifiable hot spots, so too do criminals. Though the model we propose focuses on crime, because we are beefing up police presence and strategy in hot zones, this will increase the likelihood of capture of criminals who carry out their work across a metropolitan area.

Some citizens may be concerned about crime displacement—that as crime intervention is increased in high crime areas, criminals will move into other areas—especially theirs. It should be emphasized that contemporary research increasingly shows that crime does not displace, but the opposite happens, positive benefits diffuse to other areas.

It should also be emphasized that hot spot monitoring will continue in all areas of a city, not only in hot and at-risk zones. If a crime cluster or other indicator shows that crime suddenly shifts upward in an area, the police will provide an immediate response. The response can be carried out with conventional organizational units, such as the department's robbery or gang unit.

> **Some researchers will complain that this model moves too fast, too comprehensively, without adequate testing. How do you respond to that?**

The past thirty years have been marked by the development and application of research related to police practices. As Sherman and his colleagues (1997) have noted, a broad effort to assess police practices, and indeed practices across the criminal justice system, has substantially improved our ability to understand what works in policing as well as what does not. This work also points to the need to integrate efforts across community institutions, a message we take to heart in this proposal. We witnessed broad testing in many important areas related to the current model. Research related to Weed and Seed has shown the importance of early community group involvement in successful community interventions. A broad body of research into problem-oriented policing, culminating in the widespread availability of websites focused on specific problem interventions, has helped proliferate and reenergize the problem-oriented policing (POP) movement. Felson's (2002) research on place, together with growth in environmental criminology, has spurred the understanding of micro places in the production or inhibition of crime. Bragg and Weisburd's (2010) research on hot spot policing has contributed both to a better understanding of hot spot interventions and to the research needs of the criminal justice community in the formulation of policy. In compare statistics (COMPSTAT) analysis we see the integration of contemporary models of administration with crime mapping technology to more effectively move the police into real-time crime suppression. Finally, one can see in contemporary military research the recognition of integrated population-centric models of intervention to achieve security, as well as the integrality of legitimacy for long-term security success.

Absent are efforts to integrate this broad swath of research. While books such as that by Sherman and his colleagues (1997) integrate this work conceptually, there is nothing at the level of policy or practice that actually applies it in some sort of integrated form. There is the very real concern that it might go unintegrated. Given the potential that each effort carries to contribute in a meaningful way to crime suppression or prevention, such a lost potential would be substantial. We are already witnessing some of that failure. In spite of the large knowledge we have of policing today, most departments carry on practices in investigation, in patrol, and in response for calls for service, largely as they always have.

This work—mission-based policing—seeks the integration of these models in a set of prescriptions for contemporary policing. This model argues for sweeping changes in the conception, deployment, activities, and mission of the police, based on the integration of research findings from many diverse areas of contemporary knowledge about crime. Hence, in response to the research concern, we believe that all the different areas we advocate are indeed well established in research. Mission-based policing represents the application of that research in an innovative and integrated way.

> **How about command problems across the different command units? How do you deal with the different problems created by the presence of a new command with jurisdictional authority in an area that already has a fully developed command structure?**

No uniformed commander in a large metropolitan area relies solely upon his or her uniformed officers to get the job done. Rather, the job is done through negotiation and networking to obtain the necessary resources, even when the resources being sought are within the same organization. The most effective commanders are skilled networkers outside of their own agencies. By placing the geographic command and the operational command as direct reports to the same deputy chief, we expect their goals to come into alignment and differences to be minimized.

The most likely overlap in commands will come from the precinct mobile squads and the hot zone command. In these instances, we would have the potential for units under two different deputy chiefs carrying out serious crime suppression missions in the same place. To maximize effectiveness, we recommend that the hot zone command share all its intelligence with the precinct mobile sergeants. This will facilitate interunit cooperation and increase the likelihood of tactical success.

> **If you sharply increase the military justification and basis for policing, don't you take a chance in increasing a militaristic esprit de corps, and also increase the likelihood of hostility toward the public and the perception that the police are just an invading army?**

This concern is also one of ours. Research has suggested that the development and expansion of police paramilitary units has contributed to a militaristic perspective on the part of participating officers as well as heightened unit esteem and status in police departments (Kraska, 2001). If police were to overfocus on the security component of their work without integrating it into a long-range strategy of community reinvestment, it would likely increase the insularity of the operator units involved and increase the separation of operators from local community actors.

The answer to this potential problem lies in command integrity and mission focus, and it also is closely tied to the integration of the security function with the mayor and chief, in cooperation, to reinvest and redevelop hot zones as discussed below.

1. **Command focus on the mission.** This means that commanders develop a plan, in the LOO stage of information operations, that includes the full range of LOO strategy. That is, commanders recognize and plan for the long-term goal of community development. Hence, command integrity at every stage requires that commanders always are looking toward the next stage and are developing tactics and deployment

practices that aim at fulfilling the current LOO and moving on to the next. From this perspective, the establishment of security is not the end of operations, but the platform upon which broader changes are brought into the community.

2. **Mayoral and chief responsibility.** One of our concerns is that the security model we establish in the first two LOOs—information and security operations—will become the entirety of the model emplaced to do something about crime. This would be a significant mistake. The model contained in the first two LOOs—develop an adequate informational base to do something about crime and then carry out security operations based on that intelligence—should bring crime down significantly for the short term. But the long-term presence of high levels of operators in a hot zone, without significant progress on other fronts, will backfire in the long term, building resentments against the police and delegitimizing their work.

The idea that you can end crime is utopian. How can you seriously expect to end crime? It has happened nowhere.

This is a good question. We want to emphasize that the mission-based model is based on cumulative research across different areas, combined in novel ways. It is not science fiction, but a product of existing practices and policies that have had a lowering effect on crime. The model, in this sense, is comparable to the medical notion that the use of a single agent will often not adequately deal with cancers, but that a response involving multiple agents can have a more dramatic effect. The following points should be emphasized, with this research basis in mind:

1. By ending crime, we focused on serious crime, and we focused on hot spot crime. Ending crime was defined as bringing serious crime down to levels not significantly different from a city's average. That is a less utopian goal, but in itself hugely challenging. Those who have lived in, carried out operations in, or who have sought interventions in crime in hot zones will recognize that the difference between hot zones is not some minor increase in crime. Many hot zones are characterized by profound problems of income inequality, high levels of

unemployment, gang violence, racial and ethnic segregation, and long-term disinvestment problems. Building a security base in these areas is a significant challenge. Yet we believe that, for the welfare and quality of life of community members as well as the safety of the city overall, police should focus first and foremost on establishing security in these areas. Only when this is accomplished can the significant work of reinvestment begin to take traction.

2. The notion of ending crime also is an important strategic element. The concept of ending crime should be central to the way in which the police organize, develop tactics, and deploy to deal with serious crime. At each step of the process developed, the police, at both the levels of command and line, should be thinking "How does what I do contribute in a concrete way to the goal of bringing crime down?" This way of thinking is distinct from the predominant view one encounters in most high crime areas, which is "How do we keep a lid on crime?" Police and communities become acclimated to a high level of crime and tend to quit too soon after tactics show promise, because keeping things to a dull roar is often seen as good enough for an area that will always have crime. The goal of eliminating crime entirely, on the other hand, even if not accomplished in short order, does not have tolerance for what is felt to be a dull roar. Under the mission-based policing model, the focus is on increasing safety and reducing violent crime.

The model also forces the police to focus directly on serious crime, not indirectly through large numbers of zero tolerance misdemeanor arrests. Our goal is to force a rethinking of what the police can do about crime, both by recognizing that the police in fact have a large impact on serious crime, and then by building that recognition—and the importance of the police role in the rebuilding of security where it currently is lacking—into their daily work.

You claim to be creating a new model, but in the end it is the same old liberal propaganda—invest in social programs to help poor people.

We agree that this proposal contains liberal propaganda. We would also emphasize that it contains conservative propaganda. We noted in Chapter 1 that what was needed in order to do something about serious crime was the recognition that both conservative and liberal agendas have a great deal to offer crime control, and that successful anticrime efforts, for the long term, require a great deal of both. The recommendations for mission-based policing contain quite conservative recommendations—substantially beef up the police presence in high crime areas, maximize citizen contacts, closely track anyone associated with crime, use a counterinsurgency logic combined with a more militaristic chain of command—with a broad investment in social and economic programs that aim at preventing crime.

The intense crime control component is primarily at the beginning of operations, in what we called the security lines of operation, with the more social-based programs later, in the rebuilding lines of operation. That is, the relationship between conservative and liberal elements is temporal, a segue that is carried in the progression of the logical lines of operation. A different way to think about this is that we have adopted the Petraeus model of counterinsurgency, and—not really surprising but notable—that model is wholly consistent with both conservative and liberal crime control agendas. Hence, our inclusion of both regimes does not consist of efforts to placate both political agendas, but rather in the recognition that an integrated approach—one already in place in the current U.S. Army/Marine model of counterinsurgency—implicitly contains substantial tactical elements of both.

References

Bates, S. (1987). *Spatial and Temporal Analysis of Crime.* Research Bulletin, April 1987. Chicago: Illinois Criminal Justice Information Authority.

Bittner, Egon. 1970. The Functions of the Police in Modern Society. Rockville, MD: National Institute of Mental Health, Center for Studies of Crime and Delinquency.

Black, Donald. (1980). *The Manners and Customs of the Police.* New York: Academic Press.

Block, C. R. (1995). *STAC Hot Spot Areas: A Statistical Tool for Law Enforcement Decisions.* P. 20036 in C. R. Block, M. Dabdoub, and S. Fregly, eds. *Crime Analysis through Computer Mapping.* Washington, DC: Police Executive Research Forum.

Boba, Rachel. (2005). *Crime Analysis and Crime Mapping.* Thousand Oaks, CA: Sage.

Boba, Rachel, and John Crank. (2008). A model for institutionalizing problem-solving. *Policing: An International Journal.*

Boba, Rachel, and Roberto Santos. (2007). Single family home construction site theft: A case study." *International Journal of Construction Education and Research* 3: 217–36.

Braga, Anthony. (2001). The effects of hot spot policing on crime. *Annals of American Political and Social Science* 578: 104–29.

Braga, Anthony, and David Weisburd. (2006). Problem-oriented policing—the disconnect between principles and practice. Pp. 133–70 in D. Weisburd and A. Braga, eds. *Police Innovation: Contrasting Perspectives.* New York: Cambridge University Press.

Braga, A. A., & Bond, B. J. 2008. Policing crime and disorder hot spots: A randomized controlled trial. *Criminology, 46,* 577–608.

Braga, Anthony, and David Weisburd. (2010). *Policing Problem Places: Crime Hot Spots and Effective Crime Prevention.* New York: Oxford University Press.

Brantingham, P. L., and P. J. Brantingham. (1981). *Environmental Criminology.* Beverly Hills, CA: Sage.

Brantingham, P. L., and P. J. Brantingham. (1984). *Patterns in Crime.* New York: Macmillan.

Brantingham, P. L., and P. J. Brantingham. (1993). Nodes, paths and edges: Considerations on the complexity of crime and the physical environment. *Journal of Environmental Psychology* 13: 3–28.

Brantingham, P. L., and P. J. Brantingham. (1995). Criminality of place: Crime generators and crime attractors. *European Journal of Criminal Policy and Research* 3: 5–26.

Bureau of Justice Statistics. 2006. Law Enforcement Management and Information Services. http://www.data.gov/raw/4080.

Bursik, Robert J., Jr. and Harold Grasmick. 1993. *Neighborhoods and Crime: The Dimensions of Effective Community Control.* New York: Lexington.

Caldero, Michael. (2006). Personal conversation.

Caldero, Michael, and John Crank. (2010). *Police Ethics: The Corruption of Noble Cause.* 3rd ed. Cincinnati, OH: Lexis Nexis.

Cardona, Pablo, and Carlos Rey. (2008). *Management by Missions.* New York: Macmillan.

Center for Problem-Oriented Policing. (2009). The key elements of problem-oriented policing. http://www.popcenter.org/about/?p=elements

Clark, Gerald. (1969). What happens when the police go on strike. *New York Times Magazine*, Nov. 16, sec 6, pp. 5, 176–85, 194–95.

Clarke, Ronald V., and David L. Weisburd. (1994). Diffusion of crime control benefits: Observations on the reverse of displacement. *Crime Prevention Studies* 2: 165–84.

Clarke, R.D. and S.P. Lab. 2000. "Community Characteristics and In-School Criminal Victimization." *Journal of Criminal Justice* 28:33–42.

Clear, Todd. (2007). *Imprisoning Communities: How Mass Incarceration Makes Disadvantaged Neighborhoods Worse.* New York: Oxford University Press.

Cohen, Lawrence E., and Marcus Felson. (1979).Social change and crime rate trends. *American Sociological Review* 44: 588–608.

Connolly, J. (2010). Rethinking police training. *Police Chief* (June). http://policechiefmagazine.org/magazine/index.cfm?fuseaction=display_arch&article_id=1667&issue_id=112008

Cordner, Gary, Jack Greene, and Tim Bynum. (1983). The sooner the better: Some effects of police response time. Pp. 145–64 in R. Bennett, ed. *Police at Work.* Beverly Hills, CA: Sage.

Cordes, Henry, Cindy Gonzalez and Erin Grace. 2007. "Omaha in Black and White: Poverty amid prosperity," Omaha World Herald, April 15.

Crank, John. (2003). *Understanding Police Culture.* Cincinnati, OH: Lexis Nexis.

Crank, John, Colleen Kadleck, and Connie Koski. (2010). The USA: The next big thing. *Police Practice and Research: An International Journal* 11 (5): 405–22.

Crank, John P., and Robert Langworthy. (1992). An institutional perspective of policing. *Journal of Criminal Law and Criminology* (83–82): 901–26.

Crank, John P. and Robert Langworthy 1996. "Fragmented Centralization and the Organization of the Police." *Policing and Society* 6: 213–229.

Decker, Scott. (2003). *Policing Gangs and Youth Violence.* Wadsworth Contemporary Issues in Crime and Justice Series. Canada: Thompson Wadsworth.

Donnelly, Patrick, and Charles Kimble. (1997). Community organizing, environmental change, and neighborhood crime. *Crime and Delinquency* 43: 493–511.

Dunworth, Terence, and Gregory Mills. (1999). *National Evaluation of Weed and Seed.* Research in Brief, National Institute of Justice. Washington, DC: U.S. Department of Justice.

Eck, John E. (1993). The threat of crime displacement. *Criminal Justice Abstracts* 25: 527–46.

Eck, John, and Julie Wartell. (1996). *Reducing Crime and Drug Dealing by Improving Police Management: A Randomized Experiment.* Report to the San Diego Police Department. Washington, DC: Crime Control Institute.

Felson, Marcus. (2002). *Crime and Everyday Life.* 3rd ed. Thousand Oaks, CA: Sage.

Filkins, Dexter. (2009). Stanley McChrystal's long war. *New York Times,* October 18. www.nytimes.com/2009/10/18/magazine/18Afghanistan-t.html

Fuentes, Joseph. (2006). *Practical Guide to Intelligence-Led Policing.* New York: Manhattan Institute for Policy Research.

Geller, William and Lisa Belsky 2009. Building Our Way Out of Crime: The Transformative Power of Police-Community Developer Partnerships. National Institute of Justice. http://www.cops.usdoj.gov/files/RIC/Publications/building.pdf

Gilbertson, T. 2005. "Reducing False Security Alarm Calls for Police Service: A Policy Research Note." *Criminal Justice Policy Review* 16(4):499–506.

Gladwell, Michael. 2008. *Outliers.* NY: Little, Brown, & Co.

Goldstein, H. (1977). *Problem-Oriented Policing.* New York: McGraw-Hill.

Greater Omaha Chamber of Commerce. 2010. Available from http://www.accessomaha.com.

Greene, Jack. (2003). Gangs, community policing, and problem solving. Pp. 3–16 in S. Decker, ed. *Policing Gangs and Youth Violence.* Belmont, CA: Thompson/Wadsworth.

Henry, Vincent. (2003). *The COMPSTAT Paradigm: Management and Accountability in Policing, Business, and the Public Sector.* Flushing, NY: Looseleaf Publications.

Holcomb, John, and Norean Sharpe. (2006). Calls for 911 service: A collaboration between Cleveland State University and the Cleveland City Police Department. Working Paper. http://www.stat.auckland.ac.nz/~iase/publications/17/1B3_HOLC.pdf

Jeffery C 1971. *Crime Prevention through Environmental Design.* London: Sage Publications.

Johnson, R. and Rhodes T. 2007. Urban and Small Town Comparison of Citizen Demand for Police Services. *International Journal of Police Science and Management* 11(1): 27–38.

Kelling, George., et al. 1974. Kansas City Preventive Patrol Experiment: A Summary Report. Washington, D.C.: The Police Foundation.

Kelling, George. 1995. How to run a police department. City Journal. http://www.city-journal.org/html/5_4_how_to_run.html.

Kelling, George, and H. Sousa. (2001). *Do Police Matter? An Analysis of the Impact of New York City's Police Reforms*. Civic Report 22. New York: Manhattan Institute for Policy Research.

Kennedy, David. 2008. *Deterrence and Crime Prevention: Reconsidering the Prospects of Sanction*. London: Routledge.

Kilcullen, David. (2008). *The Accidental Guerilla: Fighting Small Wars in the Midst of a Big One*. New York: Oxford University Press.

Kleiman, M. A. R., & Smith, K. D. 1990. State and local drug enforcement: In search of a strategy. *Crime and Justice*, 13, 69–108.

Klinger, David A. 1997. Negotiating order in patrol work: An ecological theory of police response to deviance. *Criminology* 35(2): 277–306.

Koper, Christopher S. 1995. "Just Enough Police Presence: Reducing Crime and Disorderly Behavior by Optimizing Patrol Time in Crime Hot Spots." *Justice Quarterly* 12:649–672.

Kraska, Peter. 2001. *Militarizing the American Criminal Justice System: The Changing Roles of the Armed Forces and the Police*. Lebanon, NH: University Press of New England.

Kromer, John. (2000). *Neighborhood Recovery: Reinvestment Strategy for the New Hometown*. Piscataway, NJ: Rutgers University Press.

Lawrence W. Sherman. 1993. "Defiance, Deterrence and Irrelevance: A Theory of the Criminal Sanction." *Journal of Research in Crime and Delinquency* 30: 445–473.

Lawrence W. Sherman and David Weisburd 1995. "General Deterrent Effects of Police Patrol in Crime Hot Spots: A Randomized,Controlled Trial." *Justice Quarterly*, Vol. 12, No. 4: 635–648.

Lasley, James. (1998). "*Designing Out" Gang Homicides and Street Assaults*. Research in Brief, November. Washington, DC: National Institute of Justice.

Lemann, Nicholas. (1992). *The Promised Land: The Great Black Migration and How It Changed America*. New York: Knopf.

Levin, Yale, and Alfred Lindesmith. (1937/1971). English ecology and criminology of the past century. In Harwin L. Voss and David M. Petersen, eds. *Ecology Crime and Delinquency*. New York: Meredith Press.

Lipton, Robert, and Paul Gruenewald. (2002). The spatial dynamics of violence and alcohol outlets. *Journal of Studies on Alcohol* 63: 187–95.

Lombroso, Gina Ferrero. 1911. *Criminal Man, According to the Classification of Cesare Lombroso*. New York: Putnam.

Marcus Felson. 1994. *Crime and Everyday Life: Insights and Implications for Society*. Newbury Park, California: Pine Forge Press.

McDonald, John, Ricky Blumenthal, Daniela Golinelli, Aaron Kofner, Robert Stokes, Amber Sehgal, and Leo Beletsky. (2009). *Neighborhood Effects on Crime and Youth Violence: The Role of Business Improvement Districts in Los Angeles*. Technical report. Santa Monica, CA: Rand.

Meier, Robert F., Leslie W. Kennedy, and Vincent F. Sacco, eds. (2001). *The Process and Structure of Crime: Criminal Events and Crime Analysis.* New Brunswick, NJ: Transaction.

Morris, Terence. (1957). *The Criminal Area.* London: Routledge & Kegan Paul.

Moskos, Peter. (2007). 911 and the failure of police rapid response. *Law Enforcement Executive Forum* 7 (4): 137–49. http://www.petermoskos.com/readings/moskos_2007_RapidResponse.pdf

Murray, R. K., and Roncek, D. W. (2008). Measuring diffusion of assaults around bars through radius and adjacency techniques. *Criminal Justice Review* 33: 199–220.

Murray, Rebecca K. (2002). Bars, brawls and blocks: An examination of the associations between the locations of liquor-serving establishments and felonious assaults. Master's thesis, University of Nebraska at Omaha.

Openshaw, S. 1984. The modifiable areal unit problem. *Concepts and Techniques in Modern Geography,* 38, 41.

Park, Robert, Ernest W. Burgess, and Roderick D. McKenzie. (1925). *The City.* Chicago: University of Chicago Press.

Parker, Michelle. (2007). Programming development funds to support a counter-insurgency. Case Studies in National Security Transformation 10.

Parker, Michelle. 2007. Programming Development Funds to Support a Counterinsurgency: A Case Study of Nangarhar, Afghanistan in 2006. Case Studies in National Security Transformation Number 10. http://www.dtic.mil/cgi-bin/GetTRDoc?Location=U2&doc=GetTRDoc.pdf&AD=ADA471252.

Paternoster, Raymond, Ronet Bachman, Robert Brame, and Lawrence W. Sherman. 1997. "Do Fair Procedures Matter? The Effect of Procedural Justice on Spouse Assault." *Law and Society Review* 31:163–204.

Petraeus, David, and James Amos. (2006). *FM-3-24 Counterinsurgency.* Washington, DC: Department of the Army.

Petraeus, David, James Amos, and John Nagl. (2007). *The U.S. Army/Marine Corps Counterinsurgency Field Manual.* Chicago: University of Chicago Press.

Pivan, Frances, and Richard Clowen. (1997). *The Breaking of the American Social Compact.* New York: Norton.

Quinlivan, James. (1995). Force requirements in stability operations. *Parameters* (Winter): 59–69.

Reiss, Albert. 1971. *The Police and The Public.* New Haven: Yale University.

Robinson, Linda. (2008). *Tell Me How This Ends: General David Petraeus and the Search for a Way Out of Iraq.* New York: Public Affairs.

Roncek, Dennis W., and R. Bell. (1981). Bars, blocks and crimes. *Journal of Environmental Systems* 11: 35–47.

Roncek, Dennis W., and D. Faggiani. (1985). High schools and crime: A replication. *Sociological Quarterly* 26: 492–505.

Roncek, Dennis W., and Pamela A. Maier. (1991). Bars, blocks and crimes revisited: Linking the theory of routine activities to the empiricism of "hot spots." *Criminology* 29: 725–53.

Sample, L., & Bray, T. 2003. Are sex offenders dangerous? *Criminology and Public Policy,* 3, 59–82.

Sampson, Robert and W. Byron Groves. 1989. "Community Structure and Crime: Testing Social Disorganization Theory." *American Journal of Sociology* 94: 774–802.

Scott, E. 1981. Calls for service: Citizen demand and initial police response. Washington, DC: U.S. Government Printing Office.

Sherman, Lawrence, Michael Buerger, and Patrick Gartin. 1989. Repeat Call Address Policing: The Minneapolis RECAP Experiment (Final Report to the National Institute of Justice). Washington, D.C.: Crime Control Institute.

Sherman, Lawrence. 1997. Policing for Crime Prevention. Ch. 8 in Lawrence W. Sherman, et al. Preventing Crime: What Works, What Doesn't, What's Promising. Report to the U.S. Congress. Washington, D.C.: U.S. Dept. of Justice, http://www.ncjrs.gov/works/

Sciarabba, Anthony. (2009). Community oriented policing and community-based crime reduction programs: An evaluation in New York City. *Professional Issues in Criminal Justice* 4: 27–41.

Scott, Michael S. (2000). Getting the police to take problem oriented policing seriously. Center for Problem Oriented Policing. http://www.popcenter.org/library/crimeprevention/volume_15/03Scott_problem_oriented_policing.pdf

Shaw, Clifford R., and Henry D. McKay. (1942/1969). *Juvenile Delinquency and Urban Areas* Chicago: University of Chicago Press.

Sherman, Lawrence. (2002). *Evidence-based crime prevention.* London: Routledge.

Sherman, Lawrence. (1997). Policing for crime prevention. In Lawrence Sherman, Denise Gottfredson, Doris MacKenzie, John Eck, Peter Reuter, and Shawn Bushway, eds. *Preventing Crime: What Works, What Doesn't and What's Promising.* Washington, DC: U.S. Department of Justice, Office of Justice Programs.

Sherman, Lawrence W., Patrick R. Gartin, and Michael E. Buerger. (1989). Hot spots of predatory crime: Routine activities and the criminology of place." *Criminology* 27: 27–55.

Sherman, Lawrence, Denise Gottfredson, Doris MacKenzie, John Eck, Peter Reuter, and Shawn Bushway. (1997). *Preventing Crime: What Works, What Doesn't and What's Promising.* Washington, DC: U.S. Department of Justice, Office of Justice Programs.

Silverman, B. W. (1986). *Density Estimation for Statistics and Data Analysis.* New York: Chapman and Hall.

Silverman, E. (2006). COMPSTAT's innovation. Pp. 267–83 in D. Weisburd and A. A. Braga, eds. *Police Innovation: Contrasting Perspectives.* New York: Cambridge University Press.

Skogan, Wesley G. (1990). *Disorder and Decline: Crime and the Spiral of Decay in American Cities.* New York: Free Press.

Skogan, Wesley G., and Kathleen Frydl, eds. (2004). *Fairness and Effectiveness in Policing: The Evidence.* Committee to Review Police Policy and Practices. Washington, DC: National Academies Press.

Skogan, Wesley, Susan Hartnett, Natalie Bump, and Jill Dubois. (2008). Executive summary evaluation of CeaseFire–Chicago. http://www. northwestern.edu/ipr/publications/ceasefire_papers/executivesummary. pdf

Skogan, Wesley, Susan Hartnett, Jill Dubois, J. Comey, M. Kaiser, and J. Lovig. (1999). *On the Beat: Police and Community Problem Solving*. Boulder, CO: Westview Press.

Spring, J. V., and Block, C. R. (1989). *STAC User's Manual*. Chicago: Illinois Criminal Justice Information Authority.

Sunshine, J., and T. R. Tyler. 2003. The role of procedural justice and legitimacy in shaping public support for policing. *Law and Society Review* 37:513–547.

Taylor, Ralph B., and Adele V. Harrell. (1996). Physical environment and crime. National Institute of Justice Research Report. http://www.ncjrs. gov/pdffiles/physenv.pdf

Tyler, Tom R. 1990. *Why People Obey the Law*. New Haven: Yale Univ. Press.

Tyler, Tom R. (2004). Enhancing police legitimacy. *Annals of the American Academy of Political and Social Science* 59: 84–99.

U.S. Bureau of the Census. 2000. U.S. Census of Population. Washington, D.C.: Government Printing Office.

U.S. Department of Justice. (2004). The Weed and Seed strategy. Office of Justice Programs, Community Capacity Development Office. www.ojp. usdoj.gov/ccdo

U.S. Department of Justice, Bureau of Justice Statistics. 2010. Sourcebook of Criminal Justice Statistics. Washington, D.C.: Government Printing Office.

Vold, George B., Thomas J. Bernard, and Jeffrey B. Snipes. (2002). *Theoretical Criminology*. New York: Oxford University Press

Voss, Harwin L., and David M. Petersen, eds. (1971). *Ecology, Crime and Delinquency*. New York: Appleton Century Crofts.

Walker, Samuel, and Charles Katz. (2008). *The Police in America*. 6th ed. Boston: McGraw-Hill.

Warner, Barbara and Glenn Pierce. 1993. "Reexamining social disorganization theory using calls to the police as a measure of crime." *Criminology* 31:493–517

Weisburd, David, and Anthony Braga. (2003). Hot-spots policing. In H. Kury and O. Fuchs, eds. *Crime Prevention: New Approaches*. Mainz, Germany: Weiusner Ring.

Weisburd, David, and John Eck. (2004). To better serve and protect: Improving police practices. *Annals of American Political and Social Science* 593: 42–58.

Welsh, Brandon, and David Farrington. (2009). *Making Public Places Safer: Surveillance and Crime Prevention*. New York: Oxford University Press.

Willis, James, Stephen Mastrofski, and David Weisburd. (2007). Making sense of COMPSTAT: A theory-based analysis of organizational change in three police departments. *Law and Society Review* 41: 147–88.

Wilson, J.Q. 1968. *Varieties of Police Behavior.* Cambridge, MA: Harvard University.

Wilson, J. Q., and G. L. Kelling. (1982). Broken windows: the police and neighborhood safety. *Atlantic Monthly* 29: 38.

Zhao, Jihong, Nicholas Lovrich, and Hank Robinson. (2001). Community policing: Is it changing the basic functions of policing? *Journal of Criminal Justice* 29: 365–77.

Index

A

AIDS in prison, 62
ArcGIS, 175
Arrests
    racial factors, 60
    resistance to, 60–61
    short-term deterrence, as, 60
At-risk zones, 73, 188
    layered deployment and, 73, 75, 77
    Omaha case example, 187–188, 199

B

Background deterrence, 58–59, 67
Balbi, Adriano, 169
Boban model, 87, 88, 94
Broken windows, 68–69
Business improvement districts
    (BIDs), 137, 138–139. *See
    also* North Omaha Village
    reinvestment plan

C

Calls for service model 911, 29
    citizens' view of, 28–29
    deployment basis, as, 28

false alarms and, 34–35
fault in, as a model for policing,
    29–30
geographic basis, 28
grid-based, 28
impediment to addressing crime,
    34
misleading measurement of
    crime, 30–32, 34
operations, 36–39
prioritization of calls, 34
rapid response as measurement
    of police response, 35–36
Case example, Omaha. *See* Omaha
    case example
Chicago Project for Violence
    Prevention (CPVP), 10
Citizen groups, 157
Citizen Observer program, Cocoa
    Beach, Florida, 41
Code 66, 98–99
Command control, 41–43
    accountability, 49–50
Command orientation for mission
    personnel, 102–103
Command-drive policing model, 21

A Call for Authors

Advances in Police Theory and Practice

AIMS AND SCOPE:

This cutting-edge series is designed to promote publication of books on contemporary advances in police theory and practice. We are especially interested in volumes that focus on the nexus between research and practice, with the end goal of disseminating innovations in policing. We will consider collections of expert contributions as well as individually authored works. Books in this series will be marketed internationally to both academic and professional audiences. This series also seeks to —

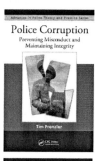
Police Corruption
Preventing Misconduct and Maintaining Integrity
Tim Prenzler
CRC Press

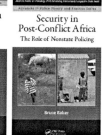
Security in Post-Conflict Africa
The Role of Nonstate Policing
Bruce Baker
CRC Press

Police Reform in China
Kam C. Wong
CRC Press

Mission-Based Policing
John P. Crank
Rebecca K. Murray
Dawn M. Irlbeck
Mark T. Sundermeier
CRC Press

- Bridge the gap in knowledge about advances in theory and practice regarding who the police are, what they do, and how they maintain order, administer laws, and serve their communities
- Improve cooperation between those who are active in the field and those who are involved in academic research so as to facilitate the application of innovative advances in theory and practice

The series especially encourages the contribution of works coauthored by police practitioners and researchers. We are also interested in works comparing policing approaches and methods globally, examining such areas as the policing of transitional states, democratic policing, policing and minorities, preventive policing, investigation, patrolling and response, terrorism, organized crime and drug enforcement. In fact, every aspect of policing, public safety, and security, as well as public order is relevant for the series. Manuscripts should be between 300 and 600 printed pages. If you have a proposal for an original work or for a contributed volume, please be in touch.

Series Editor
Dilip Das, Ph.D., Ph: 802-598-3680
E-mail: dilipkd@aol.com

Dr. Das is a professor of criminal justice and Human Rights Consultant to the United Nations. He is a former chief of police and, founding president of the International Police Executive Symposium, IPES, www.ipes.info. He is also founding editor-in-chief of *Police Practice and Research: An International Journal* (PPR), (Routledge/Taylor & Francis), www.tandf.co.uk/journals. In addition to editing the *World Police Encyclopedia* (Taylor & Francis, 2006), Dr. Das has published numerous books and articles during his many years of involve-ment in police practice, research, writing, and education.

Proposals for the series may be submitted to the series editor or directly to –
Carolyn Spence
Acquisitions Editor • CRC Press / Taylor & Francis Group
561-998-2515 • 561-997-7249 (fax)
carolyn.spence@taylorandfrancis.com • www.crcpress.com
6000 Broken Sound Parkway NW, Suite 300, Boca Raton, FL 33487